D1602110

TOWARD AN AMERICAN SOCIOLOGY

Questioning the European Construct

GORDON D. MORGAN

**Westport, Connecticut
London**

Library of Congress Cataloging-in-Publication Data

Morgan, Gordon D.
  Toward an American sociology : questioning the European construct
  / Gordon D. Morgan.
     p. cm.
  Includes bibliographical references and index.
  ISBN 0–275–94999–0 (alk. paper)
     1. Sociology—United States. 2. Sociology—Europe. 3. Sociology—
  Philosophy. I. Title.
  HM22.U5M67 1997
  301′.0973—dc20   96–20692

British Library Cataloguing in Publication Data is available.

Library of Congress Catalog Card Number: 96–20692
ISBN: 0–275–94999–0

First published in 1997

Praeger Publishers, 88 Post Road West, Westport, CT 06881
An imprint of Greenwood Publishing Group, Inc.

Printed in the United States of America

The paper used in this book complies with the
Permanent Paper Standard issued by the National
Information Standards Organization (Z39.48–1984).

10 9 8 7 6 5 4 3 2 1

Contents

Preface

Many scholars for some years have been remarking upon problems with which the discipline of sociology deals—the focus, quality, and amount of research carried out by members of the discipline—but very few persons have dealt with the discipline itself, its impact, or its future. Warning signals have been fired by such scholars as Alvin Gouldner in *The Coming Crisis in Western Sociology* and C. Wright Mills in *The Sociological Imagination*. Robert Lynd pointed out as early as 1939 in his *Knowledge for What* that the social sciences were being divided between scholar scientists or theoreticians and technicians.

The problems of the ages are not the present ones, but they belong to the coming ages. For instance, scholarship saw town life as problematic when viewed against feudal norms—when cities had such a hard time being established. When the Industrial Revolution struck, it was not industrial technology that proved problematic, but the dislocations caused by the movement of people from the certitude of feudal employment. Post-industrial society finds little argument with the mechanics of industrial life but criticizes its failure to produce the happiness that leisure and prosperity suggest.

The Great Depression of the 1930s caused the American public to have less confidence than before in the captains of industry and their ability to organize society to provide bounty for all. As the industrial giants lost favor, there was a rise of confidence in the social sciences, which were expected to suggest solutions to the human problems that impeded economic and material progress. But the social sciences were unable to rise to the challenge, even with the availability of great arrays of data on nearly every conceivable aspect of human life.

Not only the problems of the Depression caused people to question the salience of social science, and particularly sociology. Again during the 1960s, when intergroup problems once more surged to the fore, the social sciences were tested. The convergence of the civil rights movement and the Vietnam War were not technical problems such as lack of abundance and low productivity. They were the problems of the misunderstanding of groups about each other—on both a local and a worldwide scale.

When sociology was asked what it knew that was helpful, it resorted to its standard answer, "We need more data." Projects served mainly as opportunities for the refinement of the research techniques of those conducting the research. The discipline ignored the warning of C.W. Mills about its members becoming "hired hand researchers," offering support for whatever reasoning their supporters desired. From the 1960s on, sociology seemed mired in the trap of "relevancy" versus "value neutrality." Disciplines trying to say something "relevant," that is, useful, were postured as less valuable than those that adopted the language and methodology of the hard sciences. No one wanted to say anything that had much impact because neutrality would be violated and the scientific status of the sociologist would be called into question.

The quantitative-qualitative, value neutrality-relevancy, scientist-humanist debate waxed and waned under different names until C.P. Snow tried to bring some understanding by writing his widely read *Two Cultures*, which warned of the counter productivity of dichotomized thinking within the discipline. One of the most trenchant and relevant critiques of the discipline of sociology was done by Harold Nelson in *Sociology in Bondage*. In that 1981, monograph Nelson clearly foresaw the direction toward irrelevance the discipline was taking, and he warned graduate students of the paths and perils that lay before them as they sought status within the discipline.

After reading these and other critiques of the discipline and trying to assess some that were beyond personalities, it gradually became clear to me that the issue was not the orientation of the scholars toward either hard science or soft science. It seemed that the practitioners in the discipline already had a set attitude set toward any problem they faced. Nearly all of them, no matter at what institutions or on what problems they worked, approached problems similarly—out of the same mental set. Sociology seemed like a football coach who was running his players in the same formations for 100 years even though the game had changed dramatically. Differences between the practitioners were slight. They might use this or that methodology, scaling, or other data processing procedures, but they had basically the same theoretical orientations, as though they had been trained in the very same academies by the same masters.

Inquiry into this problem of similar thinking by sociologists led the author back to the roots of American sociology—Europe of the mid-1800s. Even those European predecessors had origins. These were traced back to the period of European feudalism, when there was a fascination with order. This 1,000-year period became something of a standard of thought for those seeking a model in face of the American, French, Haitian, and other revolutions, which suggested not so much order but great social change.

The feudalistic model of order, which supported a large variety of social positions (generally broadly ranked), began to be taught in American colleges when sociology was imported from Europe. Although America was more dynamic than Europe of the feudal period, it was the feudal model that gained currency, and it has held that grip up to the present time. The consequence is that sociological theory is based upon a relatively static model, whereas the society itself has been quite dynamic.

The order inherent in feudal society is traced back to Rome and before that to Greece. All these societies contained significant elements of inequality—an idea that was transferred in sociological thought to America but was contradicted in practice.

The present writings argue that a new sociology is needed, mainly because the theory bequeathed by European predecessors is largely inapplicable to the American case. The categorical and static thought of the feudal age of Europe that provided the model for European thought could not be applied to the fullest advantage in America, where change was so rapid that tradition stood little chance of developing.

The principal problem of sociology has been the question of order. As the ship sank and the band continued to play professionally, the captain of the Titanic was rearranging the chairs in the stateroom while the water rose. This exemplifies a general need for order, and there are even more recent evidences of concern with order. Tom Wicker, observing the Attica prison revolt, wrote of the necessity in the minds of the free world leaders for the maintenance of order: "The order of things must be preserved" (Wicker, 1975: 219).

Social relationships, in the thought of the Europeans, were always asymmetrical, but they were orderly. In the feudal system all knights outranked all peasants. All lords outranked all clergy. In the case of the Attica riot, there could be no toleration of the disorder of prisoners, who held the rank of peasants holding hostages who ranked above them. Would mutinous privates be allowed to hold their lieutenants and captains hostage? Neither custom nor law would approve of it because order demanded that the social responsibilities be reversed. Even if lives had to be lost to make the point, order would be preserved and, those best fit to manage the prisons were to be restored to their rightful positions.

The greatest difficulty the South faced was not being defeated in battle, but the change in the social relationships that came in the wake of the Civil War. Not all Southerners took the loss with the equanimity of a Scarlett O'Hara, who decided to swallow her pride and pick her own cotton, since there were no longer any slaves to do it. The war caused a leveling of relationships that so contradicted the long in-grown attitudes regarding social rank that the Southerners began immediately to try to rearrange society to return it to the order and predictability of the prewar structure. The stuff of novel writings of the South place emphasis upon persons out of order. The situations of individuals who are out of their places dictated by tradition give novels like *Gone with the Wind, Uncle Tom's Cabin, Huckleberry Finn,* and *Black Boy* their dynamic character.

The new sociology seeks to return general sociology to a discussion within the liberal arts tradition of topics that are more contemporary. By so doing, it will infuse excitement into the discipline. The way will be opened to approach the discipline from a variety of directions that allows degrees of rigorous thought and methodologies to be exhibited. Many of the topics in this work have been presented to students who have found them stimulating and informative. Students report that this type of sociology provides the opportunity for great flexibility in course arrangement and presentation. Material is presented as propositions rather than as canonical conclusions.

The order that the sociological view of the world demands is based upon the feudal notion of order in asymmetrical relationships. Thus, it is not Weber's (1946) "Science as a Vocation" essay that became a prescription for the conduct of science—a canon prescribing scientific and ethical neutrality. Instead, it was a neutrality that found its roots in the social relationships of feudalism. Then, a lower social rank could bring no charge against a higher one. The relationship of a higher rank to a lower one was always paternalistic, even symbolically. It took a long time before men of high rank generally had to account for their hostile actions against men of lower rank.

A famous diva soprano from a southern state felt pressure to give symbolic obeisance to her older-aged supporters whenever she went to the town. Formerly aristocratic people, they continued to "outrank" the talented singer, whose fame was worldwide. They were remnants of a social order reminiscent of the feudal structure of the encomiendas that Spain exported to the New World. In the encomienda system, old aristocratic families were given land in the New World, and the people who ordinarily worked the land became their private property. The encomendero, or head of the hacienda, was the nominal protector of the people he owned.

The author alone assumes complete responsibility for the general thesis offered herein. Several terms are used practically interchangeably in this work. They are *new sociology*, *American sociology*, and *twenty-first-century sociology*. They refer to the discipline as it separates from the older European variety. It will retain some of the old, but much of the old will be discarded in favor of the new, more distinctly American variety.

Finding that terms referring to human coloration are poor descriptors of race, the terms *Anglo, Euro,* and *European* are substituted for *white*. In many places *Afro*, *African*, and *African-American* are used to denote persons of those ancestries.

I wish to thank a few persons for assisting me in this work in ways they did not know. Although I had been gathering thoughts on the work for several years, it was only in 1991 that my work began in earnest. With the help of my chairperson, William Schwab, Dean Bernard Madison of the College of Arts and Sciences, and other administrators at the University of Arkansas, I was permitted to take off a semester to serve as Visiting Distinguished Professor of Sociology at Washington State University. It was Marilyn Ihinger-Tallman, chair of the department there, who had enough confidence in my ability to suggest that I fill that position. The reduced teaching load in a setting in which I was not so well known enabled me to do some concentrated thinking, research, and writing. Washington State University discussions with faculty members, graduate students, and occasional other visiting disciplinarians permitted further testing of my ideas. Talmadge Anderson was particularly helpful in offering very useful criticism.

I have presented papers on these ideas at various professional association meetings and these ideas have been critiqued. Harold Wilson of the University of Wisconsin, Milwaukee, has found these ideas very stimulating, and I hope useful. We learn from each other as we cross swords over interpretations at the association meetings.

I wish to thank Steven Worden at the University of Arkansas for acting as devil's advocate in the many discussions we have had over concepts and approaches to the general topic of "the discipline," of which this work is an example. Judith Hammond has been very helpful in providing alternative interpretations of ideas, which led to some sobering on my part.

Jeanie Wyant spared no effort in helping put this work into a readable, integrated, and professional form. She does not know of how much load she relieved me. I thank her for her valuable assistance. Laura Clark, at Greenwood, has been most patient through this demanding process. Generous thanks to Narraca Stubblefield and Mary Brohammer for working tirelessly on this project.

My chairperson, Patricia Koski, deserves thanks for finding funds from who knows where to allay and defray the costs of the prosecution of this work. Without her encouragement the process would have been much more difficult and certainly discouraging.

Izola Preston I save to thank last. She has listened patiently, researched untiringly, and helped with conceptualization to a degree that I cannot repay. Her encouragement toward seeing the work to completion cannot be overemphasized.

Gordon Daniel Morgan
University of Arkansas
Fayetteville

1

A New Sociology Needed

American sociology grew out of European sociology, whose concerns were with such matters as status and social class. These were important realities in Europe, where land was at a premium and where upward social mobility was almost impossible. Europeans understood their places. They were nobles, gentry, or peasants, reflecting in their stations the general system that had been in place since the Dark Ages. Tradition, rank, privilege, status, estate, and eventually class were the dominant concepts that were transferred from Europe with the birth of American sociology.

Although there had been important changes in European society before, it was probably the French Revolution that most promoted the development of sociology in Europe. More than 50 years after the revolution, Auguste Comte, a contender for the status as the founder of modern sociology, was fascinated to why French peasants revolted when they were so steeped in status and hierarchy.[1] They had so many layers of authority and tradition over them that they had little need to make decisions themselves.

The intention in this book is to show how the main features of European sociology, as represented by Comte and those who followed in his tradition, became entrenched in America and, indirectly, in much of world sociological thought. It will be argued that those features of European society which were so ingrained had little relevance in the New World context, especially in North America and the United States. The philosophical foundation upon which American sociology (essentially modern sociology) was built was more European than American and therefore made little impact upon American social thought. Because of the lack of agreement between the American and European social contexts, a new sociology is required for America. It is necessary to examine briefly the European social situation in order to understand better the claim for a new twenty-first-century sociology.

The opening of the New World in 1492 substantially destroyed the status system in much of western Europe. The process had been set in motion several centuries earlier when Europeans began to trek to the Middle East in Crusades with the hope of dislodging the Turks from the Holy Land. The Crusades were instrumental in establishing town culture, a culture of the bourgeoisie, who were not directly tied to the landlords for their sustenance. When the New World began to attract immigrants from Europe, nearly all old status arrangements were practically destroyed, or greatly modified, although there were attempts in the new provinces to reestablish the Old World order.[2]

Europe, now in the grips of the Industrial Revolution, found society in a state of transition where all previous social arrangements were in flux. European sociology, then the only sociology seeking to objectively understand the relationships of groups to each other, exhibited a primary concern with order. Any unpredictable behavior of groups of people was viewed as abnormal, to be avoided or suppressed. Any deviation from established order was thought to be an invitation to chaos.

Early European scholars hand difficulty thinking outside the confines of order as represented by rank, status, and class. Hereditary, secular, religious aristocracies, occupations based on status, and systems of religious dignity meant that Europeans were always very conscious of where they were, where others were, and what was thought to be appropriate behavior. Comte, of course, thought the central problem of sociology was that of order, discipline, and appropriateness. Everyone had a place set by custom or social rank. It made little difference which variable imposed it so long as order was maintained.

European society had been structured this way for literally hundreds of years. There was little expectation of upward mobility for most. The basis for it did not exist for perhaps the majority of the people. Classes came to be as much the thought of the common man as of the ranking lords, bishops, earls, barons, kings, and queens. Perhaps the single book which suggested European fascination with order was *Robert's Rules of Order*—published long after the idea of order and place were entrenched—which specifies the absolute procedures under which the most heated debate is to take place.[3]

In the mid-1800s when sociology was transplanted to America, although there were not the concerns of European society, there was a tendency to see America in terms in which European society was viewed. Even though there were many more opportunities for moving out of old European class and rank structures, individualism had taken hold and the question of order not so pressing, American sociology adopted the primary problem of European sociology, that of social order. That preoccupation caused Americans to focus on matters of status, class, rank, and order.

The openness of the American frontier meant that persons who did not like the impositions of New England and the Atlantic seaboard could move West and exhibit considerably more individuality. Many went into the mountains and became separated from European concerns with rank and hereditary social positions.[4] By the time that America's first great sociology department (that of the University of Chicago) made its presence felt, the emerging discipline had fully adopted the language, reasoning, and methodology of its European predecessors. Robert E. Park and Ernest W. Burgess tried to give focus to the discipline:

> The most important facts that sociologists have to deal with are opinions (attitudes and sentiments,) but until students learn to deal with opinions as the biologists deal with organisms, that is, to dissect them—reduce them to their component elements, describe them, and define the situation (environment) to which they are a response—we must not expect very great progress in sociological science.[5]

For a long time it was fashionable to bring European professors to the shores of America to teach sociology, for they seemed to have a better philosophical understanding of the nature of class and status than Americans. The harder their names were to call the deeper their understanding was assumed to be.[6]

Why Europeans were concerned with status and order is clear, but not so clear is why the Americans had the same concern. Everything seemed to change rapidly in America. Even Puritanism, with its heavy emphasis on sparse physical comforts and the rejection of personal enjoyment of any good fortune lasted less than 75 years.[7] By the 1920s Max Weber had convinced American sociologists that the Protestant ethic, the ethic of worldly asceticism, was generally operative in American society and owed its origins to the influence of the Puritans.[8] Fortunes were being made and lost in short order. Few seemed to obey the rules of status which were applicable in Europe. There was order in American society, but it was not imposed by the realities of class and status that had applied for centuries in Europe.

Only in certain parts of the country, especially the Old South, did the old European values of status, class, and rank mean much, although bluebloodism tried to get established everywhere. Southern society remained relatively static largely because of the imposition of slavery, which destroyed any motivation toward personal improvement. Even though slaves were prohibited from general improvement, there were others from Europe who objected very strenuously to any attempts to reestablish in the New World the boundaries operative in the Old World. Order had to be maintained by fearful and forceful means, for there was little inclination to follow a path of reasoning or action because the traditionalism of the past dictated it.

Americans came from a variety of cultures and there was little unanimity on how anyone should behave. America was expansive enough that people who did not appreciate the culture of others could move away into the frontier. They were trying to escape the rules of rank and status in Europe and they resisted their reestablishment in America.

Even by the mid-1800s when large fortunes began to be made, the fortune-makers did not necessarily have higher status than the more common folks. As late as the mid-1800s an American president had to stand up on a steamboat ride because no one would give him a seat.[9] Allowing common folks to purchase land, establish farms, practice trades, open businesses, gain education, and eventually the extending of the franchise to ordinary people, defeated the move to install class as a critical variable in American social life.

Sociology in Europe stressed the relatively static features of society: class, structures, norms, values, institutions, patterns, rules, culture. These do not change very rapidly. European sociology taught that culture has a high degree of predictability. Men like William Graham Sumner who so heavily influenced American sociology were schooled in European thought; he reasoned and taught in terms of the statics of mores, values which had been in existence so long they were viewed as right.[10] Emile Durkheim was so enamored of the idea of regularity in society that he argued that when values and practices change too rapidly they create a sense of anomie, a feeling of helplessness, a sense that all is lost because the old standards cannot be emphasized.[11] Even Karl Marx saw European classes harden to the extent that they could only be changed by revolution.[12]

Ferdinand Toennies was so impressed with the way that European society worked that he could offer two concepts that became part of the lexicon of American sociology students taking the introductory course. Those terms are *gemeinschaft* and *gesellschaft*, translated roughly as "community" and "society."[13] In the former, the emphasis is on feelings which are present because of close associations and appreciations of the values of those of the community. Village life, where status and rank were acknowledged and widely respected, corresponded to a *gemeinschaft*. Urban life, with its impersonal relationships based largely upon a division of labor, without people feeling for others as they do in the village community, was a gesellschaft. Although very few students utilize these terms in daily discussion or even scholarly research, they continue to hold dominant places in American general sociology classes.

Americans could not easily break away from the emphasis the Europeans brought to sociology. Indeed, as late as the 1940s, one was thought improperly trained in most fields, particularly sociology, unless some time had been spent in the classroom or in a seminar of some European thinker perceived as outstanding. American sociology was seen as inferior to that of Europe. The roots of European sociology were found in the relative statics of class, status, and rank. If these could be understood it was thought, society could be understood. With European scholars practically dictating the concerns of American sociology, it was not long before American sociology mirrored the European concerns.

But America had a more dynamic society than Europe. Rank, status, and class meant less in the New World than practically anywhere else in the world. People read books about the rich and famous because they were curious about how they lived, not because they acceded deference to their class. Scholars, nevertheless, tried to describe America in terms of the concepts the European scholars had used to describe European society, even though the conditions in which the two societies operated were vastly different. By borrowing the concepts from European scholars and applying them to the American case, considerable error was inevitable. For example, scholars began discovering social classes in nearly all places, many of them unlikely. James West discovered social classes in tiny Ozarks Mountains towns.[14] Mozell Hill found class in small towns with black sections in Georgia and Oklahoma.[15] Robert and Helen Lynd had found class systems in Middletown in the 1930s.[16] It is possible that these scholars were using borrowed but inappropriate conceptual tools by which to attempt to understand American society.

For nearly 100 years American sociology sought to become a mirror image of European sociology despite the fact that the problems of America were greatly different from those of Europe. American sociology was more problem centered, whereas European sociology focused on topics pertaining to the maintenance of status and rank. But it was with the tools the Europeans bequeathed that the Americans sought to analyze their problems. There was no single problem in America as class was thought to be in Europe where class conflict existed only in a few places, notably in France during its revolution in the 1780s and in Russia during its revolution of 1917.

The influence of the primary problem-minded European sociology caused the Americans likewise to seek a single problem, though there were many. The status of black Americans, many former slaves, became the focus of perhaps the largest segment of American sociology even though this problem did not fully excite the imaginations of the majority of American sociologists.

Sociology in America began as a subject taught by a few obscure professors in some of the more progressive schools of the time. It was interesting but evidently was not taken too seriously either by the schools where it was offered or by the students who listened to the lectures. The break of American sociology from its European predecessors was not accomplished because of great theoretical or methodological disagreements among the scholars. It was probably the loss of World War I by Germany that caused a sharp questioning of the credibility of European scholarship, even that of the English and French.

The social theories and practices that had gained the fore in Germany, in particular, are viewed as suspect or totally unworkable in America. The sociology of the Continent could not be transported to the American shores where the general environment—physical and social—was not receptive to it. Nevertheless, for some time obeisance was given to scholars trained in the European tradition. European society had tended to see its problems as matters of status and rank, and even of evolution. The social Darwinism of the 1850s was consistent with colonialism then widely practiced by nearly all western European nations. The so-called backward peoples of the world were no match for the technologically more sophisticated Europeans, and so their lands were taken over, the people largely subjugated. Reasons had to be found to justify these actions, and they were located mainly in the emergent evolutionary doctrines that held sway on into the early twentieth century.

Another important reason for breaking with European sociology was the relatively high cost of returning to Europe to study. The main force of European scholars began to leave soon before and after World War I, although many left long before. Many European scholars found ready acceptance in American colleges, where European degrees and accents had higher status than American degrees from the best American universities. Standard English was less professorial, it seemed, than broken or accented English. A number of colleges and universities had already opened in America to provide the growing population with preachers, teachers, lawyers, and doctors. Many of these were religiously based institutions, but the trend was toward secularization. Education was becoming competitive, and institutions tried to outdo each other in attracting the most exclusive clientele. A worship of European-trained teachers remained although there were not enough for all of the schools to have some on their staffs. The elite system of education in Europe meant that only a few scholars were turned out, and the few American colleges able to attract European scholars considered themselves unique. Older, more prestigious universities and colleges had relatively high proportions of European scholars or Americans who had been trained in European schools. Those colleges with more European scholars did most to preserve the idea of the superiority of European scholarship.

By the early 1900s colleges were opening nearly everywhere in the country. The Morrill Act of 1862, which gave a big impetus to public higher education, was taking hold and education was coming within the reach of the more typical citizen.[17] Large state universities began to appear on the scene as well as a variety of special schools. The demand for collegiate education was so great that little consideration could be paid to the emphasis upon European educational traditions. These hundreds of schools had to be staffed, and teachers were pressed into service without the finishing European study assumedly provided. America had to produce its own specialists, although Europe would continue to produce persons who came to America to provide some colleges with a sense of eliteness.

Sociology was an interesting field, addressing a number of questions which captivated the students. As many topics came up, sociologies of this or that became commonplace. Despite all this activity and growth, little unified the field of sociology until after World War I, when black people became rather restive in the cities and in the rural areas of the South. The social sciences were turned to for answers to some of the problems. Sociologists and social workers seemed the academics most commonly sought to provide answers to the problems.

The field of sociology received its first real growth with the entry of the first wave of black scholars who saw an opportunity to study society while applying their knowledge to changing the conditions of the disadvantaged.

When they began to study and write, mainly after World War I, sociology was connected to a major problem that all Americans seemed to face. That problem was the position, advancement, prosperity, and future of the African American population. Closely related to this problem was that of immigrants who were experiencing difficulty assimilating into American society.

The focus of European sociology upon class and caste served to build between groups and even whole societies barriers that proved extremely difficult to penetrate. Disharmony and conflict were exacerbated, developing into non-cooperation, depressions, wars, and eventual mass destruction of some societies. Class thought resulted in justification of slavery, colonialism, and classification of countries as developed and underdeveloped. This thought promoted the fragmentation of peoples into ethnic groups that bargained and negotiated, eventually fighting for their own freedom and place in the societies of which they were a part. This thought promoted the idea that no two groups could exist or work together without asymmetrical or unequal social arrangements.

Following a philosophy developed in the Middle Ages, European social thought reflected revolutions in physical science thought. The studies of Isaac Newton, perhaps the most outstanding of the new physicists of the seventeenth century, had a slow effect upon social thought. Newton's concept of universal forces such as gravity and its effects upon holding large particles of nature in place was bound eventually to be reflected in how philosophers thought about society. Social philosophy had to find a few concepts that could be applied to society. The forces of nature, the tides, the rising of the sun and the moon, the seasons, the comings and goings of heavenly bodies in their orbits, all appeared to be factors over which humankind had little control. They were facts of nature, and their regularity was so ordinary that predictability need not occur. The task for Newton was to explain an occurrence which common sense taught would happen regardless of the inaccuracy of a prediction. The tides would come in and go out if a prediction were 180 degrees wrong.

Social philosophy began to think about the seemingly unchanging and therefore most predictable features of society. Whether called castes or estates, there were classes in all societies, and they worked roughly the same way in all of them. Those at the top of the social structure received more of that which was considered desirable than those at the bottom. This large force, or class, began to have the same place in social philosophy as gravity held in Newtonian physics. Since stratification was likely to occur, the idea was easy to promote that it, like energy, could neither be created nor destroyed, even though its form might change.

European social philosophy, which developed into sociology, thus concentrated on a hunt for the elements of an enduring system in society. Scholars built social systems, even in their minds, with those elements that enabled them to explain, or more strictly, justify, whatever action they observed as taking place in the societies they studied. By the time of Auguste Comte, the influence of Newtonian physics upon social philosophy came to rest in Comte's plea to use the means of science to study and understand society. He called for the opening of sociology as positive philosophy or social physics.

Newton, who understood the harmony of the natural world, found that there were individuals who were antiscientific who insisted upon promoting the idea that nature was disorderly. Newton's unifying natural force which he called gravity, was so elemental that it could be mathematicized as a function of distance and mass. Gravity worked, but its features were fundamentally unknown.

Social philosophy, being highly impressed with the success of Newtonian physics, began to look for a few factors of social life which would have the same effect of gravity, but social philosophers were unable to divorce themselves from the social structures of which they were a part. Most were members of what they perceived as upper classes. They dichotomized society, making it disorderly and disunified. Physicists, understanding the dynamism of change, came to discuss matter in terms of electrical charges, escaping strangling ties to the statics of large particle physics. The discipline and theory of physics functioned outside the attitude and value systems of individuals. It made little difference what the values of physicists were, for natural phenomena would continue to operate according to natural laws. What they taught could effect what people thought but not basically how the physical world operated.

Controlling social science thought had an effect upon how the world was socially constructed.[18] Marx had taught long after Newton that the world was divided into two warring classes—an idea that had no analog in the natural world. Social science was frightened by the concept of a harmonious nature. Physicists could have dichotomized the world to fit their preset notions or to accord with their placement in it, but the discipline did not lend itself to this form of reasoning. Understanding the physical world could not be done on an ethnocentric basis, for it would operate according to its own laws no matter what any individual thought.

Newtonian physics stressed gravity as a universal force. Sociology stressed culture as its universal force. As gravity caused celestial bodies to behave in particular ways, the social philosophers taught that culture makes societies behave in particular ways. There was a single gravitational field in which all physical matter operated, the strength of the gravitational pull being affected by distance and mass. Social science's explanatory concept, culture, operated differently even in the same environment. To remedy this fact, social science began to add pillars to its edifice to strengthen and qualify the inconsistencies created by the application of their universal concept of culture.

There was never a major critique of European sociology in terms of its ability to answer problems germane to the American scene. Instead, U.S. scholars tended to open new fields, essentially wiring around the European paradigms. These old paradigms were left standing more out of courtesy to the Europeans than out of a belief that they had currency in contemporary American life. The European way of analysis had become part of customary sociology as presented in America.

By contrast, social science, including sociology, is not an attempt to understand the operations of society but to effect its operation by controlling its structure. Thus Comte felt that society could be controlled by the application of social science knowledge. That accumulation of knowledge became the basis of the new science of sociology.

American scholars were willing to deviate from the European paradigms to establish their own, which would speak more to the reality of the American social situation. It was difficult, though, for American scholars to attain higher degrees, especially the doctorate, without giving obeisance to the suzerainty of European sociology. As late as the 1970s master and doctoral students were structuring their thought and studies around the paradigms that had been bequeathed by the Europeans. Serious sociology was somehow conceived generally as that cast within a framework approved or utilized by the old European masters.

The European scholars' perception of the relatively static nature of European society was important in their encouragement of the major paradigms which today dominate American sociology. The functionalist perspective, for example, with its emphasis upon societal parts and their equilibrium or balance in making up systems, grew out of the basic hostility toward change that elitist European sociologists promulgated.

Men like Bronislaw Malinowski were impressed with primitive society but analyzed it roughly with concepts applicable to the European societies with which they were familiar. Malinowski practically admitted as much when he stated that primitive man is not merely a slave of custom, but like any civilized Christian businessperson, primitive man will engage in any self-gratifying behavior that he can get by with.[19] Malinowski thought there were rules of reciprocity that were always at work, necessitating that people do their duties if they wanted to receive from others. Equilibrium was kept through a system of reciprocal relationships understood and respected by the people of the society.

What Malinowski found in savage society he had already discovered in European society, namely, that people understood what they were supposed to do and, in so understanding, did those jobs and activities without much complaining. But Malinowski knew what he should do in his society just as surely as he assumed the native savage knew what to do in his. His inability to talk beyond a superficial level with the native precluded his knowing what the native thought, and so he was left to interpret the native's activities and values in his own framework. Neither anthropologists such as Malinowski nor contemporary social science scholars have been able to free themselves from the system of which they are a part in order to view more objectively their own roles, which they have, no doubt, internalized.

Talcott Parsons was a product of European social thought. He attempted to define society as a social system approximately as his European mentors had done. His focus on social order and structure reflected his deep sense of place which had been enhanced by his European experience. Parsons stressed that whatever pattern has been prevalent in a social system will seek to be maintained with mechanisms for the management of tensions within that system. He thought that the society will persist if many individuals are imbued with the basic values the prevailing culture emphasizes.[20]

Scholars such as C.W. Mills[21] and Alvin Gouldner[22] bitterly attacked the philosophical and theoretical position of Parsons who was perhaps the best representative of the entrenchment of European sociology in America. It would be difficult to summarize briefly the thought of Talcott Parsons, who authored more than twenty-four books. One thing seems clear enough from his numerous inquiries, and that is his hunt for order and structure in society. Stability, system, structure, order, and change seem dominant topics in his many books.[23] Mills and Gouldner seemed more interested in demonstrating that Parsons was personally wrong than in critiquing the edifice of European sociology.

The entrenchment of European sociology has been so strong that other scholars trying to advance alternative views of the world have been forced outside the mainstream of the discipline. The subfields slow to emphasize the primacy of European sociology were viewed as not quite sociology at all. Symbolic interaction, based largely upon the work of the interactionist school, which owed so much to American scholars such as George Herbert Mead and Charles Horton Cooley, in time, began to establish a place alongside functionalist and conflict perspectives. The meanings which actors give to events and symbols could not be overlooked in the teachings of this school. It recognized that there was a certain degree of fluidity and process involved in social relations. For the interactionists nothing was set in hard and fast boundaries. Both functionalist and conflict perspectives seemed consistent with the European concept of order, regularity, and structure. Functionalism stressed the need for equilibrium based on a very small amount of social change. Nearly any activity was found to have a function if the practice persisted over time. Institutions thus had foundations, and analysis would show that they contributed to the maintenance of the social structure, according to the functionalist perspective.

The symbolic interactionists modified the functionalist logic and stressed that meanings are processual; that is, the meaning of an act may be different from time to time. Dynamism was considered a feature of modern society and meanings could change. In contrast, both functionalist and conflict perspectives took feelings out of the social equation. People related to each other mainly out of reciprocal arrangements. People owed each other for society was essentially a quid pro quo relationship. Just as the parts of a machine have no feelings toward the other parts, depending only on them for exercise of their own function, people carry on in a similar fashion. They are basically unconcerned about the welfare of any but themselves.

Conflict likewise is impersonal, and some individuals may not realize that a struggle is taking place. It is so real and so subtle that only in unusual cases will the individuals representing the conflicting classes automatically associate a random person with the conflict. Even in the Old South, where whites often attacked blacks whenever they thought they needed a lesson in social placement, relationships did not always have all the features of conflict. Not all whites felt the same way about all blacks and not all blacks had a singular negative attitude toward all whites.

Attempts were made to summarize the characteristics of the groups—saying, for instance, "Whites do such and such and blacks do such and such"—failed. These attempts failed because neither group could be so characterized. In an ideal conflict relationship people would, like soldiers on a battlefield, need ask no questions once they saw someone in the uniform of the enemy. They have been trained to "shoot first and ask questions later." In the South conflict pitted groups against each other to the extent that there could be no resolution of the problem until one group was eliminated.

Conflict theory assumed such a rigid and inflexible social structure that American sociology had to modify the theory greatly. Social processes were introduced, possibly to preserve the conflict perspective, for there was reluctance to reconsider its cogency in the context of American society. To do so would mean a substantial revision of the thought of Marx, one of the European masters. That was unlikely. There was a great feeling that these masters had to be included for sociology to have prominence. Accommodation, assimilation, stratification, annihilation, marginality, and other adjustments were introduced to give some flexibility to the conflict perspective, which alone could not adequately describe or explain American life. Not every person in a lower class was against every person in an upper class which would be the expected relationship predicted in classic conflict theory.

The attempt to fit the concepts of European sociology to the social landscape of America was evident in the focus of European scholars on America's major social problem—that of slavery and its aftermath. Slavery had existed in the Latin American colonies for nearly 100 years by the time it was introduced into North America in 1621. Justification had to be given in Spain and Portugal, both of which had been leaders in overseas colonization. They were eventually supplanted by the northwestern Europeans, particularly France, England, Holland, and Denmark. Much of their justification came from scholars, a number of whom were clergymen, mobile in the Catholic Church hierarchy. Individual pastors might have railed against slavery, but there was no movement among them that seriously challenged the pope's general approval of slavery. Indeed, much of the wealth of the Church was based upon income from colonies where laborers were severely underpaid, if paid at all. The religious conversion of the natives in the colonial provinces had a lower priority than their working in the fields and mines to deliver the wealth needed to enhance the living conditions of the burghers back in the cities of Europe. Although scholars may have personally disagreed with the doctrines supporting slavery, they were perhaps too intimidated by the power of the Church to dare say anything against it. Martin Luther could hit the Church for its sale of indulgences but really got in trouble when he held that the Scriptures were the only basis upon which doctrines could be based.[24]

When introduced in North America, slavery was not a burning issue in Europe. It was not universally condemned by even the Quakers and Puritans—some of the first to reach American shores seeking religious freedom. Scholars, were fearful of the power of religious authorities, although some kings and queens had broken from Rome to establish their own state churches. Thus they remained silent, for the most part, on the question of slavery if they did not openly endorse it.

Religious scholarship seemed to have served secular interests by failing to criticize the institution of slavery, which it could have easily done by citing the biblical prescriptions by which so many claimed to live. Again, there was never much attempt to bring personal feelings, based on religious understanding, in line with personal practice. Slavery could be reconciled with religious teachings by separating action and thought into two compartments—the religious and the secular. Any activity became justifiable if done under the name of religion and not prohibited by law. If a man felt that he should hold slaves, the state had no right to interfere. Individual choice was said to be a cornerstone of the Protestant Reformation; there was no need to rely upon any other authority than personal interpretation of the Scriptures to justify an action the law did not prohibit. If the law prohibited an action which the group felt was correct, or forced obedience to a law that was not correct, they had a right to repeal those laws. The Reformation had helped create the atmosphere in which individuals could choose both their religion and morality.

By the time of the opening of America, the foundation had been laid for the acceptance of slavery as a matter of personal morality, falling outside the domain of religious consideration. Slavery need not be attacked by scholars, almost all of whom were religious, for the economic activities of men were not generally of concern from a religious viewpoint. It was not religion which raised slavery to a matter of conscience, though men like Bishop William Wilberforce in England were important in the anti-slavery movement.

The great churchmen, Charles, John, and William Wesley, tried to show the inconsistencies between slaveholding and religion in the late 1700s but they could not make of their view a great moral issue. Their academic language prohibited their books from reaching a wide readership, thereby limiting their influence. Harriet Beecher Stowe, the journalist, was probably more influential. Her *Uncle Tom's Cabin* (1852), sharply dichotomized the issue of slavery, making it a matter of conscience and converting it to an issue with important religious significance.

When sociology made its way to America in the period after the Civil War, there was such attention given to the European features of the discipline—concern with structure and order—that little interest was shown the most significant problem facing the nation, namely, the role and status of the former slaves. European sociology had already set the framework for thinking about this problem by bowing to evolutionary thought which had developed around Darwinism. Marx had also helped to demoralize the issue by stressing the impersonality of class struggle.

Evolutionary thought was acceptable to the Americans for it stressed the natural processes which, through competition for survival rendered various groups, if unequal, at least specialized in their struggle for existence. No animal, however weak, was without compensating survival features, and even the strongest had a number of vulnerabilities. If native peoples were not so smart intellectually or technologically, they were gifted with feelings and emotions that were the envy of the more developed peoples.[25]

The developed and undeveloped peoples then needed each other as complements. The strong could not exist without the week any more than the weak could exist without the strong. Species survival in the animal kingdom meant a relationship between the species. When scholars such as Herbert Spencer and William Graham Sumner applied evolutionary thought to the human condition, alleging that some groups were located variously on the evolutionary ladder, groups at the lower rungs were equated with being lower in evolutionary development.[26]

Social class thought was acceptable to the Americans for intellectual purposes for the same reason that evolutionary thought was acceptable to the Europeans. The data of American existence showed that many persons had risen from very lowly positions to those of great respect and affluence. They were not happy with the idea of an inflexible class structure as hypothesized by Marx. However, the maintenance of class was important in the thought of American social scientists who had greatly accepted the concepts of European thought. The erection of a conceptual caste system allowed for the maintenance of class while excluding a whole category of former slaves from ordinary association with those of supposedly higher caste.

Neither evolutionary nor class reasoning placed the problem of black freedmen on a moral level. That problem was left on a structural plane beyond the ability of groups to affect it. It was treated as a constitutional issue in which states could give the blacks as few or as many rights as they chose. Since their placement was neither a moral problem nor a problem of conscience, essentially people dictated order be preserved according to the requirements of European social science.

Certain views come to dominate as explanations of social behavior. For most of the existence of humankind, not much effort was devoted to explaining such behavior. There was occasional study, but much behavior was explained intuitively. The intuitive, self-evident, impressionistic view controlled by local concepts of good, right, and appropriate held sway essentially until the nineteenth century, when Comte suggested a positivistic or scientific study of behavior. Ibn Khaldun, the fourteenth century Arab scholar, had much earlier brought objective analyses to an understanding of society.[27] Because Khaldun did not found a school of believers and followers, the intuitive view continued until

Comte attempted to change that view to one with scientific, objective foundations. Other European scholars who thought of social behavior as having a scientific basis did not make much impact upon the people, and the intuitive view was promulgated. Social behavior was easily understood by all, according to the intuitive view, and sane people could agree upon the standards by which human conduct was to be judged. There was little to study and no need to fret over why groups acted the way they did.

The first major nonmilitary attempt to have the entire world adopt a common standard of behavior and ethics came with the rise of Christianity. The teachings of Jesus proposed a simple doctrine against which almost no one could argue. It provided flexibility to handle a variety of problems of living. The conversion of much of the world to Jesus' ethical and moral code established it as considered intuitively correct. Individual or group behavior could be judged against how closely behavior followed the cardinal teachings of Jesus. Other major religions tried the same tack, some before Christianity and some after, but few had the success of Christianity. As with other faiths, zeal led to the use of force in the conversion process, in many cases. It seemed to many Westerners that there was something intuitively correct about the moral teachings of Christianity.

Indeed, intuition became synonymous with common sense. It provided an easily graspable understanding of behavior and remained an unchallenged rationale until well into the nineteenth century. Of course, men and women not liking their lot rebelled or made life difficult for those retarding their progress or change. Most, however, disguised their dislike and put up silently, sullenly, or affectedly, with the problems they faced. Colonials, for instance, may have acted as if they supported the practices of the colonizers. They simply preserved appearances.

When after seemingly having internalized their roles people violated them, intuition was defeated and new explanations called for. When, for instance, a prince decided to consort with a commoner in defiance of tradition, or a peasant began to aspire to land her or his children might one day own, the mold was broken. People were torn from their social grooves, and a revolution occurred. Common sense said these rulebreakers were crazy, criminal, deviant, misguided, and so on. Common sense—intuition—often taught that people customarily found niches and social roles befitting themselves in which they were comfortable. Ordinarily there has been little evidence of discomfort with the roles assigned.

The intuitive view taught that people will continue to do what they have been doing unless acted upon by another force. There may be external or internal generators of force. Whenever social change threatens the impetus to it may be nullified, thereby returning the group to its former status and behavior. Thus, the British could place a price on the heads of rebels like Patrick Henry and Nathan Hale and remove the engine of revolutionary fervor from the American colonies. Britain could jail Mohondas K. Ghandi, thereby removing the driving force toward change in Indian colonialism. Yankee teachers serving to raise the ambitions of former slaves could be discouraged and eventually removed from the South causing the former slaves to return for a time to their earlier limited lives. These examples illustrate the intuitive view that change must have a generator, one most commonly external to the group. Moses' leadership of the Children of Israel is consistent with the intuitive view: Moses was trained outside the Hebrew tradition, yet by being nursed by his real mother, a slave, he early internalized the hopes for freedom of the Children of Israel.

A new pantheon was proposed by American observers who felt that the social science disciplines were not adequately describing the American social scene. Sociology, as it was practiced did not provide opportunities for enough change to satisfy American sentiments. Some wanted the order of social class, whereas others sought to persuade the people that much more change was taking place than admitted by those wed to the European paradigms.

New gods of the social sciences were beginning to dot the field as early as the 1930s. They were called muckrakers because they were so insistent in their critiques of the upper classes. Thorstein Veblen's *Theory of the Leisure Class* (1899) was only one of the important books which sought to make fun of Americans mimicking the upper classes of Europe. Veblen was quickly characterized as a nonconformist, and his mobility became shaky as he tried to teach and write within the American university setting, a setting still very closely tied to dominant European thought.[28]

NOTES

1. Auguste Comte, *The Positive Philosophy*, vol. I (London: Trubner, 1853) gives some history of the reasons why Comte was concerned with the need for a new discipline of group conduct. Theodore M. Newcomb notes that there may not be consensus as to who founded the discipline but there is certainly no disconsensus on an important aspect of the subject matter, consensus and collective features of group life. See Theodore M. Newcomb, "The Study of Consensus," in Robert K. Merton, Leonard Broom, and Leonard S. Cottrell, Jr., *Sociology Today* (New York: Basic Books, Inc., 1959), pp. 177-292.

2. The Spaniards and Portuguese, for instance, were successful in emplacing the encomienda system based on landholding and the various tenure arrangements, especially in Latin America and the Caribbean. See William Claypole and John Robottom, *Caribbean Story: Book One: Foundations* (Essex, England: Longman Caribbean, 1990), p. 14. Latin American labor problems in the highland regions of Spanish America evolved through the encomienda, repartimento, and debt peonage. In each of these stages, the workers remained in ranks tied variously to their landlords. Some of the land grants of haciendas and fazendas exceeded one million acres and some were larger in size than European states. See E. Bradford Burns, *Latin America: A Concise Interpretive History*, 4th ed. (Englewood Cliffs, NJ: Prentice-Hall, 1986), pp. 36-37. It was much more difficult to establish these arrangements in North America.

3. Sarah Corbin Robert, *Robert's Rules of Order* (Glencoe, IL: Scott, Foresman, 1970).

4. The people of the southern mountains—the Smokies, Ozarks, the Appalachians—became noted as hillbillies, monikers that were hard to dispel.

5. Robert E. Park and Ernest W. Burgess, *Introduction to the Science of Sociology* (Chicago: The University of Chicago Press, 1921), p. vi.

6. Park himself praised European sociology for being deeper, more methodologically sophisticated than the American. He writes, in reference to Georg Simmel, ". . . But Simmel's most important contribution to sociology has never been understood in this country. Although he has written the most profound and stimulating book in sociology, in my opinion, that has ever been written, he was not in the first instance a sociologist but a philosopher. . . . When these writings are fully understood, I am convinced that much of the confusion and uncertainty that now reign in the social sciences will measurably disappear." See Park's reference to Nicholas J. Spykman, *The Social Theory of Georg Simmel* (Chicago: The University of Chicago Press, 1925).

7. Kai T. Erikson, *Wayward Puritans: A Study in the Sociology of Deviance* (New York: John Wiley & Sons, 1966), is an able work which discusses the history and consequences of Puritanism.

8. This is one of the major arguments in Max Weber, *The Protestant Ethic and the Spirit of Capitalism* (1906), translated by Talcott Parsons (New York: Charles Scribner's Sons, 1930).

9. Calvin Coolidge, *The Autobiography of Calvin Coolidge* (New York: Cosmopolitan Book Corporation, 1929).

10. See especially William Graham Sumner, *Folkways* (Ginn, 1906).

11. Emile Durkheim, *Suicide* (translated by George Simpson) (New York: Free Press, 1951), contains the exposition of the concept anomie. Durkheim's work has provoked a great deal of research and commentary. See, for example, Alex Inkeles, "Personality and Social Structure," in Robert K. Merton, Leonard Broom, and Leonard S. Cottrell, Jr., *Sociology Today* (New York: Basic Books, 1959), pp. 249-276.

12. The idea of classic Marxism is that there are two warring classes, the bourgeoisie owners of the means of production and the proletariat, workers who have only their labor to sell and are always in an exploitable position. See *Karl Marx: Selected Writings in Sociology and Social Philosophy* (newly translated by T.B. Bottomore) (New York: McGraw-Hill Book Company, 1956).

13. For a good understanding of these concepts, see Carol A.B. Warren, *Sociology: Change and Continuity* (Homewood, IL: The Dorsey Press, 1977), pp. 70-71.

14. James West, *Plainville, USA* (Chicago: The University of Chicago Press, 1945).

15. Mozell Hill and Bevode C. McCall, "Social Stratification in Georgia Town," *American Sociological Review*, 15 (1950): 721-729.

16. Robert Lynd and Helen Lynd, *Middletown* (New York: Harcourt, Brace & Company, 1929).

17. The history of the Morrill Act is told in many books. For a brief but timely view of this important Act which so greatly affected American education, see Clark Kerr, *The Uses of the University* (New York: Harper Torchbacks, 1963), at many places in this small volume.

18. We use the term "controlling social science" to mean that there is a sort of hierarchy which more or less dictates what is discussed in the discipline of sociology. The control is effected through the publication process where major scholars and their schools have a disproportionate share of discipline influence. For a recent critique of this situation, see Charles J. Sykes, *Profscam* (New York: Harper, 1989).

19. See in Jerry D. Rose, *Introduction to Sociology*, 2nd ed. (Chicago: Rand McNally Publishing Co., 1974), p. 41.

20. Ibid., p. 45.

21. C. Wright Mills, The Sociological Imagination (New York: Oxford University Press, 1959).

22. Alvin Gouldner, *The Coming Crisis in Western Sociology* (New York: Basic Books, 1970).

23. A brief but valuable synthesis of the thought of Parsons regarding order is found in Mark Abrahamson, *Functionalism* (Englewood Cliffs, NJ: Prentice-Hall, 1978).

24. See Ellen G. White, *The Great Controversy* (Phoenix, AZ: Inspiration Books, 1967), p. 112.

25. It is around this idea of complimentarity that developed stereotypes of natives peoples. Any negative qualities they had were offset by some positive ones. No group was all good or all bad.

26. See William E. Leutchenburg and Bernard Wishy, eds., with introduction by Stowe Persons, *Selected Essays of William Graham Sumner: Social Darwinism* (Englewood Cliffs, NJ: Prentice-Hall, 1963), for a synopsis of the thought of William Graham Sumner.

27. Ibn Khaldun (1332-1406), *Muquddimah* (translated by Franz Rosenthal) (1958). See also Rollin Chambliss, *Ibn Khaldun: Social Thought* (1954). The author is deeply indebted to James E. Conyers for writing an excellent unpublished paper on the life of Ibn Khaldun while at Washington State University in 1958-59. A substantial literature has developed on Khaldun. See, for example, Gaston Bouthoul, *Ibn Khaldun; Sa Philosophie Sociale* (Paris: Librairie Oriental Paul Guethner, 1930), and Yves Lacoste, *Ibn Khaldun's The Birth of History and the Part of the Third World* (London: Verso, 1984).

28. Thorstein Veblen, *The Theory of the Leisure Class* (New York: Macmillan, 1899). William Graham Sumner, a founder of American sociology, was an early muckraker and polemicist who came to teach at Yale. He was much impressed with the evolutionary thought of Herbert Spencer, the English scholar who had reasoned along lines which would later become understood as social Darwinism. For a sketch of the life of Spencer, see Jack D. Douglas, *Introduction to Sociology: Situations and Structures* (New York: The Free Press, 1973), p. 43.

2

The Hold of Feudalism Upon Modern Sociology

The fundamental conditioning European intellectual experience was that of the Dark Ages. That period would not have been so psychologically devastating had not its experience corresponded to the rise of other people, especially the followers of Islam, whom the Europeans later had a need to define as somehow unequal to themselves. The 1,000–year European incubation as a backward people was unacceptable to generations of thinkers after the Renaissance. They needed to romanticize the Dark Ages to make the period psychologically acceptable, for there was no human experience that equaled that of the Dark Ages in terms of length and effect upon the psychology of a people.

The late Renaissance writers began the process of revising their view of the Dark Ages by showing that the era embodied excitement, drama, and romanticism. The feudal system, essentially a system of slavery, began to be interpreted as a chivalric, noble enterprise characterized by gallant knights, fair maidens, and courtly mannerisms. William Shakespeare and Sir Walter Scott (*Ivanhoe*) in the British Isles, Alexander Dumas (*The Three Musketeers*) in France, and Cervantes, (*Don Quixote*) in Spain were among those authors trying to present the western European Middle Age in a romantic context.

It was probably the British whom the Dark Ages affected the most psychologically. It is they who did most to romanticize the age. But they could not overcome the hold the Dark Ages had over them. Their social thought began to reflect the structure of feudalism. Even religious thought, seen in the 1611 King James Version of the Holy Bible, showed the influence of feudalism.[1]

During the 1,000 years of darkness, social categories took on qualities of rigidity that had not been seen to that extent before. In the familiar three-caste system of feudalism—nobility, gentry, and peasantry—social placement was lifelong and often hereditary, save for the knighthood and the clergy, celibate groups whose ranks had to be replenished from below. This rigid categorization continued long after feudalism had waned and the New World had opened. There were no undefined individuals in feudalism. All people had to fit into one of the three categories. An essential feature of feudalism, rank likewise became essential in the new social categorization. The categories were separated and ranked with corresponding rights and duties.

This system of thought pervaded European sociology, and when it was transferred to America in the mid-1800s, it became the cornerstone of teaching in American schools. Such thought was not often internalized, though, because there was much less agreement about social categories in America than in Europe in the aftermath of the Dark Ages. Just as science continued to teach that the earth was flat long after it was known to be spherical, so social science continued to teach out of the feudalistic experience of limited social change. Even today categorization is the basic feature of American sociology as it continues to mirror its European parentage of romanticism and rank.

Once the rigid categories were established, preoccupation with their maintenance occurred. Everyone had a place, and looking to see who was out of place became of great concern and even of research. Cinderella's attendance at a dance where she was not invited was as unexpected as Sidney Poitier's being the unexpected and misplaced guest in *Guess Who's Coming to Dinner?*[2] Even Durkheim, the old master, was so steeped in the rigidities of feudal categorization that he taught that when people were out of their assigned category, they were anomic. Catholics who married Jews, Germans who married Italians, Anglos living in neighborhoods of Hispanics, Orientals living among African Americans, and all the children who were the offspring of mixed unions, for examples, were thought to be out of category and therefore psychologically bruised and battered. In modern times, some think that Europeans who want to go to less developed countries to teach do so only under a concept of noblesse oblige. Maintaining one's place seems critical to the European, whose tradition is based on the feudal caste system and whose mind has thus been strongly affected by feudalist thought.[3]

The 1,000-year European experience in the Dark Ages clouded or conditioned thought to the extent that it was next to impossible to break out of the mold of categorization and rank. These were the intellectual tools Europeans brought to the Renaissance and to later intellectuality, and they were the ones transferred to America. Scholarship and the military are just two institutions that mirrored the religious ranks which grew out of and entrenched systems of deference of the Middle Ages.

Similar ranks are found everywhere. The question is what is the social significance of ranks? Are they socially constructed and justified? In the oldest societies, such as China and India, both of which predated Greece and Rome, we find attention to rank and its attendant—power. Rank influence is seen in many of the systems of modern society; the Catholic Church, U.S. higher education, and the U.S. military are highlighted in Table 2.1 merely as illustrations.

Table 2.1
Ranking in Some Systems

Catholic Church	U.S. Higher Education	British Higher Education	Military (U.S. Army)
Pope	Chancellor	Chancellor	Commander-in-Chief
Archbishop	Dean	Professor	General Grade
Bishop	Professor	Reader	Field Grade
Priest	Associate Professor	Senior Lecturer	Company Grade
Monk	Assistant Professor	Lecturer	Noncommissioned Officer
Friar	Instructor	Instructor	
Acolyte	Students	Students	Privates

Military ranks of chivalry had nothing to do with gracious manners and gentlemanly treatment of ladies no matter what some author said about some knight taking off his cloak and placing it over a puddle so that a lady would not get her feet wet in crossing. This story is often associated with Sir Walter Raleigh, really a pirate. Chivalry had more to do with who owned a horse.[4] Knights with horses were "Sirs," commissioned by their landlords.[5] Private soldiers were men owning nothing because of poor status or extreme youth. Young men, privates, were glad enough to run alongside the mounted men, obeying their commands, as students are to run after their erudite professors in pursuit of bachelor's degrees or as youthful law clerks are to follow their eminent barristers and judges. Most of these modern ranks and statuses could be subdivided into grades based upon such factors as tenure and recognition in fields of study.

Other groups did categorize and rank. Before the fall of Rome much of this system was in place. During its heyday the Roman Empire rewarded its conquerors with land grants on the frontiers of the empire. When the empire fell, some officers became landlords and continued the ranking system that had categorized Rome for hundreds of years. Even before, in Old Testament times, categories and ranks had existed. No better example comes to mind than the building of King Solomon's temple in Jerusalem. Operative masonry showed many ranks called Entered Apprentice (common laborers), Fellowcraft (slightly higher), Master Masons (a few highly ranked and skilled men), Grand Masters (supervising many categories of workers), Worshipful Masters, and so on, up to the supervisor of the entire job, say, a Most Worshipful Supreme Grand Master.

Nowhere did this system of ranking settle down in the minds of the people as it did in Europe, where social place became the very measure of the person. The Dark Ages of Europe impressed upon Europeans a sense of inert rigidity of thought leading to a measurement of everything meaningful in terms traceable to the feudal system of category, rank, position, and authority. The latter, authority, was a cornerstone upon which the feudal system rested. Authority was based on rank in the system.

Modern social science scholarship reflects the European preoccupation with authority. A feudal person was always responsible to someone higher; likewise, modern scholarship, for example, is preoccupied with footnoting or symbolically gaining the approval of those usually more highly placed in the academic status system, before anything is said.[6]

It will be maintained in the following section that the preoccupation with rank, authority, and status cannot be the foundation upon which twenty-first century sociology is to built, although this preoccupation was largely its nineteenth century focus. Because there are so many interferences with the system of rank and privilege, and particularly the development of meritocracy, the old standards will no longer hold. In America, where there was no hereditary aristocracy, though there were opportunities to inherit great wealth, rank could not mean what it did in Europe.

NOTES

1. See the author's unpublished paper "Social Inequality in the Gospels of Matthew, Mark, Luke, and John," where terms like *lord*, *master*, and *servant*, all very reflective of the social structure of the Middle Ages, are translated into the Bible.

2. The dynamic of the southern novel, upon which movies are often based, is traced to the violation of place by individuals whose social interaction was predicted to follow a particular pattern. This idea is elaborated in the author's unpublished paper, "Social Structure and the Southern Novel," 1990.

3. The idea of feudalism is specified in Reinhard Bendix, *Max Weber: An Intellectual Portrait* (Garden City, New York: Doubleday Anchor Books, 1960), 362-365.

4. Horses were important in battle, which in the feudal period took on the quality of a game with its attendant pomp and circumstance and display of utensils showing the splendor of the household. Ibid., 364.

5. "Sir" was a title used before the name of a knight or baronet, the latter being a man holding the lowest hereditary British title. See David B. Guralnik, editor-in-chief, *Webster's New World Dictionary of the American Language* (New York: William Collins Publishers, 1979), 779 and 114 respectively, for definitions of these feudal terms.

6. Steven Worden notes that academic tenure corresponds to the manorial system's assuring a peasant a piece of land to work so long as he did the bidding of his lord. Likewise, the tenured faculty member has a permanent job so long as the requirements of the manor, the academic institution, are met.

3

The Structure of
Sociological Revolutions

Thomas Kuhn argues that revolutions are caused when old paradigms fall under attack.[1] Modern physics could not emerge, for instance, until wise old Aristotle was overthrown and new thought was permitted to enter the arena of debate. New thought is always very threatening because it is upsetting of the old order. There was tremendous investment in the interpretations of the phenomena of the natural world which caused great difficulty for the development of science.[2]

It is difficult to bring about an important shift in the way society thinks about how it is structured largely because the persons providing the thought have not changed their attitudes. A revolution in sociological thought must by its nature proceed much more slowly than a revolution in scientific thought. If anything, the attitudes toward the way society was structured were more entrenched than those toward the natural sciences. A revolution was possible in natural science because it held out the possibility of improved lifestyles. Science would provide better homes, better means of transportation, reduced hours of work, more interesting work and better health. Even though there were institutions rejecting the new science, almost nobody argued against the potentially positive effects of an advanced natural science.

Objections to the newer scientific interpretations had more to do with who would control the knowledge generated through the application of scientific technology than with whether there would be a new science. But nearly everyone stood a chance of being helped by science, and it had much greater general support. At the upper levels there may be some esoteric argument about such theories as evolution versus creation, or of wave and particle theories of light. These disagreements did not fundamentally affect the practical applications of science. This government or that might argue about the uses to which atomic science knowledge would be put, but there was simply no way of holding back the development of that knowledge.

It is the central problems of any society that demand explanation. These are the ones with which the best thinkers have generally concerned themselves. Of course, one thinker's ideas may be totally rejected by another. The French Revolution was a central event for the very aristocratic Auguste Comte, who could not understand why French people would revolt. That was the most unlikely of all revolutions, according to Comte's thought. The unlikelihood of it continues to generate thought and commentary.

For other thinkers the American Revolution was a central world event seen as the first serious attempt at the breakup of colonial empires. Other cultures had colonized earlier, and some even longer than the period of roughly from 1619 to 1776, when the Revolution solved the matter. This was not the earliest effort of colonized people to resist their captors. The people of western and southern Europe had struggled against the encroachment of the Romans, Arabs, Turks, and Mongols for literal centuries after the fall of the Roman Empire, which itself had proved rather adept at colonization.

After the defeat of the Moslems, Spain and Portugal began their own colonial processes, claiming all the territory in the New World and some of that in the Old. Immediately was set in place resistance to this colonial domination by the local populations. When the countries of Europe saw that it was possible to swell their own coffers with the profits of colonization, they did not respect the overlordship of the Iberians. By 1588 Captain Francis Drake practically destroyed Spain's ability to hang onto her colonies by commanding the seas. The defeat of the naval supremacy of the Spaniards changed the face of the New World and opened up possibilities for the development of England as a world power.

Years later, on the heels of Drake's victory came colonization of North America with the founding of Jamestown, Virginia, in 1619. By 1621 slavery was introduced into English North America, although it had been present in the Caribbean and South America since the mid-1500s. The 250-year period of slavery, ending with the American Civil War, then became viewed as a central event in Western history. It required explanation and since then has excited commentary and serious research. Why there should be such interest in this event by so many people can probably be explained by our tendency to try to understand that which we have not understood. The Civil War tugs at American minds just as the French Revolution tugged at Comte's. Slavery was not merely a status for some persons held in bondage. It was a whole institution with underpinnings in every agency of state, custom, economics, religion, politics, philosophy, education, and even science. When it was over and people began to reflect on it, slavery could not be fathomed any more than the dimensions of the universe could be fathomed. Why it happened at all has not been answered satisfactorily. No other social event in the world has come close to having the emotional significance of North American slavery. Where the total institution cannot be studied, some aspect of it, some spinoff of it, is studied and reflected upon.

European sociology, based on Darwinism and Marxism, taught that these concepts correctly portrayed or expressed social reality around the world. For Europeans the world was that part which they controlled, really, what they considered the backward portions. Sociology was thus based upon samples of the world that did not adequately represent the cultures of the world. The "backward" places in most of Africa, the New World, and the Pacific were relatively easily taken over by the Europeans during colonization. When their missionaries, anthropologists, and social scientists began to study these subject people, they fit them into patterns that were already preset by European thought. Social Darwinism advocated largely by Herbert Spencer, William Graham Sumner, and earlier by Rev. Thomas Malthus, ranked societies of the world to conform roughly to the ranking systems already familiar to Europeans.

The ancient societies the Europeans were unable to conquer, such as India, China, including the Mongols, and some provinces of the present Soviet Union, were not the areas on which the major European paradigms were based. India, for instance, though seen as a British colony for 250 years, did not have an open class system. Instead, it featured a system hardened into caste in which the place of each individual was known and well understood. European sociology could not explain the prominence of Islam, which dominated the world for some 700 years during the Dark Ages of Europe. Nor could it not explain the cultural force the Egyptians represented even before the Dark Ages.

Social science scholarship approached the question of groups by using categorical thinking. The groups of the world are placed into three categories called races, and these are designated by color. In anthropological terms they are called Caucasian, Mongolian, and Negro. In everyday terminology they are called white, yellow, and black. These categories are forced and more properly should be thought of as continua, that is, with all groups shading into the others in the way that the colors of a rainbow fade into each other. Viewed as a continuum, there are no specific starting or end places for any color group. The designations are at best heuristic devices to ease communication but should not be thought of as accurate representations of reality.

Thinking of groups as categories led to assigning each particular qualities that all members of a given category may not possess. Everyday observation teaches that large groups consist of people of all color gradations. This same continuum effect occurs with respect to any physical or genetic quality said to differentiate the groups. There is some sickle cell anemia among whites, some Tay Sachs syndrome among blacks, and some tendency toward, say, skin cancer among Mongolian peoples. Humanity is a spectrum of colors and characteristics, and only when people are grouped broadly can the qualities be clearly seen. Even then one must be quite removed from the group in order to get the full flavor of individual differences.

Race is a very obfuscating term when used in an everyday manner. It is too laden with connotative value to be used scientifically. Although a scientific term must be highly general, it must not by its use bring greater confusion to the issue at hand. Since racial and color terms are loaded with preset values and images, they cannot provide scientific or positive social utility. To be truly useful, any reference to race must be based on reality, it must reflect the placement of the individual or group in the spectrum, not in a specific category.[3]

Terms are used to simplify communication, not to make the thinking itself simple. We say that something is round because the thing we are describing conforms closely to that definition. It is circumscribed by points equidistant from a point called the center. A round object therefore allows an infinite number of plane figures to pass through its center. But a plane figure has only length and width and not the third dimension, so it is imaginary. It is only when the third dimension is added that an object becomes real, that is, has physical qualities. We can only imagine something being round until it is rendered real, but our imagination is good enough for our purposes. We seldom have preset negative opinions of what round means because the term is used in a sense borrowed from science.

The terms *race* and *color* could be thought of as scientific summary terms, but they have been invested with so much social definition that when one says, "He is white," for instance, the intention is not to communicate that the person is from a particular end of the color spectrum. The intention, rather, is to indicate that the person has some quality that is negatively or positively valued. *Race* and *color* are not useful terms; they are merely emotion raising and may even be harmful in that their use often leads to harmful outcomes.

Setting aside terms like race and color would be sociologically revolutionary.[4] It is true that the color groups of the world constitute a spectrum from dark to light and from light to dark. The extremes of those groups could be thought of as possessing Africanicity (darkness) and Nordicity (lightness). To preserve the gradations of the group, one group being all that humanity presents, we could think of what social scientists call a Likert scaling process. Intensity of a quality could be graded from high to low. If we ranked in terms of Africanicity and Nordicity, we might think of very low, low, moderate, high, and very high Africanicity; we could take the same steps for Nordicity. The African end of the stick shades gradually toward the Nordic end, and the Nordic end shades gradually toward the African end. A full-blooded African would have high Africanicity, and a full-blooded European high Nordicity. High Africanicity would suggest low Nordicity, and high Nordicity low Africanicity. People in between could be said to have low Africanicity and low Nordicity. This kind of scaling would erase the Mongolian category by placing Mongolians somewhere between high Africanicity and high Nordicity. It would remove much of the emotion associated with ethnic and racial classification and would more easily communicate the ideas that are intended when such references are made.

CRITIQUING AMERICAN SOCIOLOGY

What few critiques of American sociology there are have not come from scholars of the mainstream; they have generally emanated on the left. In the late

1960s Joyce Ladner edited a volume entitled *The Death of White Sociology*. Its thrust was upon how the discipline had used its theoretical underpinning to buttress racism and oppression of poor people in America and the Third World. Sociology was accused of being Eurocentric and therefore had little to do with framing a program for the liberation of black people. Black nationalist sociology called for a discipline that was relevant to the conditions of suffering humanity. Nationalists were not so interested in testing of hypotheses but finding a way to ease the suffering and pain caused by a racist and oppressive economic system. In the wake of black nationalist sociology arose sociologies of other ethnic groups, women, and other categories that were not receiving their fair shares of the bounty of American productivity. Through it all there was no general critique of the validity of sociology as it was conducted. Its very foundation in the old European masters' concern with status and rank was not called into question. A key feature of European thought was that all persons had assigned social places on the basis of heredity or previous social condition. Ethnicity was prominent in determining previous condition.

Eurocentric sociology was always nominally antiethnic, though never egalitarian, for the ethnic group never had a secure place in European society. Ethnics were generally defined out of the mainstream and were therefore always problematic, whether they were called Puritans or Irish in the British Isles, Huguenots in France, Basques in Spain, or high or low Germans in Germany. Of course, the Jews in all the European countries proved to be problematic. Just as there was no ideology of their assimilation in European countries, there was none in the American context. But circumstances were so radically different in America that the old European norms could not withstand the assault and had to yield reluctantly to a move toward assimilation. Although it was most difficult to fight off assimilation of the ethnic groups, the ideology of Eurosociology was not generally receptive to the merger of all groups and cultures, even when they sought such mergers. Moreover, not only was Eurosociology antiethnic; it was at the same time ethnocentric, using a European standard by which to judge all other social behavior.[5]

The foundation for separation of society into many groups ranging in size from the dyad of two persons to multinational groups of countries pursuing special interests was found within the Euro-sociological interpretations offered up by the old masters.[6] Durkheim had talked about organic solidarity, meaning that societies were held together by common values and common ancient history.[7] People would become alienated as they moved toward mechanical solidarity, where values and personalities meant very little. Toennies gave considerably greater weight to *gemeinschaft* (community) than to *gesellschaft* (society), somewhat suggesting that the former was more desirable than the latter. He could weep the loss of *gemeinschaft* but have little to rejoice over with the coming of *gesellschaft*. Basically, these two masters literally pined for the good old days of community harmony when all those of the same coat and stripe were bound together in a tightly knit community of persons almost in face-to-face relationships. Both Durkheim and Toennies were skeptical of the ability of any society to absorb many people of diverse background. Willy-nilly, they became apologists for ethnic separation, which had been maintained in Europe for generations.

When modern sociology was born, it was neither critical nor analytical of the colonialism then sweeping the world. As one people after another fell under the sway of European domination, sociology tended to use a variety of justifications.[8] It was not really important that academics spoke to the issue because they were beholden to the very same colonial powers for their positions. Military and economic power rested with the colonialists, and that power was what the academics respected more than anything else. The studies conducted by the social scientists—by anthropologists, psychologists, and sociologists alike—supported the idea of colonialism, and as late as 1944 Gunnar Myrdal gave aid and comfort to the colonialists by talking about the existence of caste systems in America and, by extension, everywhere else in the world where colonialism existed.[9] As intelligence tests, even earlier, made their entry, they were as quick as anthropometry to use them to prove that some groups were inferior to others even though the groups could not easily be separated. Nowhere else had there been such a united front by social science to present such a negative attitude toward literally more than half of world humanity. The natives themselves had little means of resisting the teachings and some eventually accepted the prevailing interpretations of their own inferiority. The Europeans had never seen anything approximating human equality in their heavily stratified and class-based societies, and they had no framework for even thinking about it as a possibility. America provided more of an opportunity for that orientation to emerge, but the masters were set on defending the old attitudes that had long prevailed in Europe. There were a few voices pressing arguments about human equality, such as Franz Boas[10] and even romantics such as Melville Herskovits,[11] but they were lonely unheard voices crying in a wilderness where nobody was listening and few took them seriously. The tide against them was too strong. Myrdal accused Herskovits of doing yeoman service for Negro history propagandists by glorifying African culture.[12]

By the late 1960s and early 1970s there had emerged a move toward a rejection of Eurosociology mainly because it was antiblack. That movement fizzled when many of the most critical scholars were moved into prestigious schools or into high-paying jobs where in any case many were coopted and resocialized into mainstream, and valueless social science. Plugging away at testing hypotheses out of the old paradigms was what would get them better paid, and promoted and that is what they did. It did not make much difference that the requirements for an American social science were not, and could not be, the same as those of staid old Europe.

European sociology was prepared to see social life in terms of the structure that had so long prevailed in European society. Because hierarchy was a part of the thought of most of those trained in European society, they took it as a natural social occurrence. Karl Mannheim, offering lectures in England after being proscribed by Adolf Hitler in 1933, told his students that we do not consider as real people those who do not fall into our group. We treat them as categories. Thus prejudice is a kind of primitive adjustment to that with which we are not familiar. Prejudice has a natural basis in that it is an attempt to fit older generalizations into new experiences. Mobile people are more unbiased in judging others and are less prejudiced than rooted people, who are more inclined to prejudice.[13]

Mannheim's sociology was acceptable to Europeans and Americans who were looking for bases for excluding groups and keeping the organization of society asymmetrical. Mannheim came from a Germany of many small groups tied to each other for the purpose of maintaining themselves by the exclusion of other groups. It was Otto von Bismarck in the mid-1800s who had seen the limitations of the small principalities of Prussia. Wars had to be fought with Denmark and Austria for the unification of Prussia. Bismarck said these petty principalities had to be broken up and a larger, more viable Germany constructed. Bismarck became known as the Iron Chancellor because he used strong means to bring Germany into being.[14]

It is doubtful that Mannheim would ever have accepted the erasure of the petty systems of social rank that had prevailed for so long in Prussia. He had some pretensions himself to aristocratic upbringing and a significant investment in the society as it operated. Mannheim did not know the many groups that made up German society, nor did he seem to want to know them. They were outsiders and therefore suspect. A unified Germany would break down these prejudices by throwing into contact with each other people who had never met on an equal basis those with a rank higher than their own. Seeing noblemen drinking beer and eating sauerkraut in a common bar would have been very upsetting to Mannheim, who believed that social distance between higher and lower categories of people had to be maintained. Mannheim was thus fearful of democracy because it would erase the social differences among people. Of course, in all these societies there were ceremonial occasions in which the people could step out of their daily routines and ignore the rules of rank and status. For instance, in Catholic countries during Mardi Gras or Carnival, people don masks, take other roles, and discount for a few days the real meaning of social rank. After the ceremony is over, they return to their social positions, so deeply ingrained in them.

The Catholic hierarchy recognized that keeping the system intact required a way of relieving the tension that would develop under a one-sided asymmetrical arrangement. Through all these processes no fundamental change in the social order occurred, for those in authority and power believed that society was naturally stratified.

Mannheim believed strongly in hierarchically structured groupings. He thought that in-groups struggle against out-groups, and that the struggle with outsiders strengthens the in-group by promoting harmony and decreasing conflict within it. Each group develops ethnocentrism, nourishing its own pride, vanity, and sense of superiority; it exalts its own divinities and looks with contempt upon others. The nation itself is merely the extension of a large ethnocentric in-group.[15]

EUROCENTRIC FUNCTIONALISM

A central tenet of the functionalist position is that of system. A system means different things to different people. European scholars such as Herbert Spencer talked of society as if it were like a living organism. Spencer's organic analogy posed that the parts of a plant perform certain functions that are integrated in such a way as to make the entire plant a system. Spencer thought of special groups in terms of their evolutionary development. He opposed programs that aided groups not advantaged in the struggle for survival. To do so would be like feeding a wolf, a lion, or any wild animal; it would interfere with their ability to survive on their own as nature intended them to do. Spencer combined functionalism and evolutionary doctrine by showing that whatever groups were doing might be considered functional and survival inducing, survival being the principal intent of the actions of any group.[16]

Herbert Spencer's sociology was acceptable to Europeans, who had been accustomed to struggle. Through struggle the group would be maintained, if it were meant to be. Nature is parsimonious and economical. It does not carry useless species but lets them perish when they lose their adaptability for survival. For Spencer the historical landscape is littered with extinct social groups that failed to make the necessary adaptations to whatever environments they faced.

William Graham Sumner, though an American, was highly influenced by the thought of Herbert Spencer. Like Spencer, Sumner thought there was order in the competitive and often conflictive processes of nature; Sumner additionally thought that society produces norms by which order is maintained. These norms are thought of as customs, and when organized elaborately, so that they survive over time, they become institutions. Some customs are more meaningful than others and are protected as mores.[17]

Both Sumner and Spencer were products of thought that stressed status, rank, order, and the maintenance of position in favor of the continuity of society roughly as it was then structured. Their ideas helped form the philosophical basis for American sociology and allied that sociology more substantially to the social thought of continental Europe. Spencer believed that the more evolved classes had responsibility for leadership in the society, for they were the best prepared for leadership by the process of evolution. Just as a wild wolf pack would not let a weak male become dominant, a competitive society would not allow a weak leader to become dominant. Control through the force of dominance in human society, aided by the introduction of customs and institutions supporting that dominance, was the hallmark of the thought of Spencer and Sumner. Their thinking accorded well with the behavior of people of colonial orientation—bent on the making of large fortunes through the labor of men they were told were naturally subordinate.

A revolution in sociology is unlikely because there is no groundswell movement to bring it about. Many scholars are evidently committed to the discipline as it is now progressing, if it is in fact doing so. Yet a number of indicators suggest that there is no harmony within the discipline. Paradigms on top of paradigms have emerged only to be discarded, not so much because they do not describe or partially explain data but because they do not harmonize with the teachings of the masters of the discipline. The socialization of students into the thought of the masters begins with introductory sociology and is repeated in most classes until the student completes the Ph.D. degree. If along the way the scholars happen to write papers or books that do not accord with the paradigms or propositions approved by masters of the discipline, their works may be rejected. This is not because the masters are more appropriate but because of the socialization they have addressed. Durkheim has spoken on suicide, Marx on class, Toennies on societal types, Weber on bureaucracy and religion, Spencer on evolution, and Comte on the need and requirements of the discipline for a positive sociology. Leopold von Weise, Florian Znaniecki, Pitirim Sorokin, Paul Lazarsfeld, Karl Mannheim, Benjamin Kidd, Hegel, Ludwig Gumplowicz, Ratzenhoffer, Spinoza, and others of the European tradition over a period of years literally flooded the U.S. market with ideas more germane to the European scene than to the American one. Even in religion it is such individuals as Paul Tillich, Martin Luther, and Martin Buber who are studied, as if the problems they raised in Europe were somehow the ones confronted in America.[18] If religion were synonymous with values, these thinkers, like others could be placed in a hierarchy. During medieval times all values were dominated by the Church, but in modern times values became separate so that religious and other values have no vital connection with each other.[19]

Because European sociology was concerned more with social statics than with dynamics, it tended to ignore or to underplay the role of prediction. In very elegant and convincing terms it could describe how society operated. It could show the relationship of parts to the whole and how the whole was maintained through the harmonious working together of the parts. Stress was laid on how much of a positive nature each group received, offsetting any negative results, from the relationship between groups. With this focus it became difficult to offer moderately accurate predictions regarding significant social change. Order and structure were built into the thought of the scholars, perhaps a normal consequence of their belief that society would remain basically as it was structured. Change came to be seen as unusual and therefore to be treated as an aberration because its explanation did not accord with the concept of statics suggested in most European sociology.

A good example of the failure of European sociology to consider change was colonialism. For the approximately 250 years that India was under British control, for instance, there was little understanding that the people were restive or why they became so. There seemed to be an almost total overlooking of the anthropology of social life. By the time social science began to attempt to understand life in India, that life had been greatly altered; any intuition brought to that understanding was crafted to meet the conditions that seemed to most closely parallel British life.[20] Thus, as the British became more comfortable with a relatively inflexible system of class, they imbued the Indians with a much more inflexible system of caste. Since by that time colonialism had found a secure footing in European thought, supported by a strong pillar of racism, it was but a short step to the conclusion that the Indian system must be based on race.

A reading of anthropology would have shown them that color differences were not significant in aboriginal Indian society. Certain groups had evolved certain occupational niches and taboos against other work. For instance, the Aryans were cattle herders and did not believe in plowing land or engaging in much cultivation. They thought that tearing up the land was against the commandments of their gods. They would leave cultivation to other groups. Still other groups had evolved taboos against doing literary work. They would need to contact other groups who did that kind of work, for their own activities were to be placed somewhere else. Fighting was done by persons who had no taboos against spilling blood. For that occupation soldiers could come from those ranks. Groups were known to gather sticks in the forest in order to make a living. When the forests were depleted and land consolidated under colonialism, the stick-gatherers had to find jobs gathering other things in the more settled villages. The changes forced by colonialization largely, but not exclusively, meant that there was an erasure of traditional occupations and relationships in India. As groups were pushed out of their hereditary occupations, they began to jostle with each other in the new social order. Because some groups seemed preferred by the Europeans, particularly those whose values accorded more with European values, they were placed over the other groups. Brahmans thus became political and intellectual leaders in a society now managed at the highest levels by Europeans, if generally from a distance. Privileges were given to the Indians roughly according to the European perception of how they would rank in European society. Anthropologists and social science observers traveling to India would report that a racial caste system supported by the beliefs of Hinduism was in place.[21]

European sociology began its interpretation of social life with the assumption that what the Europeans reported was how life had always been and how it would remain. Caste, for example, was Hindu society as they saw it. It had the stability of the class system of England, which had grown out of the estate system of the Middle Ages. The system changed so imperceptibly that it was easy to believe it was not changing at all.

European sociology was not alone in its conclusions. In delineating class structure it had the help even of artists. William Shakespeare based many of his tragedies upon conflicts produced by persons representing different social ranks. Rather than change the ranking system, Shakespeare frequently resolved the problem by the death of a character.[22] Charles Dickens's, *Tale of Two Cities*, portrays in vivid detail the social life of the poor in contrast with the better-off classes of London and Paris during the French Revolution. The problem of the unequal distribution of wealth and opportunity in those cities was resolved in favor of a changed social structure. Instead, the poor found ways to escape their unfortunate circumstances.

In America the readiness of the social sciences to abandon a serious critique of the veracity of its theory led to important mistakes in interpretations of group actions. The discipline had little to offer to the general public, it seemed, for it was not speaking to the problems the public confronted. It ignored data that did not accord with its biases. Interpretations that seemed to support the status quo were endorsed more freely probably because the social scientists themselves had paradigms of statics in their heads and in their training. It was very difficult to internalize a sociology of dynamics by studying the European masters, as the majority of sociologists had to do during their advanced degree training.

Nowhere was European sociology found to be more wrong than in regard to race relations. The idea that even dynamic American race relations were caste relations was the prevailing myth for long years. The stage for that kind of thought had been set by the European scholar Gunnar Myrdal. Although Myrdal was severely criticized by Oliver C. Cox, the hold of caste upon American sociology would not be displaced. Not even the conflict present in the slave system, nor that which erupted during World War I and afterward, nor the social movements aimed at removing inequities in the system made much impact on those scholars whose training was grounded in the statics of caste relations.

Not only did logic and philosophy refute Myrdal but so did the data themselves. The movement for civil rights, begun even before the 1960s, had been scoring successes at various places in the country. By 1955 in Montgomery, Alabama, it got under way in a very serious fashion under the leadership of Martin Luther King, Jr. Despite the massive change taking place in America, social science held stolidly to caste and class thought, trying to fit the data of dynamics into the static molds handed out by European social science.

Other movements were in place at the same time as that for black civil rights. The women's liberation movement sought to redress the relatively powerless position women held as a result of male dominance. Although sociology had not seen women as a lower caste, clearly they had been subordinate in most general and productive areas of life. In many ways they shared the position reserved for lower-caste members, such as blacks. Throughout American society revolutions in human relations were occurring while sociology continued to try to explain the change by using concepts bequeathed by European social science.

NOTES

1. Thomas Kuhn, *The Structure of Scientific Revolutions* (Chicago: The University of Chicago Press, 1962).

2. See Andrew D. White, *The History of the Warfare with Science and Theology in Christendom* (New York: D. Appleton & Co.).

3. Franz Boas was one very prominent scholar who tried to show that the term race was more obfuscating than enlightening in its scientific accuracy. He thought it was a very dangerous idea, as did Ashley Montagu, *Man's Most Dangerous Myth: The Fallacy of Race* (Cleveland, IL: The World Publishing Co., 1950).

4. Although the author toyed with the use of the term Nordicity in 1988 to describe Europeans, it was Steven K. Worden who added the idea of the gradations by suggesting high Nordicity. Other gradations, such as high Africanicity, seemed to fall into place after that conceptualization. Instead of calling someone white, he could be said to have high Nordicity, which would mean low Africanicity. Someone black could be said to have high Africanicity and low Nordicity.

5. It was William Graham Sumner who placed the concept ethnocentrism in the sociological vocabulary. It had been known for some time that judgments about other persons and groups were usually made in terms of those of the person making the judgment who was reflecting his or her own cultural orientations. See Carol A.B. Warren, *Sociology: Change and Continuity* (Homewood, IL: The Dorsey Press, 1977), pp. 31-35.

6. The idea of the classification of human groups has been attributed to the Swede Carl Linnaeus (1707-1778), a naturalist seeking ordered relations and a unity of all living things. For an excellent discussion of the period of biological thought regarding human conduct, and a reaction to it, see William M. Newman, *American Pluralism: A Study of Minority Groups and Social Theory* (New York: Harper & Row, Publishers, 1973), pp. 250-285.

7. Durkheim was one of the early leaders against biological explanations in his *The Rules of Sociological Method* (1895), translated by Sara A. Solvoy and John H. Muller, edited by George E.G. Catlin, 1953, and in William M. Newman, *American Pluralism: A Study of Minority Groups and Social Theory* (New York: Harper & Row, Publishers, 1973), p. 259.

8. See O. Mannoni, *Prospero and Caliban: The Psychology of Colonization* (New York: Praeger, 1964). An important review of the salient points of colonialism as seen by Mannoni is found in Frantz Fanon. *Black Skins, White Masks* (New York: Grove Press, 1967), pp. 83–108.

9. Myrdal's definition of caste is well-known to social scientists and need not be rehearsed at this point. His idea is presented in his An American Dilemma. (New York: Harpers, 1944). The most persistent critic of caste theory was O.C. Cox, *Caste, Class and Race* (New York: Doubleday).

10. Boas showed from research that the differences within groups were greater than the differences between them and thereby challenged the idea of group separation proposed by the 19th century racialists. Newman, *op. cit.*, p. 260.

11. Melville Herskovits, the anthropologist, was a leading proponent of the idea that African culture was not eliminated during New World slavery and that there were many survivals of it. See his *The Myth of the Negro Past*.

12. See Myrdal, *An American Dilemma*, p. 753.

13. Karl Mannheim, *Ideology and Utopia* (London: K. Paul, Trench, Trubner & Co., 1929; New York: Harcourt, Brace and Company, 1936).

14. Otto Furst von Bismarck, *Otto Furst von Bismarck: The Man and the Statesman* (New York: Harper and Brothers, 1899).

15. Mannheim, *op. cit.*

16. Herbert Spencer, *The Principles of Sociology* (London, 1893), presents a good introduction to Spencer's encyclopedic writings about the social system.

17. William Graham Sumner, *Social Darwinism: Selected Essays*, (Englewood Cliffs, NJ: Prentice-Hall, 1963).

18. Of the many excellent works which treat of the European concern with religion, see especially R.H. Tawney, *Religion and the Rise of Capitalism*. (New York: Mentor Books, 1926, 1947 and 1961), for an understanding of the relationship between ideas and behavior.

19. Tawney, *op. cit.*, p. 15.

20. Note the influence of these scholars upon the thought of Martin Luther King, Jr. See Taylor Branch, *Parting of the Waters: America in the King Years—1954–63* (New York: Simon and Schuster, 1988), especially pp. 69-104.

21. George Coffin Taylor and Reed Smith. Shakespeare's Hamlet. (New York: Ginn and Company, 1962), reflects at many places how Shakespeare's plays paralleled the structure of Elizabethan life. The idea is fairly well established that it is difficult to see reality without doing so through the lens of socialization.

22. Of the many themes which permeated the writings of the Bard, class was not overlooked. See Ralph Berry, *Shakespeare and Social Class* (Atlantic Highlands, NJ: Humanities Press International, 1988), and Richard Burt and John Michael Archer, *Enclosure Acts: Sexuality, Property and Culture in Early Modern England* (Ithaca, NY: Cornell University Press, 1994).

4

The Lingering Influence
of Greece

European sociology has drawn its images from ancient Greek society. By positing that the Greeks had as close to a perfect society as possible, it was relatively easy to adopt that ancient model and hope that it could be applicable to modern society. But ancient Greece did not have an egalitarian society. It approved of inegalitarianism and glorified war and slavery. Its emphasis on science was not enough to discount its elitist posturing. Plato, that quintessential Greek, was elitist to the very core.

The center of modern sociology, America, could not adopt any vision of the world that had been bequeathed from the ancients and not the moderns. America was founded on very different principles than those underlying all previous societies. America was more egalitarian, in principle and practice, than previous societies. Other societies stressed structure and status much longer, and it was upon the basis of these concepts that the people of the rest of the world thought. Probably they also explain the fascination with Greece during the Renaissance. There were intellectuals who wanted get back to what Greece was about. They were bedazzled by the philosophy, art, and science of Greece but did not realize that the model Greece provided would not work in a modern technologically sophisticated state. Inequality was taken as natural within the Greek cosmos. People were fixed in classes and estates, literally by birth, without possibilities of moving out. Leading Greeks offered philosophical rationales for their system; statuses held were thought of as natural positions.

When the Romans supplanted the Greeks, they borrowed from their teachings and incorporated them into their own systems. The rationales provided by the Greek philosophers made much sense to Renaissance men, who had no concept of equality. The Greeks provided them with justifications for inequality. The Greek system was then imposed upon local peoples.

Greek philosophy supported the emerging colonialism that would sweep the Western world. Leaders could always go back to the Greeks in all things that mattered, whether science, art, philosophy, or politics. Basing all logic upon the thought of the Greeks meant ruling out alternative philosophies. None of the great revolutions of the world that were seen as forward movements for individual rights would have been possible had Greek philosophy continued to enjoy suzerainty. For instance, women were not accorded high status nor did they hold positions of power. In Greek mythology Hera was goddess of home. Athena embodied wisdom but was more noted for her beauty. The general point is that Greek society was particularly inegalitarian, elitist, and sexist.

Thus American sociology, drawing upon the European tradition traces back to the Greeks. The inegalitarianism of Plato could not, however, remain a model in western European society and especially it could not remain a model in American society. Applying any previous vision of society, save perhaps that of the Christianity of the New Testament, would be counter to the teachings of the American Revolution. The concept of human equality, which took root in America after much struggle with the remnants of European-Greek thought, was one which had no analog in past history. The focus of American social science, particularly sociology, meant those scholars finding comfort in the philosophy of the Europeans did not approve of the greater equalities portended by revolutions. The French, American, Haitian, and Russian revolutions were not defended by the Greek tradition of inequality that had become bound up in the thought of those wed to Greek concepts of social structure. European sociology or social philosophy set the stage for the legitimation of social inequality in whatever form it was offered.

It was the Italian Machiavelli who in *The Prince* made popular the notion that the ends, whether political, economic, or social, justified the means. Any practice was justifiable in terms of the ends sought. For Machiavelli, war was as defensible as any other practice. Machiavelli antedated social Darwinism by three centuries. Of course Machiavelli had been strongly influenced by Renaissance thought tracing back to Greece and Rome.

One of the most revered of all European social philosophers, Hegel, to which much later philosophy is traced, was a strong believer in authoritarian monarchical government, which easily accepted slavery and war as natural.[1] So did many other European scholars who are looked to as models of thought.

What was considered as the original thought of many masters of European social philosophy was not really original; it was a replay of Greek and Roman thought, but especially of the Greeks. The great science and mathematics and art of Aristotle, Euclid, and Sophocles, Euripides, and Aeschylus were taken as representatives of Greek society, giving the impression that such figures represented everyday life in Greece. But they were no more representative of Greek society than Nobel Prize winners are representative of modern society wherever these winners are found, or than Shakespeare was representative of his period in English history. Yet images of Greek society present a particular view and value of that society without much being shown about the abuses of human rights that were coldly characteristic of Greek society.

The fascination of the West with the philosophy, logic, mathematics, science, and even the political organization of the Greeks appealed to scholars who were not willing to recognize other frameworks and philosophies or to admit of serious weaknesses in the thought and behavior of the Greeks. There was little need to put forward any alternatives to the thought and procedures of the Greeks. Theirs was believed to have been the perfect earthly society or so it was promoted to be, particularly, during the Renaissance. That so much is traced to the ancient Greeks promotes the idea that all that they did was admirable. Today every schoolboy has heard of the Trivium and the Quadrivium, or what we call the arts and sciences, thought to be the perfect curriculum because they stressed courses that prepared leading people for citizenship and participation in the affairs of the city-state. There was practically no concern for the rights and mobility aspirations of the peasants of Greek society. No provision was made for their learning and development.

Of course, the march of Europe out of the long period of the Dark Ages encouraged thought of the past glories of old cultures, which they claimed as their own. Latching on to formerly great cultures was important psychologically to western Europeans in particular, whereas there was not much attempt by Eastern peoples to find glory in the long-dead histories of Greece and Rome. Eastern peoples were not nearly as impressed with the achievements of the European ancients as were the Europeans themselves. Thus, the scholars of the West, adopting the ancients as models, no doubt did so because there was practical value to be achieved in their adoption. The critical factor in those cultures was social inequality, and the preservation of that inequality through teaching, law, and daily practice proved to be a good reason for the acceptance of the culture of the ancients. Eastern culture, though more ancient and probably more egalitarian, was not the culture of choice of those Europeans who wanted philosophies that promoted the inequality taken as articles of faith by the Greeks. Socrates was forced to drink hemlock because of his failure to recant his teachings and accept the doctrines of those who considered themselves to be his natural and cultural superiors. His martyrdom early foreshadowed the control the rulers expected to have over those they ruled. He would do what they said, believe what they did, or face death.

The lesson of Socrates, of course, suggests that there was no real possibility of dissent in Greek society. Socrates was a professor with status higher than the rank and file Greeks in a society divided into those entitled to citizenship and those who were so-called barbarians to be treated as their masters wished because they had no civil rights.[2]

NOTES

1. See Carl Friedrich, *The Philosophy of Hegel* (New York: Modern Library, 1953), pp. xiii–xxv.

2. For an understanding of the structure of ancient thought, the foundation of modern Western thought, see Aeschylus M. Zeitlin, *Plato's Vision: The Classical Origins of Social and Political Thought* (Englewood Cliffs, NJ: Prentice-Hall, 1993). An excellent bibliography of works concerned with ancient thought is contained in this volume.

5

European Outposts Versus
Indigenous Sociology

Until quite recently American sociology has essentially been a carryover of European thought. Two of the premier scholars of modern sociological scholarship best represent the continuity of the European tradition in America: Talcott Parsons and Robert K. Merton. The intention of this section is not to review the voluminous work of these scholars but to show why the sociologies of the East and the Midwest of the United States were bound to be different, creating what we call a conflict between European and indigenous sociology.

Parsons represented the German tradition of philosophical social thought, especially of such scholars as Max Weber.[1] Merton represents the French wing of sociology, particularly the ideas of Emile Durkheim.[2] Harvard and Columbia could be thought of as outposts of European sociological thought because their scholars were so heavily schooled in the teachings of these European masters. Their philosophies were very theoretical and perhaps reflective of the problems and the orientations of Europe.

The counterweight to the European brand of sociology, represented largely by Harvard and Columbia scholars, was found at the University of Chicago, which was perhaps the first American university department of sociology to try to understand American culture in sociological terms. The Chicago brand of sociology was really an indigenous sociology. It was not from Europe, as was the sociology at Harvard and Columbia. The attempt of Chicago to undertake the building of an indigenous sociology reflected the greater distance of Chicago from European thought. After all, Chicago was basically Midwest, whereas Massachusetts and New York were just across the ocean from the German and French universities. So it is quite possible that those two schools were looking to the East while Chicago was looking to the West. In the West there was a much greater opportunity for individuality, whereas in the East there was much greater opportunity for understanding positions in terms of the parameters that had been used in Europe, namely, such factors as class and status.

The indigenous sociology of the University of Chicago reflected an opening of the social structure where previous locations and orientations did not count as much. Everything looked more possible in the Midwest and later in the Far West than seemed possible in the East and along the northeastern seaboard. It was not, of course, that the University of Chicago was attacking European sociology or the ideas of Harvard and Columbia. It was simply that location and social situation meant that the opportunity was greater for the building of an indigenous sociology at Chicago. There, academicians had no allegiance to European scholarship. There was no real attempt to explain American sociology in terms of the concepts that had been used in Europe, as had been the tendency in the East, seen most clearly in the social science scholarship of Harvard and Columbia. The University of Chicago was not alone in attempting to build a sociology germane to the emerging American case of the time; some other schools of the Midwest were doing the same. Edwin Sutherland's studies of crime at the University of Indiana seem an appropriate example. Sutherland argued about white-collar crime which was not possible within the context of European sociology. Certainly Sutherland was not the only person to realize that white collar-crime existed. He knew about histories of conflict within European culture. He was aware of the Church practices of selling indulgences. He knew about the misdeeds of royalty and their misuse of trust. He knew about certain European kings and queens who had been executed for misuse of their offices. White-collar crime did in fact exist. Nobles had practical license to commit whatever crimes they wanted without being punished. Yet the ideas brought to America about how to think about society did not leave a place for thinking about white-collar criminality.[3]

Consider cases with which we are more familiar, such as the founding of the thirteen original colonies, some being proprietary colonies, some constituting joint stock companies, and some founded on simple scams where people collected money, lied to the colonists about what they would find in the New World, got their money, and sent the people over to an exceedingly rough life. That scamming was white-collar crime, but there was no way of recognizing such crime within the framework of European sociology. It remained for an American to come to the conclusion that white-collar criminality was a violation of trust by people in high places, in middle-class positions. Such crime was not often prosecuted as such. This was an attempt to build an indigenous sociology that constituted something of a rejection of the frameworks that had been established for looking at society in European terms. Durkheim thought that criminality was a reflection of alienation. Lombroso thought that criminality meant atavistic throwbacks to earlier and inferior social types. Sigmund Freud thought that criminality was traced to early childhood upbringings and conflicts within the family structure that were mishandled by family members. American criminality was seen in indigenous sociology, particularly by the Chicago School, as having its foundation in social disorganization, not necessarily alienation and anomie, but simple disorganization of normal aspects of social operations displacement, where people had to play certain roles because of the situations in which they found themselves. There was no concerted effort to find that the explanations of these behaviors had to be found in the European model.[4]

European sociology could not be a model for American sociology because it was antidemocratic and therefore conflicted sharply with the emerging, though not fully recognized, democratic ethos of America. Where a central concept of European sociology was class and the frustration engendered, in America there was a groundswell rejection of class played out in the steady efforts of all unempowered people to gain equality. The emerging ethos of equality made America a harsh ground for the implantation of European sociology, which was imported but became syncretic. America accepted only a little of the language of the European masters and endorsed fully almost none of its basic concepts, neither Marx's class conflict, nor Hegel's dialectics, nor Durkheim's anomie. Only at the graduate level, where students had little power of resistance, did anyone pay much attention to European teachings in sociology.

American sociology developed upon its own problems. Because America never admitted that it had a serious social problem, all of the problems were treated as essentially moral. American sociology was more concerned with meliorism than with making statements that stood theoretically for all time. America became known as a land where a person could start over, at least theoretically, escaping the class-straitened societies of Europe, which would shatter before they would bend or change greatly. Everyone in America would have opportunities to rise in the social structure where class would not be handicapping. The 250 years of black slavery and the sorry treatment of Native Americans contradicted the thrust toward the making of an egalitarian society but did not halt that movement. Despite the efforts of ruling hierarchies to erect a hereditary class system, they were defeated. Yet again and again the hereditarians mounted efforts to preserve privilege by seeking to control the legal, economic, educational, and even religious machinery. Enough members of the unempowered classes got into positions on the basis of ability and opportunity to slow the thrust of the hereditarians. The overall movement in the United States has been toward democracy and wider participation of all groups, however unempowered, in the decision-making processes. Sociology likewise became reflective more of the democratic process and ethos and in so doing became more alienated from the European model.

Sociology in America, perhaps in Europe as well, has been defined on the basis of individual scholarly interest, for the most part. David Popenoe describes the matter succinctly:

> Because the sociologist is interested in all kinds of human interaction, his field of study overlaps many other disciplines. . . . We might say that sociology is not so much a unique subject matter as a way of looking at and analyzing

topics which are often familiar. To study sociology is to look for the social meanings that lie behind, and give significance to ordinary human actions.[5]

Popenoe's description indicates that it is scholarly interest that determines the character of the field, not a set of social problems for which there are no answers. The absence of an overriding few problems gives rise to a variety of sociologies leading to a claim that the field has been trivialized. Where no problems are admitted to exist, some are created by the aggressive actions of scholars, propagandists, and special interest groups. Many interests are extremely esoteric.

The interest of any scholar in a problem grows out of the sense of academic freedom long characteristic of the American university and the isolation of scholars from the rough and tumble of everyday life. The tendency was that a youthful scholar spent several years in graduate school, emerged with a Ph.D. degree, became an assistant professor at a college or university, and pursued research and publication leading to tenure. After that attainment the scholar picked an area of interest in which research and writing were continued, most of which was never published.

Often foundations or specific interest groups seek to direct or influence the nature of research by funding or commissioning work they think is necessary, and much of it is not done by academic scholars. Whether a research project is of personal or foundational interest, it illustrates the way problems are selected in the discipline. A problem may be raised to significance by its dollar funding. A $100,000 project is thought 100,000 times more important than an unfunded project.[6] The test of the quality of a project is the amount of money it costs to conduct the study, not the extent to which it seeks to answer significant theoretical questions or to offer solutions to important problems.

The problems that America faced were generally not problems of structure-technical problems in their truest sense. They were moral problems that grated on the nerves of a people who were steeped more than any other in the world in an emerging egalitarian ethic. The problems of equality, though not of class, were so precisely because the twin ethics of emerging egalitarianism and a distaste of social inequality.

European sociology, trying to posit the functionalism of a structure of inequality, despite Karl Marx, would eventually be adoptable by Americans who hungered and thirsted for the old European structures of inequality. Because this sociology made so little sense to American students, and to the general public, it had to be forced upon them, not as a plausible description and answers to problems, but as a canon. Dogma passed from one generation to the next, to be interpreted and understood by each in a similar manner.

The almost automatic adherence to the European point of view is coming under revision. Professor Allan Bloom has pointed out in his popular book *Closing of the American Mind* the loss of credibility of Marx. He thinks Marxist thought has been dead for a long time, that *Capital* is not a persuasive argument about present economics or the future of humankind. Bloom calls Marx fossilized.[7] But whereas Bloom discounted Marx, he claims the new left has gained its inspiration from another group of European thinkers: Sartre, Camus, Kafka, Dostoevski, Nietzsche, Heidegger, and Rousseau, to name a few. Bloom illustrates that Americans merely put down one set of European masters only to pick up another.[8] Americans remain enamored with Europe's ability to produce the consequential thought for America. It was the same in nearly every liberal field. Education sought its roots in such Europeans as Froebel, Frobenius, and Rousseau. Political science tried to connect to Thomas Hobbes, John Locke, Nietzsche, Machiavelli, and Otto von Bismarck, for instance. Economics copied the thought of Adam Smith, David Ricardo, John Stuart Mill, and latterly John Maynard Keynes. Art looked to Michelangelo, Da Vinci, and even Picasso for norms and standards, while music tried to copy Bach, Beethoven, Handel, and Haydn. The list could be extended indefinitely, but the proposition stands that Americans were afraid to do their own thinking and creating even though they claimed to be the freest thinkers in the world because they were less restrained by old culture and tradition.

Sociology was very much influenced by European thought. The Europeans did not always have freedom of speech. They could not be very critical of the government, so when they disagreed they talked around the issue. They offered disclaimers as did Wilhelm Reich during the rise of fascism, stating that fascists were not interested in political action but were concerned only as scientists. Even Albert Einstein had to demoralize his work and claim that he was merely a disinterested scientist carrying out his studies without concern for the political uses to which his findings might be put. Value-free social science was a political necessity despite the fact that findings and analyses could be used for political purposes.[9] As long as the findings supported the regime in power, they were acceptable, but when they called for a change in the operation of the society, particularly with important alterations in it, the idea of value-free science came to the fore. Einstein knew that with nations at war or threatening war, experimenting with guided missiles and atomic power would give a decided advantage to the country that got there first.

Social science was as dangerous in the long run as misguided atomic science. It could be used to promote and reorder the social and economic priorities of the time. It was therefore necessary to make sure that any social science that could not be used to support existing structures and regimes not be given much of a hearing. It is a simple fact that a large number of impediments to the spreading of research knowledge have been erected. One of the most important of these is the use of the peer review process.[10] More is at stake in the process than the simple publication of research papers in learned journals. A clear function of the process is to ensure that no radical knowledge gets into the system. Radical not in the sense of advocating the overthrow the government or trying create social chaos but in the sense of making a significant departure from accepted dogma.

European thought was never divorced from political practice. Thus it was important to exercise political control of professors and other thought-makers. Professors, in their turn, influenced others. They were thought to have the most disciplined knowledge and reliable facts of any people in society. They were the gods of knowledge akin to priests, politicians, and royalty, who were gods in their particular spheres. Most European countries had very few professors, and the professorial jobs were contested heavily. Such a job could mean inroads to the highest levels of influence in the country. Mass education in Europe did not spread as rapidly as it did in America, where the physical need for professors became so great that it was not possible to give all of them high status. Some 500,000 college teachers meant that category of people could not be so outstanding. In order to get the numbers, it was almost necessary to give up any meaningful political influence. In America a professor was simply someone who taught classes at a local college or university. He or she need not have any more or less to say about any pressing public topic than anyone else.

Mimicking European social thought became such an American preoccupation that intellectual thought in the United States became almost meaningless. As a result, very few academic books written by Americans have had any important political consequences. Novels such as *Uncle Tom's Cabin, Huckleberry Finn,* and *Gone With the Wind* probably had more effect on American thought than the weightiest of intellectual tomes. Everyone seemed to know that American intellectuals, represented most clearly by the professorate, were air-headed people; they were simply good people who did not need to be taken very seriously. The state would pay them to play their little mind games, harass the students, and stay out of trouble. Basically, they were expected neither to produce nor to engage in heavy thought of political or social consequence. It would be much simpler to get deep thought with political implications from the Europeans. Someone with something to say that deserved a hearing could be hired by industry and the activity engaged in safely monitored by those higher up in the social and economic hierarchy, but neither in Europe nor America did scholarship have all that much respectability. Scholarship was engaged in by lower-middle-class people without high status within the European system of thought, which was highly status bound and tied to landownership and hereditary privilege. Early European scholars were monks and priests, who did not have titles of nobility. The eventual titles of professor and doctor indicated persons who did a certain kind of work at the behest of their feudal lords.

NOTES

1. Weber's important *The Protestant Ethic and the Spirit of Capitalism*, published in 1904 and 1905, was translated by Parsons in 1930. A foreword to the 1958 edition is by R.H. Tawney. New York: Charles Scribner's Sons. See also Talcott Parsons, "Max Weber and the Contemporary Political Crisis," *The Review of Politics* 4 (1942) 168, 169. Parsons devoted a good part of his professional life to understanding Weber, who influenced him heavily. See his translation, with A.M. Henderson, of *Wirtschaft und*

Gesellschaft, by Max Weber, as *The Theory of Social and Economic Organization* (New York; Oxford University Press, 1947); Reinhard Bendix, *Max Weber: An Intellectual Portrait* (Garden City, NY: Anchor Books, Doubleday & Co., 1960 and 1962) is an excellent reference work on the writings of Weber. Howard Odum reports that Parsons considered the work of Max Weber to be of sufficient importance for it to dominate his own contributions up to 1949, when he headed the Department of Social Relations at Harvard and served as president of the American Sociological Society. Howard Odum, *American Sociology: The Story of Sociology in the United States Through 1950* (New York: Longman, Green & Co., 1951), p. 49.

2. Robert K. Merton has been most concerned with the issue of alienation in modern man and woman, a problem central to Durkheimian sociology. Merton's influence on American sociology is notable. See especially his *Social Theory and Social Structure,* revised and enlarged (Glencoe, IL: Free Press, 1957).

3. The concept of white-collar criminality has become firmly ensconced in American sociology mainly through the work of Sutherland. Neither the idea nor the data identifying this form of criminality were original with Sutherland, but his conditions for presenting them were. White-collar crime could not have been exposed in the context of European sociology, for doing so would have meant an attack upon the more aristocratic classes. See Edwin H. Sutherland, "White Collar Criminality," *American Sociological Review*, 5 (1940): 1-20.

4. The standard approaches to an understanding of criminal causation are presented in a variety of readily available texts. Good overviews may be found in Sue Titus Reid, *Crime and Criminology,* 6th ed. (Fort Worth, TX: Holt, Rinehart & Winston, 1991).

5. David Popenoe, *Sociology* (New York: Appleton-Century-Crofts, 1971), p. 1.

6. Studies of journals showed that there is a growing tendency for funded research to be published. Unfunded research evidently carries less weight within the structure of the discipline. Research that is not funded will be discounted faster than that which is funded. The size of the grant will to a greater extent determine the placement of the scholar in the discipline. This unpublished research is in the files of the author.

7. Allan Bloom, *The Closing of the American Mind* (New York: Simon & Schuster, 1987).

8. Ibid.

9. It was probably Max Weber who argued in Germany for ethical and value neutrality which had to be claimed if academic work were to be carried on. Close reading of the works of Weber will indicate that he was not nearly as value free or as ethically neutral as might be supposed. Read especially Reinhard Bendix, *Max Weber: An Intellectual Portrait* (Garden City, NY: Anchor Books, Doubleday & Co., 1962), in which many aspects of Weber's work are explored.

10. In this process scholars evaluate the work of other scholars and consider it for publication. The number of articles and books failing to be accepted for publication is enormous and some of these could make outstanding contributions to understanding. Peers may not always want to see new ideas introduced into the marketplace because they may overturn current ones. Peer review may serve as "gate keeper" to prevent ideas from competing with those already approved by those who count. The process is reminiscent of the Catholic Church's efforts to set the standards by which orthodoxy and heterodoxy would be determined; this process lasted from roughly 1517 to 1534 in the seventeen-year meeting known as the Council of Trent.

6

Weber: Some Unanswered Questions

No sociologist other than Marx has had a greater impact on sociology than the German sociologist Max Weber (1864–1920).[1]

Why is Max Weber so important in American sociology? His writings are close to 100 years old. There have been so many changes in all societies that his understanding of so many of them could not be as great as seems to be attributed to him. In nearly every subfield Weber shows a degree of preeminence, or the Weberians certainly have their impact. This is probably not because of Weber's understanding or catholicity. Weber was quite ordinary in many respects, but he towers intellectually over most sociologists, then and now. Marxist sociology is greatly discussed and his ideas are attacked as well as supported. But not even Isaac Newton held as tight a hold over thought in physics as Weber had held over thought in sociology.

Weber is just one of the scholars of the European tradition whose ideas are practically to be discussed on a mandatory basis in any sociology class. It is not that the ideas of these scholars do not merit discussion, but there seems to be an almost inordinate concern with them. Their sayings and understandings are the substance of many courses. There is no denying that Weber and a few others addressed many topics and amassed many pages of work, but their conclusions are like those of all other writers, not always more compelling, belonging to their times. Because of history and tradition their ideas and writings are continually combed for gems of understanding.

In this section we want to ask a few questions of Weber and of a few other scholars of the European tradition with the intention of seeing if there is merit in fascination with their work. Do they have real answers to societal problems or are they deferred to out of history and tradition?

Weber would seem to be a name representing a Semitic background, even if that background were long ago. Just when the older Webers converted to Protestantism is unknown, if they did. Was Max trying to deny his heritage by moving in a more cosmopolitan environment? His father evidently had also worked himself up from involvement in the Jewish subculture in which his own father might have been enmeshed. There is scrupulous lack of recognition at any level in the works of Max Weber, the author, regarding his own religion. There is little evidence of Weber's participation in any religion, only his study of it. But as pious as his mother was, which required some participation in services, why is there such little evidence that Weber was or was not active in religious services? His brightness was not an excuse for his noninvolvement since many of his peers considered some degree of participation as a sign of normal social development. And why was Weber so withdrawn while he was a younger child? Could it be that he saw himself as marginalized even then? Even bright children would have been encouraged, more or less, by their parents to show some degree of religious development. Since Weber liked his mother so much, is it not possible that he would not only have been impressed with her Calvinist piety, but the strong tendency is that he would have tried to please her by participation.

His sense of ethical neutrality which he demanded in academic work may have had more to do with his rejection of his own background, which had little status in the Germany of his time, than with formulating a requirement for the conduct of sociological studies. Ethical neutrality gave him an excuse to deny his own social background, if some of it were Jewish, to reject that it had any influence on him. Could Weber have pressed for ethical neutrality for practical reasons? He knew that there was substantial discrimination against Jews and if he could deny any connection with them he could move more freely within German society.

Weber's family probably had not made a complete break from Judaism and even when the father tried to escape it, its pull showed in his behavior. He never felt comfortable around Jews for he had rejected them, possibly not wanting to be reminded of his origins. Nor did he feel comfortable around Gentiles for the status system was such that he was rejected among those whose attention he craved. So the senior Weber withdrew and engaged in the type of lower middle class behavior which Max did not approve. This is probably one reason he and his father had a poor relationship.

Max Weber was a marginal man, on the record. When he went to the University of Heidelburg he was not accepted by the men of the school and compensated by engaging in drinking and dueling. At the university Weber went from a skinny youth to a portly man with what was defined as a typical German beer gut, perhaps from drinking so much beer. If he were successful at these endeavors perhaps he would be accepted by those whose attention he desired, and they would not hold his background against him. The group that Weber was a natural member of, if our hypothesis is correct, he rejected but was unable to find a group which replaced it in a satisfactory way.

Ethical neutrality meant that he was seeking a social situation in which he would be accepted for what he thought he was, not for what he was not. If the academic and social community would not approach him with their minds made up he would have a much better opportunity for reaching his own goals of personal satisfaction. Weber understood that there was nothing he could do about his background. The next tack was to have it discounted by trying to get agreement that prejudice was not a scientific attitude.

Value neutrality was not simply an attitude toward scientific data and conclusions. It was an attitude Weber hoped would be used with respect to individuals such as himself. People who are secure in their own personalities, politics, power and social status do not argue for ethical neutrality. If anything that is what they do not want for the present structure is favorable to them. No one wants to relinquish an already favorable status to acquire an unfavorable one.

Weber found fault with Catholicism. He remembered how Catholic popes had used their offices to extend their control over the Prussians and the Dutch. The Catholic faith was thrust upon them as much as Islam had been thrust upon the Spaniards and Portuguese in earlier centuries. When Charles Martel defeated the Moors at Tours in the 700s, opening the way for the spread of Catholicism to the Low Countries, Prussia and to Eastern Europe generally, it became clear that Catholicism would spread by means similar to those which had been used by the Moors. Trade and the sword were the two principal means by which any religion spreads. Missionaries have been relatively unsuccessful in changing whole populations of people without the support of tradesmen and armies. Not only were ideas and values at stake, but territory and trade as well. The Catholics did not want competition and it was important to Catholicize as many people as possible to bring them under the trade control of the Catholic hierarchy. The excesses to which the faith went to assure converts and control of them moved men like Martin Luther to object and eventually to foment the Protestant Reformation in the first third of the 1500s. The control of the sea, and much of the land by the Iberian Catholics meant that Jews and others had very little option but to knuckle under or suffer extremely at the hands of the Catholics.

Weber's criticism of Catholicism was couched in academic terms. It came about after he had argued for ethical neutrality, literally to establish that his attitude toward the Catholics was mainly a product of his academic understanding of its fundamental values. Of course, the best argument against Catholicism was an answer to the question, "What had the Catholics contributed to the life and culture of the world?" At the time Weber began his inquiries into religious values the world had shifted from Catholic to Protestant control. Sir Francis Drake had done most to defeat Catholic control of the sea by sinking a great deal of the Spanish navy in 1588, more than 50 years after Luther had penned his thesis against Catholic suzerainty.[2]

By the mid–1800s the Catholics had been defeated in most of the countries of the world. Spain and Portugal had been reduced to second and third rate powers. Italy had not the means to save Catholicism but had to throw up barriers around the Vatican, reducing its influence to that of a small power without other than titular recognition. Catholicism would hold on only among the poorest people of the world, in the backward colonies of Latin America, the Pacific rim countries and a few places in Africa. There would remain bastions of Catholic membership in all the countries but the influence of the religion was greatly reduced. Without an army Catholicism was all but finished as a faith with the ability to bring about change or to make a difference anywhere in the world.

Weber studied religion after the shift had been made from Catholicism to Protestantism. Now the best examples of economic success were found in the Protestant countries, where, if during the centuries between 1300 and about 1600 the economic achievements of the Catholics would have been as impressive as anything the Protestants could put forward after about the 1700s. The spectacular achievements of the Protestants led Weber to conclude that there was something in Protestant values which encouraged their economic upmanship. He would find those underpinnings within Protestantism, within values of Calvinism and Lutheranism. He would stress that individualism, not groupism, best explains economic success. By cutting away from the holds of a group, Weber thought that an individual would be freer to follow a sense of acquisitiveness.

At bottom Weber was anti-group for he realized that there could not be individual freedom while there was adherence to a group. The Puritans were a group but the last had been dead 200 years when Weber wrote his *Protestant Ethic and the Spirit of Capitalism.* There were few people left who adhered to Puritan values. The great fortunes made in the last quarter of the nineteenth century by the Robber Barons[3] had little to do with the realization of Protestant values, as Weber claims. It was the absence of such values which promoted their behavior. But Weber wanted to see some group other than the Catholics make progress on a world economic scale for he was as much anti-Catholic as he was anti-Semitic and rejecting of his own implicit background.

American sociologists have their European favorites and perhaps one of the all-time favorites is Max Weber for his work spans so many of the major features of sociology. Weber is important methodologically for his advocacy of value neutrality and the use of ideal types and *verstehen* (insight into that which is studied). He is important theoretically for his concepts of bureaucracy, charisma, and in demonstrating the influence of values upon behavior. And he is important for showing that a breadth of knowledge of history, psychology, and empirical data are all necessary to bring about a comprehensive understanding of that which is studied. But Weber has another function as well and that is his role in demonstrating the hold that European thought has upon American sociology. If any of these topics is approached there is a tendency to try to find the answers to hypotheses in the thought of some European such as Max Weber.

That there is little new under the sociological sun is evident from the readiness of practitioners to try to reduce answers to those posed by Weber, Durkheim, or some other European thinker. Whether these thinkers are correct or incorrect is not really the problem. The idea is that answers must be posed in the terms they suggested. Weber offered the Puritan Ethic as an operating mode for capitalists but ignored that the ethic had lost most of its meaning long before Weber began to try to integrate his understanding of capitalism as an institution under its rubric. It is no doubt true that many large fortunes were made because men were driven to overcome limited backgrounds and prove that they had arrived by acquiring fabulous fortunes. In America there were many fewer regulations and restrictions on opening businesses and expanding them than existed in Europe. Where families controlled business in Europe, they were long in gaining a foothold in America, although they finally did. But there was not the degree of control that existed in Europe. There were various niches that entrepreneurs could get into as late as the mid-twentieth century. Fortunes were being made but not so much because individuals were exhibiting Protestant values. Many fortunes were simply added to as the economy expanded. The rules of inheritance permitted the passage of substantial fortunes from one generation to the next so that the inheriting generation, by holding onto its wealth, could often become fabulously rich without literally "hitting a lick at a snake."

The influence of Weber's thought on how wealth is accumulated and what values drive that accumulation is so strong in American sociology that there is little attempt to press for the reality of Weber's contention. Harmonizing thought about this behavior is a part of the folk culture of American sociology. There is really no credible thought about capitalism unless Weber or some of the European masters are brought up and hypotheses tested, even informally, within the parameters they set. It has to be done so that Weber will be recognized and his overlordship acknowledged. It is almost as though nothing has happened since Weber's *Protestant Ethic*, his bureaucracy, and his studies on religion.

Weber could not know that as the rules for societal conduct developed it would become more difficult to exploit and therefore more difficult to develop fortunes. For instance, child, female, and minority group labor could not be exploited as easily as during the period before and immediately following the Civil War, although all were taken advantage of. Railroad companies could build railbeds at low cost because of the presence of Oriental workers. Common labor at low cost continued to fuel the factory employment rolls.

By about 1905 when Henry Ford agreed to pay automobile workers $5 per day he almost caused an economic revolution. But Ford understood that holding the workers in thralldom was not a stratagem for increasing the wealth of any. They needed to buy homes and furniture and cars with their new earnings. Following Ford's lead Detroit became one of the most prosperous middle-class cities in America for it was there that a laborer could work for a decent wage and have a decent standard of living. Some of the most energetic workers of

Detroit were the former sharecroppers of the South. Although they did not become great capitalists, they did accumulate beyond their dreams when they were still a part of the stagnant South. None of this had anything much to do with the presence or absence of a Protestant Ethic. Their progress was due more to the openness of the social structure which allowed them to work and to use their earnings as they desired.

While Detroit and other cities were developing middle classes because of more open opportunity structures, the sociologists were continuing to teach Max Weber and his preachments about the Protestant Ethic. Reality and interpretation were nowhere in agreement. Weber's hold, as well as that of European sociology was still very strong.

NOTES

1. James W. VanderZanden, *Sociology: The Core,* 3rd ed. (New York: McGraw-Hill, 1993), p. 14.

2. In 1507 Martin Luther issued his challenge to reform to the Catholic church at the chapel in Wittenburg, Germany. See Kai T. Erikson, *Wayward Puritans* (New York: John Wiley & Sons, Inc., 1966), p. 34.

3. The term *Robber Barons* has been applied to the American tycoons of industry of the nineteenth century. They founded large companies using the predatory tactics of feudal warlords. Rugged individualism seemed to have been their guiding philosophy, which accorded with social Darwinism. See Harold M. Hodges, Jr., *Conflict and Consensus: An Introduction to Sociology* (New York: Harper & Row Publishers, 1974), pp. 300–302.

7

Questioning Durkheim

At a major university a prominent basketball player sat in a corner, cap over his eyes, almost asleep. The lecturer droned on about some old master of thought. The player woke up, forgetting where he was and blurted out, "Why do we have to learn this (expletive deleted)?"

In his very unconventional way, the student asked a most profound question whose answer may greatly affect sociology specifically and the social sciences at large.

Emile Durkheim, an evolutionist and great scholar of religion, thought that, as man became more rational, there would be a diminution of the influence of religion. There was consensus in religion, something every society needed to be held together, Durkheim thought.[1] But Durkheim seemed not to fully appreciate that nearly any activity which so captivates the minds of individuals that they no longer need to think in order to act can become a religion. Whenever people worship a practice, it becomes a religion, a deity, a god. And all the trappings of religion are soon manifest in it.[2]

Religion, like other parts of society, is not static. All parts of society are always changing, though not always in a clearly visible way. Old ideas die out and are replaced by new ones. Static old ideas harden into religious dogma and survive long after they have lost vitality among the newer and younger members of society.

Durkheim's proposition that rationality leads to a reduction in the influence of religion can be partially tested by resort to historical and contemporary evidence. By rationality is meant that scientific reasoning takes the place of normative or customary justification for action. There are good reasons for an action or an institution, not merely that they are obedient to the forces of custom and tradition.[3]

Now, if rationality reduces religious influence, and religious influence is another way of supporting the cake of custom, then, in a very scientific society, religious conflict should be minimized. A rough index of the rationality of a country is its number of scientists per 1,000 of population. In the U.S. that number is perhaps the highest in the world, probably because of the extensiveness of the higher educational system which is instrumental in the production of scientists.

Durkheim, of course, would not agree that formal training ensures rationality in all matters, for rationality itself is socially constructed. Complete rationality would mean the value of emotion would decline to zero. As Durkheim himself suggests, no society can exist without the opportunity for its participants to express emotion. But emotion and rationality are incompatible in the Durkheimian scheme of reasoning.[4] The greater the movement toward rationality, the greater it is toward atheism. Thus new cults must supplant the old religions, for man has long had, and probably always will have, a god or perhaps of several of them.[5] Specifically, all people use rationality, or their best judgment, in their daily lives and work. When rationality becomes very widespread, the culture might become like Pitirim Sorokin's sensate society.[6]

But Durkheim's proposition may be questioned because it is not in agreement with observational data. Germany was very scientific at the outbreak of both World Wars, but especially before the Second. Being so did not prevent Germans from using religion to give support to the holocaust. Japan's rationality did not deter her from concluding it was her religious duty to seize Chinese territory and to make war on the U.S. America's concept of "manifest destiny" provided a religious justification for spreading her empire from the Atlantic to the Pacific Ocean and beyond. Nor does rationality prevent her treating free enterprise as a religion and communism as the work of a people with no taste for human freedom. South Africa is very technologically sophisticated but uses religion to justify the suppression of the indigenous peoples of that land. Rationality has not mitigated fights among and within countries, nearly all of which seek justification for their actions in religious terms that cannot easily be separated from the political and the economic.[7]

Durkheim claims to have found a relationship between group solidarity and suicide. Solidarity is used as an abstract concept. Mechanical solidarity stresses the commonness of values, norms, and social history. It develops in groups sharing a common world. Organic solidarity grows out of differences where values of groups are literally in competition. It is a function of the division of labor. People do different things because they inhabit different social and economic worlds and interpret those worlds differently.

Durkheimian reasoning poses a trap because of his attempt to integrate the logic of the mechanically organized village with the organically structured urban environment. His solution to the dilemma is to propose evolutionary development such that the urban organically integrated society appears more rational. While suggesting the growth of rationality, Durkheim does not give evidence that urban decisions are more rational than those of persons in villages. They may be more bureaucratic, of course. Whether in villages or in cities, these persons have their own religions, traditional or modern.

Closely related to his discussion of relations is Durkheim's understanding of group solidarity. For Durkheim, social integration develops among groups that are homogeneous. He is not clear on what produces the homogeneity. Most likely, it is value consensus. His reasoning is tautological in that he is saying that groups which live and interact together closely come to have the same values and are then defined as homogeneous and integrated. Durkheim becomes a critic of pluralism, believing that harmony and morality break down under organic solidarity and a decline of homogeneity.

Durkheim's France was hostile toward pluralism, leading him to see pluralism as a threat to the very existence of society. His writings suggest that the natural state of mankind is homogeneity brought on by the similarities of values and outlooks. Achievement of value similarity and social integration would be accomplished in societies that did not have many strains or outside influences. Long isolated villages and communities which maintained their distinctiveness were the ones which had the best chances of reaching mechanical solidarity and a common morality.

Although Durkheim was an avid seeker of data to demonstrate the validity of concepts he thought meaningful in the social sciences, he remained rigidly abstract and did not produce actual evidence of groups that were mechanically organized. These remained concepts of the mind. Mechanical solidarity made sense theoretically, but Durkheim himself did not illustrate any society which was so organized which had the degree of social harmony and moral integrity he required. The concept of moral integrity of society dogged him throughout his career, and he was unable to reconcile the problems of mechanical solidarity with the lack of it which was present in France even at the time Durkheim wrote. He was forced to use ideal types because he could not find empirical support for his proposition. Because of his lofty position as an academic, and because of the freedom he had to think whatever he wished, it was not necessary that he talk specifically about particular cultures exhibiting mechanical solidarity.

It was only within a homogeneous culture that mechanical solidarity could be achieved. France itself was not mechanically integrated. It was broken down into too many groups by language, culture, and tradition. Parisians differed from those from Alsace-Lorraine or the French Alps. The Belgians, speaking French, were not a part of the moral universe of the French. Posing group integration as one of mechanical or organic solidarity revealed that Durkheim was more in favor of traditional groupings than of groups which were crosscut.

Differences cause strain under Durkheim's concept, and they are not encouraged. But Durkheim does not call for assimilation of different groups. His solution is to argue that the loosening of moral ties occurs when groups are no longer mechanically integrated. The more similar the groups the greater the likelihood that they will share a moral common ground. Mechanical solidarity is not shared with those categorized as "they." There is little space in Durkheim's sociology for organic solidarity to have the psychological benefits of societies solidified mechanically. "They" were organically structured and their stability a lot less than the almost natural stability which was a function of mechanical solidarity.

Durkheim's emphasis on mechanical solidarity identifies him as a functionalist. He teaches that certain cultural practices maintain the equilibrium of the society. Durkheim did not like the tension created by differences in values and moral standards. He thought groups would experience less tension if they did not move out of the moral universe in which they were born and socialized. So protective of the moral order of the group was Durkheim that he thought a group could not hold together when the bond was merely organic, based solely upon a division of labor. Since Durkheim abhorred instability, he was not hopeful for those groups not having a large degree of mechanical solidarity. Any "we" group had more to recommend it than any organically solidified society.

The promotion of mechanical solidarity became a necessity for keeping a group tightly bonded. Mechanical solidarity would be advanced by the promotion of ethnocentrism, territorial exclusiveness, endogamy, religious homogamy, and other factors. Even political factors would be used to proscribe and limit the contact of groups which were different. Support and perpetuation of the group became reasons for being of individuals tightly integrated into it. Myths of the past greatness of the mechanically organized culture would be used to help assure that the group did not stray from its boundaries or permit others into those boundaries. In short, Durkheim's argument for mechanical solidarity was a plea for group exclusiveness of the kind which led to modern fascism.

The United States is probably the first large nation to be forged out of a variety of small states with individual identities. Through a revolutionary and later a civil war, they merged into a federal society in which each state retained some autonomy but at the same time became a part of a greater whole. It took the heavy handed Otto von Bismarck to forge the petty states of Prussia into a modern more comprehensive Germany. India attempted unification but was unable to achieve it for it could not overcome the "we-they" dichotomy posed within the context of Durkheim's mechanical and organic solidarity. Where mechanical solidarity was greatest, the call was for nationalism and territory so that all the like people, those with similarities of speech, morals, values, history, and even looks, could be together. For them, nation could not include those persons outside the group with whom there was no moral harmony, no mechanical solidarity.[8]

NOTES

1. See in George J. Bryjak and Michael P. Soroka, *Sociology: Cultural Diversity in a Changing World* (Boston: Allyn and Bacon, 1992), p. 305.

2. In the place of traditional, organized, and doctrinal religion, there arose secularization, or civil religion, which meant obedience to the rules and dogma of the state. This idea is explored in Robert N. Bellah, "Civil Religion in America," *Daedalus*, vol. 96, no. 1 (1967): 1–21, and in Ronald L. Johnstone, *Religion in Society*, 4th ed. (Englewood Cliffs, NJ: Prentice-Hall, 1992), p. 325.

3. Cults seem to spring up in all societies whether they are more or less rational. For instance, among politically liberal people, the cult of the choice of the mother to decide whether to carry a fetus to term opposes the cult of the rights of the unborn portrayed by the conservatives on these points. The members of Jim Jones' Jonestown People's Temple were modern, very rational people in most of their dealings but fell under the sway of the charismatic Jim Jones. Some 912 of them committed suicide by drinking cyanide laced Kool Aid in 1977 in the jungle of Guyana. Similarly, in 1993, some 90 people lost their lives as they gave obedience to David Koresh, the leader of the Branch Davidians, in Waco, Texas. Followers of the Reverend Sun Myung Moon, "Moonies," were defined as white, working-class and middle-class individuals under age 30, with some college education. The critical variable was that these people were lonely, not that they were irrational as Durkhemian theory would predict. See T. Robbins et al., eds., "The Last Civil Religion: Reverend Moon and the Unification Church," *Sociological Analysis*, 37(2): 111–125 (1976, Summer).

4. People who are perfectly rational have been known to give up their freedom to be members of communes where their lives are largely regulated. They maintain that modern society, with all its regulations and requirements, encourages many to try to get away from it all, even by involvement in living situations which structure life so that to others who do not understand them they have less freedom. See William M. Kephart, *Extraordinary Groups: The Sociology of Unconventional Life-styles* (New York: St. Martin's Press, 1976), p. 286.

5. For an understanding of the role of newer cults since the 1950s, see Arnold W. Green, *Sociology: An Analysis of Life in Modern Society*, 5th ed. (New York: McGraw-Hill Book Co., 1968), pp. 448–449.

6. As a cyclical theorist, the claim was made, ostensibly upon the basis of research, that sociocultural factors are related to three mentalities: the ideational, the idealistic, and the sensate. The ideational mentality embodies religious, otherworldly qualities. The sensate mentality is more scientific, objective. The idealistic is located somewhere between these extremes, making use of some of the features of both. See Pitirim Sorokin, *Social and Cultural Dynamics* (New York: American Book Company, 1937, 1941), four volumes, wherein the idea of these mentalities is elaborated. A brief synopsis of their meaning is found in Robert K. Merton, Leonard Broom, and Leonard S. Cottrell, Jr., *Sociology Today* (New York: Basic Books, 1961), pp. 221–222.

7. In the Near East and in the old Soviet Union, technical rationality is at a high premium, but fighting continues. See Samir al-Khalil, *Republic of Fear: The Inside Story of Saddam's Iraq* (New York: Pantheon Books, 1989) and R.G.D. Laffan, *The Serbs* (New York: Dorsett Press, 1989).

8. One of the most insightful critiques of the sociology of Emile Durkheim is found in Charles H. Anderson, *Toward a New Sociology* (Homewood, IL: The Dorsey Press,

1974), pp. 5–7. Durkheim's idea of the division of labor as holding individuals in the bounds of society was not sufficient. A moral system is required which is reflective of the social order of the time. Whatever the prevailing social order, the moral order generally adapts to it, reducing the strain or anomie between the individual and society. See also John Horton, "The Dehumanization of Anomie and Alienation," *British Journal of Sociology*, 15 (December 1964): 283-300.

8

Contradictions in Merton's Anomie and Science Models

Robert K. Merton is probably the best known American representative of the Francophone style of European sociology. A central idea in Merton's sociology is that of anomie, which he evidently borrowed from Durkheim. At the same time Merton acknowledges his debt to Weberian sociology by discussing science as flowing out of Protestantism as Weber had essayed earlier that capitalism developed best in a Protestant environment.

The present essay notes certain inconsistencies in Merton's analyses of the idea of anomie and that of the role of Protestantism in the development of science.

Its assumed neutrality and even potential utility are what makes science acceptable to almost any group. But even it has the potential for corruptibility, as seen in the Amish and Mennonite cases. They believe there is no way to improve upon the relationship between man and nature.[1] For them this relationship is sovereign and permanent and opens opportunities to live the most satisfying lives by treating man and nature as one. The relationship of man to man is as much a natural relationship as that of man to nature for neither can be separated from the other. For these groups, as for others similar, neither science, sociology, other knowledge or influences which disturb this relationship are needed. These groups, for example, might not want telephones for there is no need to contact or be contacted by anyone beyond the sound of one's voice. People working and living together have all the communication they need. The bringing in of telephones might be as deleterious to those societies as the introduction of marijuana, cocaine, alcohol or cigarettes. Unless the group could control the generation of power to run the machines, their way of life would be imperiled if these innovations were introduced. They would have to work at outside jobs to earn the money to pay for the technological innovations. Already there are encroachments forcing the dependence of these groups upon the outside world for sustenance.

Merton of course cannot account for the Amish and Mennonites and people like them. They fit none of his anomie categories.[2] They are not people unable to compete successfully for the values of the middle class who react by becoming deviant. They are not retreatists trying to withdraw from a world of which they disapprove. They are not seeking to create a world of their own while dropping out of the competition in the real world. These are not alienated people with agendas for changing the world to meet their specifications. Nor are they apocalyptic or millenarian prophesying the destruction of the present world upon whose ashes will be built a new and more perfect one. And yet it is difficult to socialize each new generation to the old values. The forces of change are too great for even these strict groups to resist. Others before them had tried and had failed. Their young people fell to the influences of modern technology and then to the attractions of modern values. Experience has taught that values cannot be separated from technology, at least, not on a basis of permanency. Science and technology could modify values so that controllers of these former would also control values. Logically, then, the forces dedicated to the control of values would seek to control science and technology. Groups which do not want a corruption of their values resist the introduction of science and technology. Thus the Amish and Mennonites keep a very simple technological base, resisting and disdaining mechanical innovations as long as possible.

There are many groups for which the Mertonian scheme of anomie fails to account. Consider the Father Divine Peace Mission Movement. This movement begun in the aftermath of World War 1, spread from Baltimore, Maryland, to Valdosta, Georgia, to New York, Jersey City, and Philadelphia, involving hundreds of thousands of people following after an uneducated preacher thought to be born George Baker from around Savannah, Georgia, between 1860 and 1888. Dates of his actual birth and childhood are obscure. His parents were believed slaves. He changed his name to Major Jealous Divine, and later was known as Father Divine. He died in 1965.

The Peace Mission movement was made up of persons not all of whom were down on their luck. The movement cut across a broad spectrum of the people. Members joined the movement because it gave them something they wanted. They sought pleasure and gained it by association with Father Divine.[3] Anomie theory does not account for psychological or sociological motivations for behavior for motives cannot be easily categorized. Neither can the teachings of society be conveniently dichotomized as goals and means. To do so ignores the complexity of human behavior.

Anomie theory has been applied most often to studies of delinquency. Scholars such as Albert K. Cohen, Solomon Kobrin, and Walter Miller have been most vigorous in applying the thought of R.K. Merton to this phenomenon.[4] The juvenile gang, as it appears in America, does not seem to have a counterpart in other countries of the world. To be sure there is delinquency in each of the countries, but only in a few of them is the issue of status a factor. In Denmark the closest thing to gang delinquency was in Christiania, an old military barracks where persons dissatisfied with middle class life followed life-styles of engagement in drugs and sex. They were not dangerous and were not harassed by the authorities. Some participants in the Christiania subculture held jobs in legitimate fields and were only part-time in that subculture. They seemed to be rejecting the high standard of living typical of the Danes.[5]

Although Sweden and Norway do not have living standards as high as that of Denmark there is not enough alienation for youth to form gangs to prey off others, to protect turf, and to secure status within their private culture.

Japanese deviancy may occur for much the same reason as that motivating Danish deviancy. The level of living is high and the opportunity to extend it so unlikely that youth may drop out of the competition. These youth may become hard to manage by their parents and teachers who are unable to imbue them with traditional Japanese values of hard work and upmanship. The postwar generation of Japanese found themselves with the task of rebuilding a destroyed economy and culture. A generation later they had virtually accomplished that task. Their children may not know much of the struggles of their grandparents and would not be impressed with the need to promote Japanese nationalism through economic imperialism. Already there is a high incidence of Japanese teenage suicide, some arguing because of the inability to uphold family honor through school or economic success. But there seems to be nothing like gangs roaming the streets of the cities or defending turf within them as is done in the American case.[6]

In the countries of Latin America there is considerable youth delinquency but most of it is theft. Youth in Brazil sleep in the streets, rummage in garbage heaps, and steal.[7] It is similar in the Caribbean islands, Egypt, and throughout India. Stealing gangs are located in most of the African cities. It is perhaps in South Africa that the gang most resembling the American gang is found. There the gangs seek the same economic values as the American gangs but there is the additional factor of politics. Those representing rival tribal groups, now translated into political factions, may be in serious conflict with one another.[8]

It is probable that the American gang is fairly unique on a world scale. In most other countries the ingredients for gang behavior do not exist to the extent they exist in American society. Poverty is certainly a factor in them all, but not all poverty groups have the same characteristics. American poverty differs from that of most other countries in the respect that U.S. poverty is most likely to be broken home poverty. In no other country is the family as decimated relatively as that of the U.S. where nearly 25 percent of all children will be born out of wedlock or live in homes with a single parent. In the slums and ghettos the rates are double or even higher. The absentee father is a major factor in the formation and continuity of the juvenile gang. In other countries, even if the family is poor but intact the likelihood is greater that the father will not permit the son to be a gang member.

MERTON AND SCIENCE

In 1904 Max Weber published his widely discussed and influential *The Protestant Ethic and the Spirit of Capitalism.* From that time forward there was considerable discussion on how to account for the development of the modern phenomenon called capitalism. Weber associated growth with the presence of asceticism, a part of the Puritan ethic. This set of values also stressed cleanliness, time consciousness, upward mobility, and rationality, to name a few. Protestantism, represented most clearly in Puritanism, suggested that success was an expectation of the good man who would be successful in his worldly calling, generally in an honorable field. Goodness and success would be evidence of salvation to be granted in life after this world.

In the late 1930s Robert K. Merton, of Columbia University, wrote an important and widely read paper entitled "Puritanism, Pietism and Science."[9] In that seminal work Merton argued that modern science could also be attributed to the presence of an ethic which dictated that scientists follow many of the practices of Puritanism. As Weber had found nearly 40 years earlier, namely that the Puritan ethos promoted capitalism, Merton found that modern science had essentially the same origins. Accordingly, Merton's was a prediction that modern science would most likely arise within a Protestant or Puritan tradition as Weber held that capitalism was to be expected mainly within a Protestant tradition. Essentially, both capitalism and science were to be found in Puritan/Protestant cultures.

The development of modern science may be dated from roughly about 1500 A.D. There was science before then, found in all of the ancient cultures: Greece, Egypt, Babylon, Rome, Persia, India, China. Emphasis on the mastery and understanding of the natural world seems to be characteristic of the world's oldest people. Even modern primitive people stressed this understanding as they sought to make their lives less directly dependent upon nature. Even though their tools have been simple, they have illustrated a focus on the principal of rationality and practicality.

IMPERIALISM AND SCIENCE

From the beginning of the New World after Columbus's discovery in 1492, there was an ushering in of a period of European domination which lasted until at least World War II. Within that time, some 450 years, the great discoveries of the world were attributed to persons of the European tradition. Ordinarily, these persons were Protestant, at least predominantly. So long did this domination last that it was easy and tempting to expect that science could emerge only in a European, largely Protestant, tradition. Merton's argument could not be refuted for he was predicting and explaining within a tradition which had gone on so long that any scientist seen was immediately associated with the European tradition. Thus Merton came to emphasize the ethic, the tradition, rather than other factors that might help explain the origin of modern science.

Although all cultures contained elements of scientific reasoning, and considerable scientific headway had been made before 1500, it must be said that many of the cultures of the world, perhaps those with the least to offer in modern scientific achievements, were the groups most likely to fall under the influence of colonialism and imperialism. As great physical resources were lost during the period of imperialism, there were important arrests made of the scientific development of the colonies dominated.

Merton's hypothesis has enjoyed widespread sociological popularity and his article has been practically required reading by those students interested in the development of science as a rational enterprise. What Weber did for capitalism, Merton now had accomplished for science. Ascetic Protestantism has been considered the progenitor of orientations such as science and capitalism, both stressing altruism and a detached personal orientation toward science.

However, since World War II much science has emerged from non-Protestant, non-pietistic sources, as has much capitalistic endeavor. The most damaging evidence to the credibility of the Mertonian/Weberian hypothesis is the rise of Oriental science which is comparable in every way to the science of the West. Oriental science is represented largely, but by no means exclusively, by the achievements of Japanese scientists.

The ability of the Japanese to wage war on the scale they did in World War II, using the most sophisticated scientific orientations and technology, should have alerted western academics to reconsider the Mertonian hypothesis. And yet, Orientals do not claim to operate within rationalistic and ascetic frameworks somehow connected to expectations of otherworldly salvation. Indeed, the dominant religion of Japan is Shintoism which places little emphasis on afterlife in a world rendered more perfect than the present.

If Japan were an aberrant case, perhaps Merton's hypothesis could be sustained. But there has been a general burst of scientific creativity and applicability throughout the former underdeveloped world. India, Iran, Pakistan, and Nigeria (not Oriental) are just a few countries which developed scientific frameworks very rapidly after World War II. Each has the capacity at the present time, inhibited only by politics and economics, to develop atomic bombs, or to conduct heart transplants. The technology and attitude exist practically throughout the formerly backward world to undertake scientific work the equivalent of any found in the West.

It may be argued that it was not the religious orientation of non-Western peoples which determined their attitudes and achievements in science, but the presence of colonialism which deterred achievements of the colonized and subjugated peoples in nearly every walk of life. As the example of Japan illustrates, removing the restrictions upon the thoughts of the people released energies which even they did not know they had. In India and Pakistan holy men, and even many scientists, still take baths in the waters of the sacred River Ganges while recording notable achievements in all the quantitative, empirical, and technical fields.

Merton himself should have seen that by 1957 when he published his revision of his 1936 paper, there had been a significant movement of non-Protestant students into the field of science in the premier universities of America.[10] Few of them changed their religion but most of them caught the vision of science. By 1989 there were about as many Orientals and non-Protestants receiving doctoral degrees in the natural and quantitative sciences as there were of all Western students—Protestant, Catholic, or Jew. But there was no significant attempt to reorder the thought of the eminent Dr. Merton for the hypothesis he had promoted was consistent with the European thought of Durkeim and Weber and the hold that their thought had upon American sociology was practically unbreakable. Data would be interpreted to fit the existing thought and not thought to fit the existing data. Our point, of course, is not to debunk Merton, nor to undermine his contributions, but to simply show that once ideas get emplaced they are difficult of displacement or modification, largely because of tradition, inertia, and even a belief that these ideas are unassailable.

NOTES

1. For an appreciation of the lives of these groups see William M. Kephart, *Extraordinary Groups: The Sociology of Unconventional Life-styles* (New York: St. Martin's Press, 1976).

2. Merton's categories—conformists, innovators, retreatists, rebels, and ritualists—are well known in sociological writings. See Robert K. Merton, *Social Theory and Social Structure* (Glencoe, IL: The Free Press, 1957), pp. 131–160.

3. See Kenneth E. Burnham, *God Comes to America: The Father Divine Peace Mission Movement* (Boston: Lambeth Press, 1979).

4. For biological, psychological, environmental, and sociological approaches to juvenile delinquency, which earlier was considered a special form of deviance of young persons, see a representative work such as Martin R. Haskell and Lewis Yablonsky, *Crime and Delinquency* (Chicago: Rand McNally & Co., 1970).

5. The author studied Christiania in the mid–1970s and fully understands that the circumstances have perhaps changed greatly from then. The point to be made, though, is that Danish society at large did not feel that the behavior of these Danes was contravening values it held sacred. Thomas Mathiesen's *Politics of Abolition: Scandinavian Studies in Criminology* (New York: John Wiley & Sons, 1974), will help with an understanding of how the Scandinavians approach their problem of criminality. Their approach, of course, is entirely different from the American approaches. The best of anomie theory seems inappropriate in the American case.

6. Japanese gangs are beginning to be found in the cities there. They have the *ochikobore* (in-school dropouts), *bokozoku* (deviant young people), and *yakuza* (criminal gangs). A good brief overview of the growth of deviant behavior in Japan is found in George J. Bryjack and Michael P. Soroka, "Crime and Deviance in Japan: Youthful Rebellion in a Peaceful Society," in *Sociology: Cultural Diversity in a Changing World* (Boston: Allyn and Bacon, 1992), pp. 270–273.

7. See James Brooke in *The New York Times, International,* November 13, 1900, for an brief understanding of the problem of slum children in Brazilian cities; also see Bryjack and Soroka, "Crime and Deviance in Japan," p. 273–277.

8. Mark Mathbane, *Kaffir Boy* (New York; New American Library, 1986), gives a good modern interpretation of delinquency in South Africa; there it is associated with the fight to eradicate apartheid.

9. Robert K. Merton, "Puritanism, Pietism and Science," in his *Social Theory and Social Structure* (Glencoe, IL: The Free Press, 1957), pp. 574–604.

10. Robert K. Merton, revision of "Puritanism, Pietism and Science," in Ibid.

9

Collapse of the Old Sociology

For close to a century the old sociology served its purpose based upon the teachings of the Enlightenment, namely, that individuals and groups were valuable and free in their own rights. It then bowed to the concepts of geneticism that swept the land and held sway until well into the twentieth century. Evolution explained differences in groups, and history was unkind to those failing to adapt to changed environmental requirements. It is not coincidental that one of the leading founders of American sociology, William Graham Sumner, endorsed evolutionary thought and applied it to social groups. Sumner, abetted by such natural sciences as there were, physiology and anthropology, held on to evolutionism, taught it, and infused it into American sociological thought.[1]

Sociology did not defeat evolutionism because its practitioners failed to ask Sumner and his colleague Alfred Keller to renounce insupportable hypotheses about group development, which they published in a book entitled *The Science of Society*. Of course, they had borrowed heavily from Herbert Spencer, whose *Principles of Sociology* mirrored Darwinism.[2] If anything, sociology later promoted its own brand of evolutionism in the caste hypothesis stressed by William Lloyd Warner and his colleagues but made even more famous by Gunnar Myrdal in *An American Dilemma*.[3]

The first large-scale test of evolutionism came forward in World War I when the U.S. Army Alpha Tests showed that northern blacks scored higher than southern whites. The next came in the early 1930s when Adolf Hitler began posturing Aryan supremacy basing his logic upon the science of the time. The military powers of the colonial governments were such that no test was needed. Hitler did not invent the idea of European (Aryan) supremacy. It had been invented after Columbus discovered America in 1492 and needed an excuse to justify the exploitation of the native peoples conquered.[4]

Common sense taught that it was not evolution that explains group differences. Opportunity and culture seemed to explain much more. Hitler had to revise his hypotheses in 1936 when Jesse Owens and Ralph Metcalf outran Europeans in the Olympics. Near the turn of the century Jack Johnson had defeated Jim Jeffries to become the first black heavyweight champion and to drive an early nail in the coffin of evolutionism and social Darwinism.

By the time of the publication of Myrdal's *An American Dilemma* (1944), sociology was established as a supporter of the status quo ante in the major universities where it was offered. It adopted and supported paradigms that did not permit much social change. Women had gained the franchise and the temperance movement had lost out to the relegalizing of alcoholic beverages. Neither of these changes owed much to social science, which was becoming irrelevant to all matters of great social concern. The social scientists, including sociologists, laid back waiting for the natural scientists, especially the evolutionists, Lamarckians, Mendelians, endocrinologists, psychologists, and others to adduce evidence in support of the colonial hypothesis of the differences between groups defined as races. Contrary data made no impact upon the evolutionists, who had seized upon Darwinism as support for their positions.[5]

This judicial practice of genetics and anthropology by the U.S. Supreme Court helped cause the old science to be called into dispute. At the same time license was given to natural and social science to promote any values they chose and to ensure that there was no retreat from *Plessy v. Ferguson*. Science was now revealed to have a political agenda and was no longer value-free. Natural science became more like social science, and both ended up moralizing to support values the scientists themselves already held deeply. Sociology became what the sociologists believed and what was inevitably supported by their research. What sociologists said or wrote made little difference, for their sterile and commonplace insights simply supported the status quo.

It was not a contest of the saliency of paradigms that caused a fragmentation of sociology and its virtual collapse. There were plenty of sociological problems that were on the same level with AIDS, the common cold, and cancer. Pressing problems whose solutions would have made important differences in the lives of the people were scarcely addressed. Instead, legions of sociologists attacked problems whose solutions had low demonstrable utility. Candidates for advanced degrees settled on more esoteric and narrow-gauged topics and much mega-research had the same ends in mind. It was not necessary that all sociologists work on single problems such as, say, cold fusion in physics. Whatever was found out would reasonably be expected to have some value, if no more than that the research experience would make the sociologist a better teacher.

The scientific pretentiousness of some disciplinarians and their esoteric studies, especially when publicly financed, did not sit well with the public. Few save other sociologists in something of a peer review process could make sense of what sociologists were saying in their writings. Once the writings were deciphered, the receivers found that they were neither better nor worse off as a result of having reviewed the reports. The writings simply did not make much difference one way or the other in anything that mattered.

As early as the 1940s sociology was in trouble from the standpoint of support of its major propositions. Melville Herskovits and E. Franklin Frazier jousted on the relatively innocuous problem of the presence or absence of Africanisms in black American society.[6] Their argument was diversionary in that its settlement had little more than psychological meaning for the people involved. A few Africanisms retained would mean a culture truncated.

The argument between Oliver C. Cox and Gunnar Myrdal on the matter of America's caste system was much more vital.[7] If academics could show that a racial caste system existed with which both groups were in agreement, the status quo would be well served. When old-line sociology could not win the caste argument, the discipline quickly began to lose credibility. Sociology was split internally, and members began to attack and discredit each other without understanding that the discipline itself was under serious assault.

During the McCarthy cold war years of the 1950s, social scientists, especially sociologists, were thought purveyors of liberalism and communism. A hunt for campus communists was later found to be an excuse to silence social scientists, especially sociologists, who called for a more egalitarian society.

The general public was always suspicious of sociology, for it seemed to have no paradigms that accorded with experience and common sense. Even so, armies of students enrolled in sociology classes. Most people thought a good sociology course would introduce students to much knowledge from which they had been protected. Most of all sociology would challenge their provincialism; it would broaden their horizons but would not be a field in which the majority of its students could make a living. For some, sociology was proving to be a liberal philosophy undermining conservatism.

Into the 1960s sociology helped to liberalize students, in the process often alienating them from their parents. Students drifted into drugs and counter cultures that stood in opposition to the values of their parents. Much of this opposition was masked under disagreement with the Vietnam War.

If the discipline was to continue to enjoy public support, liberalism had to be changed to conservatism. Sociology was then expected to find a framework in which to hold people in their old places. Ideas of equality gave way to ideas of cultural pluralism, which taught that all cultures had value of which their members should be proud.

To mount an open attack upon sociologists was now politically unacceptable. To do so would have tested free speech in the university setting. In another tack sociological research became tied to foundations and government, making it difficult to conduct research not sanctioned by these funding sources. The peer review process would weed out all research that did not meet government and foundation standards, especially research that did not promise to support prevailing values regarding social structure. Dissident voices were practically driven out of the field; their articles and books were relegated to the shelves and never heard from again.

The old status-driven sociology was discarded as soon as possible by the new wielders of power; who had been trained in the 1950s and 1960s. They relied little upon their training in the liberalizing disciplines, falling back upon bureaucratic procedures to establish their control and credibility. These new leaders were most unimpressed by the ability of the old sociology to provide a theoretical or practical basis upon which a more just society might be erected. They understood the liberalizing potential of a well-taught and critical sociology versus the traditional conservative old status- and place-based sociology. They felt more comfortable with the old, even if it were seen by the students as irrelevant to anything meaningful. The old sociology, now mainly a little game of word definitions and name identifications, became useful mainly as a means by which students could augment their grade point averages. The change value of the discipline was practically lost.

Out of the classrooms, at the highest levels of the discipline, the irrelevance of the discipline was seen in internecine arguments over definitions, such as those of poverty and the underclass. Very little change was implied as discipline leaders clashed and augmented their own bibliographies in clarifications of clarifications, spinning arguments about "how many angels can dance on the head of a pin" at some specifiable level of probability. It was all very exciting to those doing the arguing, but those needing help would need to look elsewhere for relief, for it evidently was not to be found in sociological theory.

NOTES

1. See especially Cynthia Eagle Russett, *Sexual Science: The Victorian Construction of Womanhood* (Cambridge, MA: Harvard University Press, 1989), pp. 141–142.

2. William Graham Sumner and Alfred Keller, *The Science of Society,* 3 vols. (New Haven, CT: Yale University Press, 1927) and Herbert Spencer, *Principles of Sociology,* 3 vols. (New York: D. Appleton, 1925).

3. Gunnar Myrdal, *An American Dilemma* (New York: Harper, 1944).

4. See Oliver C. Cox, *Caste, Class, and Race* (New York: Doubleday, 1948), wherein is found Cox's clash with Myrdal and where the essence of the exploitation hypothesis is posited.

5. One of the key cases that sought to place people in racial categories was *Plessy v. Ferguson* (1896) when the U.S. Supreme Court opined that if one had any black ancestry, one was black. A line had to be drawn in the sociological sand across which none would be allowed to step. Any black blood at all made one black, while gallons of white blood did not establish whiteness.

6. The Frazier-Herskovits feud continued for many years in the various books of these distinguished scholars. See E.F. Frazier, *The Negro in the United States* (New York: Macmillan, 1949) and Melville J. Herskovits, *The Myth of the Negro Past* (New York: Harper, 1942), for some impression of the position these scholars held on the issue of Africanisms in New World black culture.

7. William Lloyd Warner, "American Caste and Class," *American Journal of Sociology*, vol. 42, no. 2 (September 1936): 234–237, was not the first to talk about the caste-like features of American race relations. His work made the concept popular, however. Cox began to criticize the concept in the early 1940s. See O.C. Cox, "The Modern Caste School of Race Relations," *Social Forces*, vol. 21, no. 2 (December 1942): 218–226. It was Gunnar Myrdal, in *An American Dilemma* (New York: Harper & Row, 1944) established caste thought in American sociology. Cox's thesis was criticized by many who did not approve of the capitalistic need for cheap labor, which gave rise to race relations. See, for example, N.D. Humphrey, "American Race Relations and the Caste System," *Psychiatry: Journal of the Biology and Pathology of Interpersonal Relations*, vol. 8, no. 4 (November 1956), pp. 379–381.

10

Americanizing Sociology

By the end of World War II, sociology was a discipline concentrated mainly in the United States, although it had its modern nineteenth century birth in Europe. The discipline spread somewhat rapidly after colonies became independent in the postwar period, but old colonial countries failed to permit the general spread of the discipline within their confines. In typical European countries a few professors practically monopolized sociological teaching and research until well into the 1950s, largely because educational opportunities were not available on a non-elite basis.

Opposition to the total educational dominance of elite schools and professors forced the opening of more school places to a wider segment of the population. New schools were opened in old countries and newly independent ones. Sociological teaching became widespread and more internalized in this way.

Modern sociology followed the American model, which had sharply challenged and practically overthrown the European focus. It called for research on relatively local environments and problems. The internationalizing of sociology led to the localizing of it by the use of paradigms, language, and methods commonly used in American sociology. International sociological bodies began to proliferate, but they were unable to get far beyond the problems, language, and methods commonly used in American sociology. There, was not a true internationalizing of sociology, but the spread of American sociology to other countries.

But the problems of other countries were not those of the United States and so the transfer amounted to foreign peoples' readily studying America's social problems. American books, when not simply transferred to other countries wholesale, were translated into local languages, with the result that sociologists in the rest of the world became more knowledgeable of American cultural and social problems than they were of the culture and problems in their own countries. For many of them sociology had little applicability in their countries but was produced for the American market.

Drawing upon the paradigms popular in the United States international sociology came to focus on social class, the principal problematic in America mimicking the old European emphasis that did not apply to most of the other countries of the world. A class structure was nothing unusual in these old countries and even in some of the new ones, for neither wealth nor opportunity had been equitably distributed despite the protestations of Karl Marx. Peasants were as comfortable in their poverty as scions of wealth and privilege in their assumed "natural" roles and stations. There had been no longstanding ideology of the equality of peasants and gentlefolk in the Old World. This same inequality had generated revolutions and civil war in the previous two centuries and continues to provoke unrest and change in the present.

American sociology was a study of the poor, the deviant, the entrapped, and the exotic in their myriad institutions.[1] Persons in the international contexts often assumed these groups to be nonproblematic. International sociology would deal with the same types of problems, using essentially the same methods as were used in the United States.

The disaffection of Americans with a rigid class structure led social scientists to countless and detailed analyses of every facet of that structure. Its very underpinnings were laid bare, its functions and unanticipated consequences examined under the cold lenses of intellectual scrutiny. Class became one of the most descriptive and explanatory variables in American sociology and in international sociology as well. This was inevitable with the increasing use of American paradigms.

An American preoccupation with European sociology worked against the development of a genuinely American sociology, one which fit the American scene. Only a single American school of sociology emerged, and that was the Chicago school of the 1920s through the 1940s. However, the main part of the Chicago school gained its strength from the thought of the European masters. The primary theoretical focus of the Chicago school was upon class, status, and caste, and it was within these parameters that most of their studies were conducted.[2] The school was given a degree of distinctiveness by its willingness to concentrate upon everyday features of society by use of the relatively uncomplicated methodology of participant observation. The Chicago school's methods and its willingness to study the underside of life—pimps, prostitutes, criminals, marijuana users, gangs, hobos, the slums, and so on—were soon being followed in other schools by scholars trained in the Chicago tradition. Soon Chicago professors began to feel a little sensitive about their students' turning out dissertations and theses on the denizens of Chicago's seamy underside. The academics tried to gentrify their studies by using the same methodology to study the upper and middle levels of society. It was more difficult to get data on the highest levels of society, but they did go as high as they could. School teachers, principals, superintendents, and other accessible middle-class aspirants such as medical interns were studied. Louis Wirth, a representative of the Chicago school, used the same methods to study the assimilation of Jews into American society, as did students and professors studying a variety of ethnic peoples who were making the transition to American life.[3] The Chicago school basically adhered to the requirements of European sociology by its focus on the class or status of the groups they studied. The school was essentially descriptive but derived its theory from the older European models.

The conflict, neo-Marxist, and mathematically radical empiricist wings that developed in the United States following World War II could not lay claim to status as genuine innovations. They had drawn their inspiration from the European continent and were more or less trying to find favorable environments for their work in America. Followers of the tradition of Marx, such as Ralf Dahrendorf, Richard Quinney, Austin Turk, and George Vold, the latter three in criminology, tried to form schools of thinkers that would critique the American social system, or at least the parts of it in which they were interested. The old scholar Otto Pollack, showing his obedience to Marxist thought, had proposed that women would be as criminal as men were the system not sympathetic to women to the extent that they are protected, for the most part, in regard to crime. Attempts to bring European thought to American understanding of crime continued in the work of George Rusche and Otto Kirchheimer, who sought to relate punishment and social structure.[4]

No matter how much the scholars emphasized the primary European concepts regarding conflict, functionalism, and statics, however, they found little acceptance in the United States. No one really believed that there was class conflict in America, even though they were told many times that there was. They were not prepared to accept the plantation system, the ghettos, and even the practices of ethnic discrimination as viable examples of class conflict. Nor would they accept the functionalist proposition that these and other structural features of society helped to maintain the order of the social system. Whatever one believed about the mingling of people, their general suffering was not a part of their training.

TEACHING THE OLD MASTERS

What is the impact of the old European masters on the teaching of sociology in modern American institutions? Perhaps it is prudent to begin at the high school level, where a few schools offer students an elective course or two. There, sociology is taught much differently than at the college level, although, where the teachers have graduate degrees, they sometimes tend to make the course they teach like the one they took in the college they attended. High school sociology focuses less on the nomenclature of the discipline, nor does it stress familiarization with the names of individuals and their theories of human society. The students are not much concerned with who said what, when, and where. The high school course is, rather, an introduction to the operation of society as the student sees it. Such an introduction allows many opportunities for discussion.

Many school districts discourage the teaching of sociology by having social sciences taught instead. In the social science approach, there is a focus on each social science in turn. The approach is generally topical under the time restraint of a single semester. With four our five of the traditional social sciences to be covered, sociology gets perhaps even less than its share of discussion in favor of the disciplines that are concerned with much less controversial material.

Sociology textbooks used in high schools are often the same as those used in college, although in the 1960s and perhaps afterward a few texts were written specifically for the high school market. Today the books targeted for the junior or community college market, where the growth in enrollment seems to be, are the ones used in the high schools. Again, the tendency is to water down the course to the extent that it is not very challenging to the students, who enroll in great numbers. In high schools, junior colleges, and community colleges the emphasis is not on teaching the old paradigms and the old masters.

At the standard four-year college level, the old masters are brought back in. This is possible because the general sociology course is taught on a topical basis. The idea is that the course can be sliced up and dealt with as a series of topics. Whether these topics are called institutions or problems or are given other titles, when they are addressed they are accounted for on the basis of theory. Table 10.1 lists some topics and theorists that might be covered in a general sociology class. The topics suggested are not intended to be exhaustive. The asterisks are used to indicate that for the category given,there are too many persons of European extraction to name at this time. The names chosen are merely illustrative of the influence of European thought.

There are American versions of these problems and topics, and notable advances have been made by Americans in all these fields. The knowledge accumulated is of a stair-step variety, each addition growing on the previous base; thus it is understandable that with America emerging later than the other countries, its contributions are built on those made earlier in time. The foundation of American society rests heavily upon Europe. The contributions of other peoples to American life and culture are only recently being recognized.

American scholarship attempted to compete with the more established European scholarship. In most of the sciences and in many of the arts American ingenuity soon matched or surpassed that of Europe. America was more dynamic and permitted the exercise of the talent of relatively more of its people, whereas in Europe traditionalism prevailed leaving only the most polished minds to make its major advances. Aristocratic thought continued to plague Europe and affected the Continent's ability to change with the times.

In America it was in the social sciences, particularly sociology, that the hold of Europe was most noticeable. European thought was, not something to build on, but a platform on which to rest. There was little incentive to move beyond the thought of the European masters. The holistic way Europeans approached

Table 10.1
Fields, Authorities, and Ethnicities

Topic	Authority	Ethnicity
Art	Michelangelo*	Italian
Suicide	Emile Durkheim	French
Economics	Karl Marx	German
	Adam Smith	English
Social Class	Karl Marx	German
Race	Gunnar Myrdal	Swedish
Bureaucracy	Max Weber	German
Personality	Sigmund Freud	Swiss
Population	Thomas Malthus	English
Religion	Emile Durkheim	French
General Statistics	Karl Pearson	English
Intelligence	Alfred Binet	French
Criminality	Cesare Lombroso	Italian
Evolution	Charles Darwin	English
Primitive People	Claude Levi-Strauss	French
	Bronislaw Malinowski	English
Genetics	Gregor Mendel	English
Law	William Blackstone	English
Theater	William Shakespeare	English
Music	G.F. Handel*	German
Physics	Albert Einstein	German
	Isaac Newton	English
Medical Science	Marie Curie*	French
Novels	Feodor Dostoevski*	Russian
Education	Johann Pestalozzi*	Swiss

*Representative of the categories.

their subject matter was lost on Americans, who were more likely to approach their work topically, although they used European concepts. Europe was homogeneous by class, the essential sociological variable, whereas America showed greater variability in its class structure and composition.

There were so many groups of differing orientations that America had the problem of assimilating them all. Assimilation turned immigrants into Americans and then placed them on the same class ladder that all other Americans were on. Even former slaves eventually became assimilated and therefore took their place on the American class ladder. Since European social thought assumed populations were homogeneous, the transfer of that thought to America generated such concepts as assimilation and its antithesis, cultural pluralism. When Americans teaching sociology at the college level told themselves they were going deeply into sociological content, they were really turning to the thought of old European masters who provided them with the theoretical underpinnings of their discipline, thereby causing them to approach American society with essentially the same orientation as the Europeans.

R.P. Cuzzort and E.W. King bring home the symbolic importance of European mastery of sociological topics as they warn students of the importance of knowing names: "If we are discussing religion and we have both read Durkheim, then we do not have to engage in prolonged discussions to make clear the knowledge that we already share."[5] It seems to be understood that there can be no discussion of religion unless it is addressed from a Durkheimian framework, widely recognized by sociologist as a functionalist one. Durkheim has already set the parameters for discussion by those highly impressed by Durkheim's thought. In their thought, practically everything of sociological relevance regarding religion has already been said by Durkheim. A major task is to find out what he said and to understand it. This process passes for an understanding of the sociology of religion. Nearly all else on the topic is anticlimactic, for the classic statement on the matter is by Durkheim.

The same attitude prevails with respect to many other sociological topics. From the European standpoint, American sociology is not really sociology because it is so superficial. It is reduced to a technology, one of gathering, sorting, and processing great amounts of data with the hope that the information will speak for itself. Thus anyone with technological sophistication can become a sociologist. Topics may be made smaller and more specific, yielding a smaller understanding of the total picture of society, which itself is never so segmented. Superficial study, including the use of questionnaire data, amounts to tests of the hypotheses of the European masters even when resolution of those hypotheses will not yield much more knowledge than is already known. A concern with hypothesis testing of the "theories" of the European masters, through the means of technology, takes thought out of the study and prohibits its asking and answering hard sociological questions.

TEACHING THE OLD SOCIOLOGY

The old sociology was intimidating to beginning students. A special nomenclature had to be learned in which to discuss social science events. Unless a student learned this language and memorized it, there was little likelihood of getting a good grade in the course. German, French, Latin, and Greek words were liberally dispersed throughout any sociological writing adhering closely to the old school rules. If foreign words were insufficient to confuse students and to turn them away from reading, a very technical language of statistics and physics was substituted, the gist being that students frequently said they did not understand what a writer was trying to say.

Sometimes the old sociology was translated into English, and the words, where clear in ordinary senses, became quite confusing in sociological use. For instance, the word *distance* is easily understood in English, but when prefixed by *social*, the term becomes unclear; social distance is not distance, for the space between objects is not the same when measured from two opposite points. If A is one group and B another, the social distance from A to B is different than from B to A because of how the two groups feel toward each other. Another word is *assimilation* which in plain English means "absorption." For example, food is assimilated into the body via the digestive processes. But there are some nine different types of assimilation when a sociologist discusses how two groups become one.[6] Of course, the use of special languages gives the impression that the subject matter is mysterious and more difficult to understand than it really is.

The old sociology conveyed the idea that one knew how society worked when one knew the language in which society was discussed. There was an implied match between knowledge of society and knowledge of the language of society. So students spent more time learning language than by observation and analyses of how society works. Social system models became words on paper with lines drawn from word to word, suggesting that social relationships were straight-line ones.

American sociology was different from European sociology in that it used more statistics. Where the Europeans were more esoteric and ivory-towerish, the Americans sent students into the field to "get data." With these data they answered all manner of questions. A fifty-item questionnaire, answered yes or no or even ranging from, say, strongly approve, approve, undecided, disapprove, and strongly disapprove could turn into a thesis of 50(49)/2 possible tables with a page or two of discussion of each table. By the time the researcher got through holding this and that constant and explaining this much or that much variance and declaring that this or that hypothesis was believable at this or that level of significance, it would appear that this was no ordinary student talking randomly about society; this was a scientist armed with the tools of science. This was a knowledgeable and believable person.

The problems of the discipline are seen in the problems of teaching general sociology. After four or five lectures on the basics of sociology and the history of the discipline, students begin to lose interest. The material becomes repetitious. Students experience déjà vu in the furious leaping from topic to topic, for the topics discussed do not represent a stair-stepping of skills and knowledge necessary to understand the additional material. Topics are covered because they are interesting to some publisher or to a book writer, or to the teacher and those are the ones foisted on the students.

James Herndon contends that there is not enough challenging material in a semester-long course to hold the interest of student; that most of the work could be done well in five or six weeks.[7] Although Herndon was talking about secondary schools, the situation is much the same in many sociology courses in colleges and universities. After the first few weeks of school, the classes become dull and students begin to take every opportunity they can to miss the lectures.

The old sociology was characterized by convention and form dictated not by the concerns and requirements of the data with which the discipline dealt but by those imposed by persons who controlled the discipline by their personalities rather than by the cogency of their observations or the accuracy of their predictions or explanations. The old sociology promoted a degree of dogmatism that militated against approaching subject matter without adhering to the required form. It limited the number of questions posed by insisting that answers advanced fit a special format, not merely that they meet what were thought of as statistically rigid criteria. Increasingly, propositions had to be derivable from frameworks set by the European masters in their theoretical schema. Sociological studies quite often then became a matter of testing some small number of hypotheses said derivable from some scheme such as Durkheim's anomie theory, Marx's conflict propositions, or perhaps Weber's preachments and impressions about bureaucracy, or certainly from the propositions of scholars who consider themselves intellectual descendants of the masters.

One reason the old sociology came into being was because of the concerns the old masters had with controlling various populations. As a discipline, sociology was to be a branch of the natural sciences. It had as its goal understanding and then controlling the social environment as the natural scientists understood and manipulated the natural environment. Like all sciences, sociology was to be so esoteric and difficult to understand that it would be interesting only to those who chose the discipline for study. Its tools, techniques, and theory were to be unavailable to most people but would become the property of a relatively small elite who would plan to use the discipline for whatever purposes they had in mind.

As natural science could be sold to willing buyers, sociology was to be sold to those who needed or who could profit from the knowledge and control it offered. Its emphasis on value neutrality was aimed at convincing others that its subject matter was indeed the equivalent of that of the natural sciences and that ideas, feelings, and thoughts could be put aside in the interest of finding the best way of predicting, explaining, and controlling the social environment.

By the time the United States became a social and economic force in the world, the emphasis had changed from control to understanding. The American population was too diverse to provide a formula for control such as that suggested by such old European masters as Auguste Comte. Control was possible in European countries because of their long histories of subjugation and entrenchment in caste and estate arrangements, in their hardest, and social class in the more flexible situations.

In the United States the question focused on why the people were behaving as they were, often when social control was not implied. Many Americans did not understand such things as slavery, Indian subjugation, property and gender requirements for voting and officeholding, and the imposition of social structures that seemed dysfunctional to all. Not even the fuss over religious tolerance made much sense. People who did not like the available pattern of worship available could start their own churches. Freedom of speech, assembly, and worship were conditions the government could not control, even if it wanted to. The constabulary was too small and disunited to do so, particularly over great amounts of territory.

Of the old branches of sociology, theory and methodology, theory was most controlled by European thought. The basic concepts of the discipline derived from mentalities that reflected the influence of the most successful discipline in Europe at the time—theoretical physics. The language of sociology became effectively appropriated from the vocabulary of physics, which had experienced such success in predicting and explaining the phenomena with which it dealt. It became relatively easy to attach the word *social* to any concept used in physics and use that word in a similar way in regard to human society. There was generally a physical analogy to a sociological problem. This tendency derived not so much from a direct emulation and imitation of physics but out of a belief that the social environment could be controlled in the same way the physical environment offered the possibility of control through technology.

Subfields of sociology drew their major concepts from the old European masters. Demography may be used as an illustrative example. Thomas Malthus, the pessimistic English preacher, thought that population control was necessary lest the world become overrun with people who would then exhibit all the well-known problems of misery and poverty.[8] When Malthus wrote, he reflected the growing overpopulation of European countries in the late 1700s, but he failed to envision technological advances that would permit the feeding of populations several times the size of those he estimated. He thought in terms of limits characteristic of Europeans of the time, not in terms of the expansiveness that would face the people of the New World, particularly Americans. Malthusianism was adopted as the framework for discussing American population problems even though the density of the United States was less than forty persons per square mile by 1900. As late as 1970 when the U.S. Commission on Population Growth issued its final report, *Population and the American Future*, the thrust was clearly upon the assumed negative aspects of population growth. At that time the Commission wrote: "The United States today is characterized by low population density, considerable open space, a declining birthrate, movement out of the central cities–but that does not eliminate the concern about population. This country, or any country, always has a 'population problem,' in the sense of achieving a proper balance between size, growth, and distribution, on the one hand, and, on the other, the quality of life to which every person in this country aspires."[9]

The contest between European (old) and American (new) sociology is seen clearly in the population issue of abortion. Again, the old sociology stressed governmental control of the population in the same way that it had been suggested in Europe. The New World had provided Europeans with new territory to which they could ship their surplus and unwanted people. It was the idea that some people were unwanted that is of most significance here. The class, estate, and other systems of defining social status so prevalent in Europe had taken hold in America, particularly among the more privileged classes, because they believed that European thought was not only correct but always appropriate. They began to conceive and perceive of the problems of America in terms dictated and bequeathed to them by the Europeans. The slow-growth populations of Europe became the models favored by American scholars, who had received much of their training in the European academies.

Criminology, another long-time subfield of sociology, never fully repudiated Lombrosianism, a broad school of thought stressing that the criminal population could best be controlled by means up to and including execution, since the stigmata of criminality were largely uncorrectable because they were in-born.[10]

Environmentalism, which seemed more consonant with the causation of crime in America, came to be viewed as the theory of the liberals, who gained brief recognition in the late 1960s and early 1970s when mistreatment of prisoners in the jails and penitentiaries was condemned and the death penalty finally outlawed in the momentous Supreme Court decision *Furman v. Georgia*.[11] But that victory was only partial and short lived. By the late 1970s *Furman v. Georgia* had lost much of its impetus as new appointees were named to the Supreme Court. It shifted back to conservative and signaled a return to the domination of the old European concept of social control through the dominance of force and power.

Not only was it impossible to mount a serious critique of American sociology because there was an unwillingness to critique the assumptions of European sociology for fear of confronting the thought of the masters and finding it wanting, but there was no viable counterculture developed in America. During the 1960s for a brief time the hippies and the back-to-the-landers tried to make statements against the crassness of materialism by rejecting it and taking solace in deviant lifestyles associated with the drug culture. By adopting the behavior and appearances of members whom they perceived as being of the lumpen proletariat, they thought they could make league with the poverty-stricken persons of the slums and ghettos and, together, they could assault the bastions of capitalism.

The hippies found that they were not alienated for the same reason that poor people were. When relatively affluent whites dressed in rags, wore long hair, maintained no permanent employment, ate out of trash barrels when they could do better, the poor folks became disenchanted with them and rejected them. Being deprived of a class of persons whom they felt had genuine complaints against capitalism, the hippies retreated and after a few years gave up their deviant lifestyles to become yuppies, now working harder than the old middle class to make up ground and reclaim their middle-class status.

For a while the hippies thought of themselves as a counterculture because they stood against the major values of the materialistically oriented American culture. After a while the ideologues of the counterculture, such as Professor Timothy Leary of Harvard and Tom Hayden of Berkeley, were discredited. The counterculture began to die, and its supporters and participants began to drift back into legitimate society. The few counterculturists left had no forum and after some years were very strange middle-aged people who looked as if they had never grown up.

The newer contenders for the establishment of a viable counterculture were merely people who enjoyed drugs and irresponsible sex but who were making no ideological statement through their actions. In many cases they were persons trapped by the realignments of the economic system. Some were no longer supported by their parents, and they opted to exist as well as they could on the fringes of legitimate society or in the underworld altogether.

With the decline of the hippie movement and the aging of Herbert Marcuse and Benjamin Spock, criticism of American culture emphases came to a virtual halt, and Russell Jacoby could write that there were no intellectuals in America who are under forty-five years of age.[12] Sociology, likewise, became less critical as empiricism again began to rule the discipline, at least as it was manifest in the publication of articles in the leading journals.

Sociology seemed more and more unconnected to anything that mattered in society. The general course became one of the fun of familiarization of naive students with a variety of exotic cultures and their unusual problems, tied together by a vague concept of relativity that attempted to get them to appreciate these exotic cultures. The students were accused of being ethnocentric when they devalued the exotic and Third World cultures as well as the culturally deviant features of American society.

After racing through the concepts of culture and a few ideas about science and methodology, the class degencrated into a discussion of practically anything anyone wanted to discuss. Stratification was always a popular topic because it allowed students to discuss aspects of the class system and to debate the criteria for being lower class along with the values of that status. Some order was returned to the discussion when population problems provided the opportunity to use a few mathematical formulas regarding birth and death rate calculations, which lent a sense of definiteness to the subject matter.

NOTES

1. Persons familiar with the structure and concerns of American sociology through a study of its major offerings will verify that these are the types of problems with which the discipline customarily deals.

2. The Chicago school of sociologists sought to use processes such as cooperation, competition, accommodation, succession, invasion, and dominance to describe urban life. For a concise appreciation of the logic and methods of the Chicago school, see Richard P. Lowry and Robert P. Rankin, *Sociology: The Science of Society* (New York: Charles Scribner's Sons, 1969), pp. 380–383.

3. See Louis Wirth, *The Ghetto* (Chicago: University of Chicago Press, 1928), which has become a classic on the assimilation of Jews in American culture.

4. George Rusche and Otto Kirchheimer, *Punishment and Social Structure* (New York: Columbia University Press, 1939).

5. R.P. Cuzzort and E.W. King, *Twentieth Century Sociology,* 4th ed. (New York: Holt, Rinehart and Winston, Inc., 1989), p. 3.

6. See Milton Gordon, *Assimilation in American Life* (New York: Oxford University Press, 1964). The literature on assimilation is extensive. A good starting point to understand the process is a reading of William M. Newman, *American Pluralism: A Study of Minority Groups and Social Theory* (New York: Harper & Row, Publishers, 1973).

7. James Herndon, *How to Survive in Your Native Land* (New York: Simon & Schuster, 1971).

8. Thomas R. Malthus, *An Essay on the Principle of Population,* 2 vols. (London: Dent and Sons, Everyman's Library, 1958).

9. Commission on Population Growth and the American Future, *Population and the American Future* (Washington, D.C.: U.S. Government Printing Office, 1972), p. 13.

10. Cesare Lombroso, *L'uomo delinquente* (Torino, Italy: Bocca, 1896–1897), was the book in which the thesis of born criminality was most elaborated. Lombrosianism remains in the thought of many prison administrators and much of the public. One administrator suggested that 15 percent of the prison population is not reachable, that is, they show no possibility of rehabilitation. If their problems were environmental, they could be reached by changing their environment. The assumption implicit is that their problems may be beyond environment, that is, inborn. See Mara Leveritt, "Retaking Control," *Arkansas Times* (January 7, 1993), p. 14–17.

11. *Furman v. Georgia,* 408 U.S. 238 (1972).

12. Russell Jacoby, *The Last Intellectuals: American Culture in the Age of Academe* (New York: Noonday Press, 1989).

11

Eastern Rites Sociology

The purpose of the old sociology was to see how social order could be maintained, for order achievement was the principal goal of the feudal arrangement upon which old European sociology was built. Scholars set on a linear structuring of social life thought scientific knowledge meant control, whether of the natural or social environments. The old sociological gods of order had to be served, for sociology itself had become an apologist of little change in the way society was structured. It was important that departments of the schools of the first rank, long represented by Harvard and Columbia, teach in such a way as to preserve the status quo of the old masters who had themselves said so much about the preservation of order.

The concept of order was installed as the principal problematic in the Eastern Rites of American sociology.[1] It traveled to the Midwest, where it was diluted to some extent. It migrated to the Far West when newer universities sprang up with professors in charge who were too far from the center of the Eastern Rites that they were to a large extent ignored.

Leaders of the Eastern Rites were interested in naming safe people for important places in the emerging field of sociology to preserve deference to the old masters. Some of the newer schools would become larger than those of the Eastern Rites and would process many more students who would take leadership roles in the discipline and society.

The old sociology legitimized the ranking systems bequeathed as correct by the European masters. When those systems came under even mild attack, through the addition of alternative paradigms, leaders of the old sociology reacted by hiding behind the barrier of greater scientific rigor. A scientific sociology would help preserve and control the social order, which had been the hope of the old masters. Tests of scientific rigor then became the new dogmatic basis upon which sociology was accepted by members of its emerging inner circles. Dona Richards notes that the self-image of Europeans was at stake if control of the social order were lost. Control was to be maintained through the teachings of anthropology at first. Later, that intellectual task shifted to psychology and sociology. The paradigms of the old masters were studied through newer and younger eyes, and European society itself was placed above intellectual and ethnological scrutiny.[2]

The old sociology in its transatlantic Eastern Rites tried to maintain its hard science status. Its basic intent was control by the imposition of order dictated by its theoretical paradigms. The posture of scientific respectability became closely held as a value—almost a dogma—by sociologists most wed to the old school. Where Comte and Weber had called for "value neutrality," even when the predominant values of their own major works stressed control, students schooled in those traditions thought they could achieve "ethical or value neutrality" by hewing closely to a set of procedures that came to be known in the lower reaches of Eastern Rites sociology as the scientific method. Ethical neutrality meant a demoralization of all values except those already in place. Never neutral, the old sociology advocated continuity of society as it operated.

Within the context of the dictatorships in which old European sociology came to life, it is understandable that ethical neutrality would be called for. No political regime would countenance a critique of the system by professors being paid by that system. Professors offering regime support were the only ones who would be allowed to achieve prominence in the profession.[3]

Eastern Rites sociology continues to promote ideas that have already been defeated. A good example of this tendency is for a group of these scholars to teach that criminality is in-born, constitutional, or genetic.[4] The implication of their research is to locate potential criminals early in their lives, even in the womb, and erase them from society. If genetic analyses prove that individuals are defective, by associating that genetic characteristic with criminality, even statistically, the argument can be made to remove or isolate the person. When science is allied with politics, the stage is set for someone like Adolf Hitler to grossly misapply these findings.

Scientific methodology, strived for most earnestly by second- and third-tier scholars, not only would assure academic respectability but also would be a yardstick for foreclosing ideas that would otherwise not be discounted. Methodology and ideology became mutually reinforcing such that there could be no counter to ideology because there was no way of getting past the methodology. In sociology, methodological wars were fought, for there was less need to challenge the ideology often operating behind methodological procedure. These wars were carried out within the discipline that was separating itself from more everyday concerns. The Eastern Rites of the discipline had settled the ideological issues, leaving methodology and technology the only areas to be contested.

Eastern Rites control of the discipline meant easier control of the problematic elements of the population. As in feudalism, when knights elaborated their own means of controlling each other, utilizing such schemes as the honor system, group loyalty, and fealty, Eastern Rites sociology made similar appeals to those in the discipline. No Eastern Rites sociologist dared launch an idea without asking approval of the leaders of the Rites.

Fear of Eastern Rites sociology of losing ideological control led to an even greater imitation of the scientific process, but even more to the certification mainly of that work which had been approved by the grant-awarding agencies. Work that was not funded had a much more difficult time gaining the stage, to say nothing of center stage. Even when research was not threatening to ideology and control but was for the general development of society, it was often rejected if it did not come from the right sources. The work in biology of Ernest E. Just,[5] in the natural sciences of George Washington Carver,[6] and Oliver C. Cox in sociology amply attest to this fact.[7]

A Darwinian conflict between Eastern Rites scholars was set off to see who could gain the approval of the granting agencies that by now had become closely allied with the federal government. Together these sources would make or break sociological careers, although other disciplines were even more involved in and dependent upon the process. The larger the grant, the greater the likelihood the scholar was a supporter of Eastern Rites thought. This support was seen in their desires to conduct research on whatever topic was needed. Whenever control was thought to be breaking down, more money became available to study how greater control could be implemented. Where granting agencies did not define the parameters of research through a selection of topics, the lesser Eastern Rites scholars, anxious for recognition, provided their own impressions of problems with which grant-awarding agencies might be concerned.

The Eastern Rites of American sociology desperately seek ways to keep the old masters propped up. The discipline is being purged of dissidents and fellow travelers objecting to mainstream sociology.[8] Purging is done by denying degrees to trainees who do not display the proper orientation toward the old masters and their apostles. Because of the peer review process, unapproved ideas and values may not be published in the major journals of the discipline. There is some suggestion that journal articles correctly placed may be weighted more heavily than books, even those released by the right presses.[9]

What is the appeal of the old masters? Earlier they were to be read in the original, which proved a student or professor's erudition rather than ability to ferret out grains of truth and insight. The social world has undergone a radical restructuring since they wrote, but those most steeped in Eastern Rites sociology find little need to seek knowledge elsewhere. Exploration for new understanding is discouraged in many departments; answers are to be found in the writings of the masters. The political aspects of the raising of saints in sociology and the conversion of acolytes to catechists have been much discussed.[10]

Decline of Eastern Rites sociology did not occur mainly because the protectors gave in. The rites were protected by assuring that diversity did not occur. Faculty were hired for their compatibility with present faculty, which assured that old paradigms were promoted. At Columbia, where Robert K. Merton presided, persons of the eminence of C. Wright Mills could not teach at the graduate level in the sociology department.[11] Lewis Feuer had to teach three to four hundred students in an integrated social science course at Berkeley in the early 1960s.[12] When Nathan Glazer moved to Harvard, though with solid credentials and experience, he was assigned to the Graduate School of Education.[13]

There were no sociology departments in European universities before World War I; but some of the most important writings had taken place by men in other positions, usually outside the universities. Ideas that could not be supported by administrators or universities were little tolerated. These institutions were part of government, and their heads highly respected members of the ruling cliques. In Europe, bureaucracy heads supported and represented the upper classes. As they faced the Marxist dilemma, they found that the spread of literacy made the discord between the upper classes and the working classes more glaring.

It was always dangerous in Europe to criticize the rulers and rules of society. Even in England, where freedom of speech was assumed, persons without independent means who criticized the rulers or the government could find themselves at risk of losing economic support. In some countries critics could be jailed. European royalty kept themselves entrenched, but they could not restrict the growth and economic power of the bourgeoisie. Unless allied with royalty or with the ruling class, the bourgeoisie would become a serious counterweight to the authority of the rulers.[14]

There are three main concerns within American sociology, and each grows out of the experiences of the people represented by practitioners of the discipline. The first concern is the Jewish experience. Jews have been preoccupied with their history and rights as they have tried to function in societies hostile toward them. Their social distinctiveness has been both a challenge and a disadvantage. The long history of Jewish bondage and freedom, of achievement and disappointment, has equipped the Jewish people with a peculiar intellectual way of trying to make sense of their history.

The second concern in American society is the black experience. Black Americans have, like Jewish Americans, had a major intellectual preoccupation. Their wrenching from Africa and the subsequent 250 years of rejected status equipped the black scholar with both an interest in and a need to understand that experience. Whatever that scholar's research, the underlying intent was to make sense out of that long interlude of inequality. The effect would lead to many explorations, detours, and discoveries that would never allow the scholar completely to abandon the quest to understand that long and personality-stamping experience.

A third concern dominating American sociology is the mainstream culture's need to justify the actions taken by their forbears with respect to the mistreatment of the Jews and Africans. Somehow these actions were rationalized into a theory that would give its proponents psychological relief, thereby allowing them to retain a sense of humanity. This rationalizing took the form of flight into the formalities of logic and scientific methodology. Each new solution only generated more problems; as for the Jews and the Africans, the problems created by history seemed eternally unsettling. The old sociology was unlikely to satisfy the main problems presented.

NOTES

1. We use the term *Eastern Rites* to refer to the sociology taught at the two leading departments of the eastern seaboard: Harvard and Columbia. The professors of these schools brought forward a brand of sociology most like that of Europe, where the emphasis was upon order and control. The long domination of Parsons at Harvard and Merton at Columbia meant that students at these schools might as well have been seated in academies at the feet of old Europeans themselves. The sprinkling of their students around the important newer departments pushing for prestige and eminence was a gambit to preserve the paradigms, concerns, and emphases of the old masters. Alternative sociology was viewed at first as heretical, for it did not derive from or support the old paradigms.

2. See Dona Richards, "The Ideology of European Dominance," *The Western Journal of Black Studies,* vol. 3, no. 4 (Winter 1979): 244–250.

3. At Harvard, under the leadership of Talcott Parsons, Pitirim Sorokin could talk about Vilfredo Pareto's "circulation of the elite," and Robert Michels about the "iron law of oligarchy." At Columbia Robert K. Merton's students continued to push Durkheimian sociology of anomie flowing from failure to maintain roles associated with social place.

4. Lombroso's famous position is elaborated in Cesare Lombroso, *L'uomo delinquente* (Milan, Italy: Hoepli, 1876, and Torino: Bocca, 1896–1897). C. Ray Jeffery was a strong believer in biosocial criminology. For an important discussion of this perspective, see S.R. Balkan, R.J. Berger, and J. Schmidt, *Crime and Deviance in America: A Critical Approach* (Belmont, CA: Wadsworth, 1980); and James Q. Wilson, *Thinking About Crime* (New York: Vintage, 1975). Wilson is an Eastern Rites scholar carrying on the work of Ernest Hooton, who tried to revive Lombrosianism. See Ernest A. Hooton, *Crime and the Man* (Cambridge, MA: Harvard University Press, 1939), p. 130, and his *The American Criminal: An Anthropological Study* (Cambridge, MA: Harvard University Press, 1939).

5. The Eastern Rites of the old sociology took group inequality to be a normative feature of the social structure. See John H. Stanfield in "Race in Science," *Contemporary Sociology: A Journal of Reviews,* vol. 13, no. 6 (November 1984): 684–685; and Kenneth R. Manning, *Black Apollo of Science: The Life of Ernest Everett Just* (New York: Oxford University Press, 1983).

6. Linda O. McMurray, *George Washington Carver: Scientist and Symbol* (New York: Oxford University Press, 1981).

7. Oliver C. Cox, *Caste, Class and Race* (New York: Doubleday, 1948).

8. Students who do not adopt the prevailing theoretical orientations purveyed by members of their departments may not receive their final degrees even though they may show all the other abilities that are normally required of sociologists. Between the Russian Revolution and the cold war, Marxist or radical scholars had hard times finding positions. See Herbert M. Hunter and Sameer Y. Abraham, eds., *Race, Class, and the World System: The Sociology of Oliver C. Cox* (New York: Monthly Review Press, 1987), for the story of one of America's most controversial but rejected sociologists; also

see Jeffery M. Masson, *The Assault on Truth: Freud's Suppression of the Seduction Theory* (New York: Farrar Straus Giroux, 1984).

9. As more scholars found publishing outlets, a move was made to assure that publishing was done in the right media. The scholarly journals were ranked and higher status given for publishing in them. Scholars from the more highly ranked departments dominated the journals. The vast majority of the nation's leading scholars and scientists are found in the major universities. The most outstanding scholars in outlying places are being constantly recruited to the more prestigious institutions. See Theodore Caplow and Reece McGee, *The Academic Marketplace* (John Wiley & Sons, 1961), p. 11.

10. Some of the most notable sociologists tell of their lives and influences on them in Bennet M. Berger, ed., *Authors of Their Lives: Intellectual Biographies by Twenty American Sociologists* (Berkeley: University of California Press, 1990), p. 203.

11. Ibid., p. 199.

12. Ibid., p. 207.

13. Ibid., p. 208.

14. The English solved this problem through the creation of an hereditary peerage, which was the backbone of the aristocracy. See David Cannadine, *The Fall of the British Aristocracy* (New York: Anchor Books, 1992).

12

Natural, Old Sociology, and Poststructuralism

All social social science begins with certain premises assumed fundamental to the viewpoint held by the formulators of the science. Those defending specific subdisciplines in the social sciences often defend the value premises of their disciplines as well. These practitioners are often closest to the centers of their disciplines, where thought about the discipline is constructed. Peripheral members teach what those at the center propose or impose upon them.

The basic or primitive propositions of a discipline are not matters that may be settled empirically. Minor propositions lend themselves to easier resolution by empirical means. It is the minor propositions to which ordinary social science, including sociology, is oriented. The bigger the proposition, the more likely it is to be resolved in philosophical rather than empirical terms. The smaller the proposition, the greater the possibility that the rules of ordinary science may be used in its resolution.

In the writings of Karl Marx, a primitive proposition is "the history of mankind is that of the struggle between the haves and have nots." That this is a value or philosophical proposition is clear from the fact that we do not know the beginning of humankind and so do not know its human history. Even with a good record of the activities of certain groups, little could be said about those groups for which no record exists, making generalization hazardous. Enormous gaps make such Marxist statements quite suspicious from the standpoint of veracity.

Social science has sought for a long time to find basic differences between groups. One of the enduring philosophical ideas is that groups differ by color or race. Sociologists delight in comparing racial groups, suggesting that there is no way of resolving differences attributable to race. If a problem is due to race, it has no solution, since change of race is impossible. Even though formal social science is more tentative about adducing evidence to support such differences, there are also many who persist in presenting data as though there were credibility to the argument supporting racial differences. They have reduced primitive propositions to empirical ones and in so doing have erased the very basis on which their argument is structured.

If we say, for example, that blacks earn 58 percent of what whites earn yearly, we have not said much because we have no way of knowing who is being discussed when the color concepts are used. Common observation confirms that some who are classified as black are not and some classified as white are not. Determining who is being discussed is a matter critical to the resolution of the proposition. There is not total accord of the category and the individual so defined. Research on matters such as the differences between racial groups requires invoking a value premise. One must believe that races exist in the first place. That they do is a primitive proposition that is not deducible from data. It is that belief, not certain knowledge buttressed by data, that generates the idea that races exist. Oliver C. Cox points out that race meant little before the expeditions of Columbus to begin the conquest of the New World.[1]

Races are not natural categories but are the result of social, economic, and political construction. They are statistical categories supported by artificial and weak empirical criteria for their definition. The weaker the natural criteria, the more the definition must be propped up artificially. The addition of artificial criteria continues until the entire edifice is artificially supported. It is, therefore, not inexplicable that political, economic, educational, behavioral, and other criteria are used to force a definition of race, for there is no natural dividing line between humans and assuredly not one based upon some biological or genetic constant.

Natural sociology begins from the assumption that there are no important differences between large groups of humans and that very little is to be gained, or even understood, by reference to these differences. Natural sociology assumes that the normal state of humankind is equality in terms of concerns with things that matter to all humankind. Natural sociology reflects the greater communication that today exists between groups, which reduces the social distance between them. With the erasure of these differences, the framework is set for greater cooperation of men and women from whatever cultures they represent.

A primitive proposition of Marxism was that the economic values of life are most important. Natural sociology makes no such assumption but recognizes that the internalization of such values is a matter of training. Economics are not more important than any other value except in our paradigms. It is fully recognized that people ordinarily make their living in economic pursuits.

European or traditional American sociology saw problems of society as due to personal shortcomings of individuals. Europeans were more likely than Americans to see class as a factor. When a class analysis was used, there was little need to focus on the problems of individuals. If individuals were the problem, there was little need to address the issue of class. European sociology stressed the workers and the owners, which enabled Marx to conceptualize in terms of conflict of the classes. Basically, there was no middle class in European society, or if there were, it was very small and allied with the upper or ruling class. When there was a shift from the estate to the class system, there was not necessarily a shift in mentality by Europeans who continued to think in terms of the old, more rigid estate categories.

Believers in the old system of rank and privilege began to conceptualize problems as matters of people being out of their natural positions. European sociology had taught that estate categories were natural and that individuals who violated their positions were badly out of step and were destroying the social landscape. The old sociology projected that lower-class persons could be reformed by adopting the values of the higher classes. If they did not, they would be erased from the ranks of society.

Change of the lower class was conceptualized as a problem in assimilation. During the period following the Civil War, immigration of eastern and southern Europeans to fill the requirements of an expanding and partially destroyed economy meant the introduction of a sociological lower class. These persons did not understand the values of American life, were discriminated against, and had to be converted from their old ways, which had no status in the New World. They were forced to give up their language, mannerisms, values, and much of their culture to conform to the requirements of the new culture.[2]

Making sure that newcomers became assimilated was a value inherent in the old sociology. Old World values would not be widely tolerated in America except in a few esoteric areas such as music and food. The wider older culture was generally devalued.

European-driven sociology opposed significant change in the social order. It was much concerned with patching up, painting up, and restoring society to its former state. It was like a museum director who wanted specimens preserved in their original states. For the old sociology, as for the museum director, the past was very special.

American sociology taught the smaller the groups on which it could focus the better. This attitude gave rise to a large variety of particularistic studies. The assumption was that society was divided into increasingly smaller groups, each promulgating values of others, at least to recognize interdependency.

American sociology was wed to European sociological theory from its very beginning. The single book that did most to unify the field in the 1920s was Robert E. Park and E.W. Burgess's *Introduction to the Science of Sociology*.[3] They drew heavily upon European traditions, especially those of Germany and France. As the Europeans had done, they called for highly empirical investigative work into the social processes, into interaction, and into the nature of social organization. Believing that the social sciences could have the same degree of control and predictability as the natural sciences, while escaping the speculations of the social and moral philosophers, the founders followed the pattern of Europeans in divorcing the content of the discipline from the problems faced by the people.

There were never enough European universities to provide a significant fraction of the people the opportunity to attend. University matriculation was always on a highly selective basis, and the persons selected were separated from the people and their problems. They could spend time in the "Ivory Tower." There they could speculate, for very little was expected of the scholars. If they wanted to argue among themselves over abstract theories and concepts, the state would be happy to provide them with the stipends they required. The knowledge they accumulated had little significance beyond impressing others of the disciplines.

As late as the late 1600s when Isaac Newton was doing his most significant theoretical work on gravity, optics, and the calculus, very few persons saw any practical benefit derivable from his studies. So what if Newton found a formula to predict the location of certain planets at certain times, or the strength of the tides, or the length of light waves. These facts were interesting to those who had the leisure to contemplate them. They had little to do with people in the country-side, in the cities, or wherever.

As important as were the laws of gravity, more than 200 years passed before powered flight was possible. Despite all that work of Hermann Helmholtz on electrical stimulation of body parts in the mid-1800s,[4] it was late in the century that a garage tinkerer named Thomas A. Edison was able to use electrical knowledge in a practical way to produce an electric light bulb.[5]

The attempt of American sociology to become the plaything of academics ensconced in the universities was a carryover of the European style of disengagement from that which required thoughtful solutions. University professors were privileged people in the European context. They had the leisure to speculate and concern themselves literally with the most esoteric of problems, letting their own values decide their importance. American sociology was not the only discipline that sought to divorce itself from practical applications.

Another reason for the small emphasis on a practical thrust in European scholarship was the entrenchment of the status quo. Too many scholars were beholden to the structure of opportunity to do much more than endorse what was already said and done. They had not forgotten the lessons of Socrates and Copernicus and Bruno.[6] They remembered how dangerous it was to adduce alternative ideas that did not have the support of the decision-makers and rulers. Of course, some, perhaps a large percentage of the professors, were located in the ruling groups themselves. Had they wanted to bring forward thought that was different, they most probably would not have.

The old sociology has been very inflexible, unable to anticipate or allow for changes in the general society. Attempts to explain as the old masters did, within their theoretical frameworks, has led to discouragement toward exploring new alternatives. Arguing a case within a framework already set takes away from the options the new arguments produce, giving the advantage to the users of the old arguments. Poverty, to be explained, must happen within a Marxist, functionalist, or interactionist context. Other paradigms explaining poverty are almost summarily dismissed.

Crime is explained within the frameworks set by these parameters and a few others. Each generation of students argues about the biogenetic, psychiatric, psychological, or sociological definitions of criminality. After Durkheim, Marx, and Freud, throwing in a little of Lombroso, professors move on to a discussion of crime as a sociological phenomenon and spend the rest of the semester talking about anomie theory, weighing down students with Merton's paradigms of adjustments to societal expectations.[7] Then all that is said about crime causation as a sociological reality is ignored as individual cases and interesting data fill out the semester. Occasionally students are taken to a prison or go on their own. They come back with what they see as insights into the nature of criminality when what they have gotten mainly is some idea of the physical structure of the prison.

Nearly every concept of sociological thought may be traced back to old European masters whose paradigms were inapplicable to the conditions of American life. Robert K. Merton was very much influenced by the thought of Emile Durkheim, especially with respect to Durkheim's ideas on alienation and anomie. When, in 1938, Merton formulated his ideas that began to influence thought on deviance, he drew very heavily upon a tradition that was not applicable in America. Merton's concept stressed adherence to group values, the assumption being that society was practically all-powerful in making its impressions on individuals.

Merton differed with old thinkers such as Thomas Hobbes[8] and Machiavelli[9] who thought that the struggle for survival implied great conflict, and who believed that the law of tooth and nail would prevail. Machiavelli believed that any action that achieved the goal of management and control was acceptable. The goal dictated the quality of the means, giving rise to the idea of "use any means necessary."

There was a fierce intellectual struggle among Durkheim, Hobbes, and Machiavelli. The latter two thinkers erased morality from the equation of human conduct, allowing the actors to seek their goals literally by any means they could get away with. Durkheim brought morality back into the equation, leaving room for action based on how individuals felt about a condition. Merton could see this conflict, and he tried to integrate morality and rationality into one theoretical schema. He did so by posing a means-goals continuum—conceptually, that is, though he treated these as discrete variables. One could agree or disagree with either the goals or the means. When Merton conceptualized the goals-means dichotomy, he suggested that society tells us what goals to seek and what means to use to reach them. Likewise, society teaches members to agree or disagree with the goals and the means. Merton was trying to build individual choice into the structure to reflect the societal value of personal choice. He was trying to convey, probably, that men and women are not wholly social in that they retain a few choices in decision making.

Although Merton utilizes only five adaptation modes—conformist, innovator, ritualist, retreatist, and rebel—there are six logical possibilities within the system he suggested. Two combinations, agree and disagree, to each of the goals-means schema would yield six possible reactions: (4 x 3) / 2. What happened to Merton's other mode of adaptation, if he were to claim a logical, quasimathematical means of predicting adaptations? It seems that Merton has shortchanged us a logical mode of adaptation. But it was not so much that Merton could not produce another logical mode of adaptation as it was his unwillingness to attempt to explain outside a Durkheimian framework. The parameters had been set within which even the eminent Merton had to make his decision. Thus Merton himself became something of a conformist to the prevailing sociological thought of the day, that thought being heavily dictated by the Europeans.

POSTSTRUCTURALISM

Poststructuralism means a decline of criticism, a seeking of the approval of those to whom one is subservient. It uses an impersonal, almost scientific language that separates the writer from the group written about. The assumption is that specialists are required to fully understand what is said by one scientist to another. The writer in poststructuralism speaks to an audience of other writers of the same orientation, never directly to the people.

Poststructuralism constitutes a sharp change in the general attitude toward the purpose of scholarship or educational work. At first, scholarship saw as its mission the upmanship and liberation of the people. This made such scholarship always practical and having a social meaning. Poststructuralism would not have been possible even in the period after Reconstruction. Then education was not so much for personal aggrandizement; it was for the opportunity to render service to the people in the struggle toward upward social leveling. There was not much time for internecine fighting, even over relatively important matters of methodological sophistication.

Under poststructuralism, artistic and literary efforts would have become mired down in semantics. There would have been no Richard Wright or John Steinbeck because criticism would not have been possible, even through realistic literature. Bigger Thomas would not have been allowed to literally go crazy with alienation caused by a society that denied his fundamental humanity. There would be more Celies,[10] for scientism would supplant the confronting of obdurate structure using any tools possible.

Was Rosa Parks really being discriminated against when asked to move to the back of that Montgomery bus in 1955, or was discrimination merely a picture in her head, a concept that did not have 100 percent coincidence with reality? A poststructuralist would maintain that Parks was bound by law to obey it, the same as anyone else, since, in a democracy the will of the majority prevails. If Parks did not like where she was seated, there were legally acceptable ways to change the law. Simply organize the people who do not like the law, contact the representatives and bring pressure on them to change the law, or vote the politicians out of office at the next election. There is no need for defiance of the law; when that happens, there is a breakdown of law and order. If people are not allowed to vote, they can take away from the system things that will force the system to recognize those not participating.

Of course the poststructuralists are as much concerned with law and order as they are concerned with order in literary criticism and other literary work. In the poststructuralist way of thinking everything has a place, and by keeping to place, order is preserved. Just as words out of order lose their meaning in this line of literary criticism, people who are out of order lose their meaning in the social world. Meaning can be fathomed only in an ordered world. Society by nature abhors disorder. The societal tendency is always to create order, not to promote disorder, according to poststructuralists.

Under poststructuralism fewer writers would be in the field, for it would be dominated by canon-makers, a literary oligarchy that carefully and certainly define what work is permissible and admissible. The canon-makers would become like the hymn society that thoroughly controlled entry into the hymn books. The result was a tremendous cleavage between the images created by the hymns and the social realities of the people. The idyllic rural pastoral scenes—the little church in the wildwood—for instance, have not existed for years.[11] Some 80 percent of the people live in cities. The requirements that the poststructuralists impose upon writers will force adherence to form and will ignore process and change, which the tools of poststructuralism cannot handle.

There has been little to write about in America, only something to fuss about. Any writing or artistic creativity has a double meaning. Even that which ostensibly is to entertain can be thought of as social criticism. Entertainment is a luxury that only secure people can afford, and that makes entertainment a leisure class prerogative. There can be no ethnic literature if it is admitted that literature is a form of protest, to show the absurdity of some situation, to allude to certain inconsistencies and cleavages that separate groups in the society. Literature can neither be created nor can it exist outside a social context. If it has no evanescent meaning, one will be given to it, and that meaning will not satisfy all members of the society. Poststructuralism therefore becomes a negation of the fact that serious gaps exist in the society and significant unhappiness and social disgruntlement are real. It ignores the political and therefore the class nature of even literary creativity and productivity.[12]

NOTES

1. O.C. Cox, *Caste, Class and Race* (New York: Doubleday, 1944).

2. William I. Thomas and Florian Znaniecki, *The Polish Peasant in Europe and America,* 2 vols. (New York: Alfred A. Knopf, 1927).

3. Robert E. Park and E.W. Burgess, *Introduction to the Science of Sociology* (Chicago: University of Chicago Press, 1921).

4. Raymond E. Fancher, *Pioneers of Psychology* (New York: W.W. Norton & Co., 1979), pp. 87–125.

5. The story of Thomas A. Edison's making the electric light bulb is a classroom instance of the resistance of the status quo to new possibilities, even in the practical sciences. See Henry Schroeder, *History of Electric Light* (Washington, D.C.: Smithsonian Institute, 1923), and Robert Silverberg, *Light for the World: Edison and the Power Industry* (Princeton, NJ: Van Nostrand, 1967).

6. These scholars suffered painful deaths for holding fast to their conclusions. The story is told in Andrew D. White, *The History of the Warfare with Science and Theology in Christendom* (New York: D. Appleton & Co., 1896).

7. The Mertonian focus is seen in a variety of sociological writings on deviance. See, for example, Charles H. McCaghy, *Deviant Behavior: Crime, Conflict, and Interest Groups* (New York: Macmillan Publishing Co., 1976).

8. Thomas Hobbes, *Leviathan* (Oxford: Clarendon Press, 1909), argues that men are basically selfish and desiring of power. Without a ruler with absolute power, the lives of men would be nasty, brutish, and short. Men require a natural ruler and protector.

9. Niccolo Machiavelli, *The Prince*, written in 1513. Machiavellianism has come to connote deep, dark, and treacherous politics where the end justifies the means used to accomplish purposes. Whatever one does to reach one's goals is permissible. See Alfredo Bonadeo, *Corruption, Conflict, and Power in the Work and Times of Niccolo Machiavelli* (Berkeley: University of California Press, 1973).

10. Celie is the heroine of Alice Walker's best-selling novel *The Color Purple* (New York: Meridian Books, 1981).

11. A. Stephen Stephan, "Hymns: Making the Irrelevant Relevant through Ecology," *The Hymn*, vol. 25, no. 1, (January 1975): 6–9, called attention to the dysjuncture between hymn lyrics which reflect idyllic and pastoral images when America and much of Europe are today highly urbanized.

12. Theodore O. Mason, Jr., "Between the Populist and the Scientist: Ideology and Power in Recent Afro-American Literary Criticism Or, 'The Dozens and Scholarship,'" *Callaloo*, vol. 11, no. 3 (summer 1988): 606–615.

13

The Continuity of Paradigms

The major sociological paradigms, or theoretical frames of reference, have not undergone modification for nearly 100 years. Karl Marx is still being talked about today more avidly than perhaps at any other time, probably because more students are being exposed to his line of reasoning, although there may not be as much credibility in class struggle as was formerly thought. Class struggle belonged to another period, an industrial age when wealth was very scarce and literally and figuratively out of reach of much of humankind.

Today, especially in the United States, there is much cooperation between the classes in the production of wealth. Poor people readily agree to be led by persons of the economic upper class, and upper-class people accede to the leadership of poor people who achieve that leadership through the usual electoral processes.[1] Ralf Dahrendorf claims that the conflict is now not between owners and workers in modern capitalism but between managers and workers and that workers themselves may be part owners of companies because they hold shares in them.[2]

Durkheimian sociology remains strong, not wholly because it is explanatory but because it is driven, like Marxism, by inertial forces that dictate that it continue along its same path even though its credibility is neither questionable nor highly discussible. It has become imbedded into the sociological ritual, and like any ritualized process, the reason for its continuity is difficult to find.

Old paradigms do not die out simply because they are old. Like any change, they lose their hold because they are found unable to explain data, reality, and conditions. Aristotle was not overthrown because people did not like him but because new ways were found of confronting the data that Aristotelian logic had foreclosed.[3] The test of the quality of any paradigm or system of reasoning is the extent to which it explains and describes. It must be able to do the job literally better than any other paradigm, or it will be replaced. In a sense, then, paradigm establishment is very Darwinian, and there is furious competition among the makers to see which one gains hegemony.[4]

The old sociology consisted of a set of paradigms that together sought not so much to explain human behavior but to control thought about behavior.[5] Its paradigms were domineering, demanding that thought conform to the concepts it bequeathed for thinking about human behavior. Marxian sociology would not permit any thought other than that which stressed a conflict perspective that pitted class against class. Meadian sociology was equally dogmatic in that it insisted that roles and expectations were the only things that mattered in social life. Functionalism emphasized the role of institutions, values, and behaviors as they contributed to the ongoing of society. Ironically, each of these paradigms was saying virtually the same thing, namely, that society has a vested interest in its own survival. Neither the Marxists, the Meadians, nor the functionalists were willing to predict the destruction of society. Nor did they predict its substantial reorganization. Marxist sociology is basically a sociology of anarchic equilibrium–the ruling class versus the working class. Meadian sociology also stresses equilibrium so long as persons internalize and enact the roles society thrusts upon them or gives them leeway to choose. Functionalism is unabashedly equilibrium maintaining, for all parts of society relate to each other in a highly ordered and regularized way.[6]

That the old sociology have predictive and explanatory accuracy was not as important as that it be presented as sociological canon—which is to say that the way the old masters viewed society was the proper and only acceptable way to view it. As in religious dogma, interpreting outside the canonical framework was analogous to sociological heresy. The consequences were similar in that a teacher laid himself or herself open for substantial rejection and reduced mobility options if accepted interpretations were not recognized.[7]

The old masters thought in terms of rigid categories, ignoring that the world is structured along continua, at least in terms of most meaningful social variables. This rigidity gave rise to rigid thinking among those sociologists taught the concepts of the old masters. The masters tried hard to build process into their models but were so bound by structural and psychological restraints themselves that they were generally unable to think and write beyond the categories they conceived.

Marx knew that he was lower class just as surely as he knew that class existed.[8] The categories of the working class and the bourgeoisie would not leave Marx's thought, no matter how he tried to push them out. Herbert Spencer could not get over placing groups on an evolutionary stepladder, no matter how he tried.[9] He refused to believe, for instance, that some pygmies may be more evolved than some Europeans called the most evolved. Even when they were highly impressed with Darwinism—which is processural, that is, eschewing statics—they returned to categorization. Emile Durkheim's subjects are alienated if they fail to agree with the norms and values of society. Of course, in status-conscious France, everyone had a place and most generally agreed with the placement offered. A man or woman was socially placed just about where he or she should be. Alienation arose only when the individuals failed to internalize their station in life, according to Durkheim. Alienation was as much a function of misplacement as of misunderstanding the requirements of the role one would like to play.

Durkheimian thinking led to a condition called alienation partly because of a conceptualization of social place.[10] In a society where there is no set place for any individual, the degree of alienation would be predictably smaller. If one is trained to recognize alienation as a consequence of inability to accept or feel comfortable in a social place, the idea of alienation would seem perfectly natural. Place could be meaningful only in a rigidly set categorical society. Place is reinforced as a pattern of elite or leisure-class living.

The analogy of a table setting is appropriate.[11] In a properly set table every utensil is located in its socially defined proper place. To a person who has internalized the idea of place, it could be quite upsetting to see a spoon, knife, or fork out of place. In the social world it could be equally nerve-wracking to see an individual socially out of place. For example, no one would want to see a former U.S. president polishing shoes or sweeping floors. Such work would be a serious violation of social place for those who are steeped in the idea of place. It would be beneath his dignity, some might think, even though there is much emphasis placed upon the dignity of labor. If a former president decided to undertake these tasks, he would be defined as alienated or even worse. Nor would some people be comfortable seeing, for instance, a sharecropper at a socialite black-tie affair. Where fluidity is not built into the system, or even into the thinking, the individual has a chance of becoming alienated and therefore appearing strange to those steeped in the idea of place.

Although American society shows some degree of rigidity, it is far less rigid than most other societies, and movement from one social category to another may not produce the alienation possible in, say, England or France where there is less mobility. Without rigid categories, passing judgment on behavior becomes more difficult; for there will be no inflexible standards by which to judge.

European sociological masters were trying to do more than reach a dispassionate understanding of how society works; they were much closer to offering prescriptions for social control, to maintain the social system as it was, probably because they could not perceive of alternatives that did not accord with their own biases. Their connection to government and power was a lot less disguised than is the case with American social science scholars. It is true that some social scientists in the United States are highly placed, but there are so many of them and relatively much greater opportunities for criticism that it is unlikely their positions will be accepted uncritically, even by government. More likely, government will show tendencies toward control as a result of the inputs of U.S. social scientists and not because of such direct programs as might have been found in Europe at earlier stages of the development of sociological science.

European sociology's attitude corresponded to the elitism of the professors who supported it. The structure of continental universities was such that the lines of thought followed the lines of rank. Those with aspirations of ascending the ladder to a professorship in an academy were cognizant of how they were viewed by those ahead of them. Their thinking was likely to conform to that of the established professors, making it difficult to infuse new thoughts and views of the world. European worldviews were seldom independently reached; most often they reflected the structure of the Church, which was always hierarchically arranged. Just as religious dogma came down from the pope, knowledge in the academy came down from those at the top and became dogmatic academic knowledge. Since so many academics were also associated with the Church, not unexpected was a virtual fusion of the two knowledges. There was such congruence between church knowledge and school knowledge that one could practically be taken as a representative of the other.

Because church knowledge stressed a high degree of social control through the application of its moral principles, and also because academic knowledge and church knowledge were so closely related, academic knowledge became, in effect, moral knowledge, which again led to control. Breaking free of the Church's hold upon academic knowledge was difficult. In most European universities it was a long time in happening and in some, it has not happened even today. Beyond all else, a knowledgeable person was a moral person.

Judeo-Christian theology and the Catholic Church and its offspring, the various Protestant groups, stressed male rulership and therefore became noted for their gender discrimination. Females were given almost no formal positions within the Church. This Church protocol extended to the academy, where the low position of the female was retained. Even if females did not internalize their positions, they were not willing, in general, to rebel against the males in power. There probably was not a female professor in a European university until well into the 1700s, although these universities were established as early as 1200. Old sociology, reflecting this traditional hierarchy, hardly recognized women at all in its analyses; nor did it raise the issue of the loss of female talent that resulted from holding women down in the lowest social positions, hiding them, as it were, behind what William Graham Sumner called the "cake of custom."

Of course, the old sociology had taught that the most elemental division of society is by age and gender. It took as its models the remaining preliterate societies open to general observation, ignoring that by this time the structure of these societies had changed drastically and it was necessary to greatly restrict roles even to survive in much restricted ranges. For examples, there were at one time many more Bushmen than there are today. When they were much more numerous and had much greater territory in which to operate, Bushmen had many more role opportunities; there was not the need to restrict members to specific roles. An expanding society undergoes role expansion, whereas a decaying one has increasingly fewer roles that individuals may enter. Durkheim, Marx, and Weber thought in terms of division of labor and the growth of bureaucracy when the societies they discussed were constricting opportunities for role expansion.

The old paradigms continue partly because of inertia and familiarity with them by those who are responsible for teaching them. They are convenient; they serve to help organize lectures and student term papers. Any hypotheses for further study and research generated by the paradigms are often post hoc explanations; there is no set of logically derived, interrelated, and deductively connected postulates and hypotheses within the paradigms themselves. Basically, we study the old masters because they represent the academic tradition in which we ourselves have been socialized.

NOTES

1. Minority peoples from quite inauspicious backgrounds are found in considerable numbers in state houses and in many levels of local and national leadership. Although some might call them token leaders, this kind of representation is not so widely found in any other country today. Their participation shows that patriarchy, status, and class have decreasing value in American society. Geoffrey Hawthorn, *Enlightenment and Despair: A History of Sociology* (Cambridge: Cambridge University Press, 1976), pp. 192–193, believes that this is so because of the absence of such historical realities as the feudal system, an established Church, and a lack of that which corresponded to what was taken for granted in such cultures as England and China.

2. See Ralf Dahrendorf, *Class and Class Conflict in Industrial Sociology* (Stanford, CA: Stanford University Press, 1959).

3. By Aristotelian we refer to a tendency to use philosophical methods rather than those of experimentation and measurement. Many of the disciplines, including sociology, were philosophical until well into the nineteenth century. Protodisciplinary knowledge was present in the form of folklore, magic, and other basically unorganized understandings that were untested. See Robert E.L. Faris, ed., *Handbook of Modern Sociology* (Chicago: Rand McNally & Co., 1964), pp. 1–34, for an appreciation of the origins of the discipline of sociology.

4. Protoscience as well as modern science strives to achieve the most likely explanation of phenomena. Primitive peoples are rational enough to see the value of better explanations and in that sense are not stagnated nearly as much as they are perceived to be.

5. Some of the variables used in the making of concepts in sociology were measurable, but the concepts composed of the variables themselves are not. For example, social class may be composed of the variables of income, occupation, house type, and education, using a modified version of William Lloyd Warner's concept of class. See Joel B. Montague, Jr., *Class and Nationality: English and American Studies* (New Haven, CT: College and University Press, 1963), pp. 38–42, for an impression of the influence of Warner's thought about class on American sociology. When these variables used in the definition of class are brought together to indicate class, the concept itself becomes difficult to measure exactly.

6. Kenneth R. Hoover, *The Elements of Social Scientific Thinking* (New York: St. Martin's Press, 1988), pp. 134–138, stresses nonscientific factors that might enter into

the offering of the conclusions of scientists. In other words, scientific work is a human enterprise and, as such, is subject to many of the vicissitudes of all such work.

7. It is noted by Hoover (p. 135) that a master-apprenticeship system works in the fashioning of academic careers. Those studying with the most famous masters gain the best positions and the greatest access to means of communicating their views.

8. There is a very large literature about Marx's basic proposition, namely, that power is used in the making of social decisions largely because the world is divided into the powerful and the powerless or, in Marx's own thinking, between the owners of the means of production and the workers or the bourgeoisie and the proletariat. For a good overview of Marxist thought, see T.B. Bottomore, ed., Trans., *Karl Marx: Selected Writings in Sociology & Social Philosophy* (New York: McGraw-Hill, 1964).

9. Inherent in the idea of evolution, as seen by Spencer, was the concept of progress. Spencer, of course, became identified with social Darwinism. A very useful essay on the idea of progress, as seen in the social sciences at the turn of the century, is found in Robert E. Park and Ernest W. Burgess, *Introduction to the Science of Sociology* (Chicago: University of Chicago Press, 1921-1924), pp. 953-1011. Spencer had written much earlier about the problems of evolution and progress. See his "Progress, Its Law and Cause," *Westminster Review* 67 (1857): 445-485. His thought is contained substantially in *The Principles of Sociology* (London, 1893).

10. The idea of alienation is so commonly associated with Durkheimian thinking that attribution to him is almost automatic. It is, of course, Durkheim's *Suicide*, originally published in 1897, that receives so much attention for its contribution to the elaboration of theory from factual data. For a brief presentation of Durkheim's thoughts on suicide, see John E. Farley, *Sociology: Annotated Instructor's Edition* (Englewood Cliffs, NJ: Prentice-Hall, 1990), pp. 28-29.

11. Books of etiquette have long been popular in the United States. They really tell persons without the best of upbringing how to behave more like their social betters. The standards of acceptable behavior are generally set by the upper classes. See Anna Steese Richardson, *Standard Etiquette* (New York: P.F. Collier & Company, 1925), for some idea of the importance of proper behavior as determined by the definers in a number of settings.

14

Modernism and Postmodernism in Sociology

Postmodernism is a reaction to the modernism that has dominated sociological thought since around the 1950s. Modernist sociology was concerned with order and predictability on the model of the natural sciences. It encouraged sociological practitioners to think categorically, often in dualisms and hierarchies. The hunt for invariant correlations between variables was the technical means for promoting modernist sociology. If the proper variables could be found that were consistently related, the value of one variable could easily be predicted from another.

Modernist sociology was quite rigid in insisting that students secure and evaluate data from particular theoretical frameworks, whether functionalism, ethnomethodology, symbolic interactionism, conflict, or other models. Modernism, therefore, was much more inflexible, in fact, almost dogmatic, in insisting that there was no knowledge until that knowledge was contained and constrained within set theoretical parameters. It sought to validate the knowledge gained by appeal to authority and hierarchy and not to the data of the natural world and social reality.

Manipulation of modern social science, especially, was a part of the agenda of those who sought power and control within the general society. They would be willing to provide modern sociologists with some economic security in exchange for their theoretical support of their agendas. Modernist sociologists knew who their supporters were and were unwilling to advance theories and hypotheses that might alienate that support.

Modernist sociology was based upon seventeenth-century concepts made popular in the nineteenth century by philosophers such as Auguste Comte, Karl Marx, Herbert Spencer, and William Graham Sumner, all later identified with academic sociology. Some variations in this attitude were found later as such men as Emile Durkheim and Max Weber entered the debates. Key concepts in their reasoning were the ideas drawn from Newtonian mechanics. Force, power, mass, velocity, equilibrium, closure, and change were talked about in sociology as though they were precisely quantifiable.

The ideas that were not directly amenable to manipulation and measurement assumed the same positions in sociology as those not so directly measurable in the natural sciences. Values tried to gain some popularity as concepts but were driven to the edges of the discipline and almost asserted to be metaphysical. Modernist sociology sought to justify its existence by posturing mathematical precision as a substitute for strict reasoning.

As much as a prescribed social relations agenda was characteristic of modernist sociology, its political agenda was not far behind. Imbedded in this sociology was a prescription more favorable to the status quo than to change. Social problems were viewed as deviations from socially accepted upper-middle-class values, although they had been characteristic of the upper classes for years. It was not so much that people objected to the behavior of the deviants but that their behavior was not formally endorsed by the class that considered itself the guardian of behavior and morality. The correction of social problems was approached as political problems that largely reflected the morality of the middle class.

Modernist sociology provided the opportunity to use politics to solve social problems by focusing on groups and their relationship to the larger middle class. A model was used and comparisons made against that model. For example, after Max Weber's *Protestant Ethic and the Spirit of Capitalism* (1905), the middle class became the standard against which the classes below were measured.[1] Later, speech, family values, work ethic, attitudes toward the hereafter, educational values, and nearly all else were related to the middle-class measuring rod. Even science was thought not possible unless under Protestant middle class culture.[2]

Weber noted that cultures that were not Protestant were poorer than those that were. By this time much of the world was under colonial domination and the people unable to make normal changes. The countries that were not actively colonial had practically been destroyed or sharply reduced in the effort to become colonial or to resist becoming colonized. Weber's estimates were made upon cultures that were not equal from the beginning. He failed to note that within cultures that followed the Protestant ethic, whole groups were not as prosperous as those Protestants who were located higher in the social structure. Weber could not explain, for example, why there were poor southern mountaineers and ghetto-dwelling Protestants who held more closely to the Protestant ethic than even the more successful Protestants.

As with some other forms of theoretical work, modernism forced constituents to choose up sides based upon categories that were not always other than the ideological postures of the modernist members of the social science profession, nearly all of whom vied to become representatives of the ruling class. Modernism became justificatory, not just by the data collected but by the analyses of its practitioners as well. Scholars of this stripe were more attuned to studying the "less powerful" members of society, identified in the terminology of modernism as lower class, although in the upgrading of their terminology they became members of other categories such as the deprived, the homeless, the addicted, criminals, the problematic, and the handicapped.

The principal method of the production of modernist scholars was by apprenticeship. The case of sociology may be used in illustration. The acolyte usually enrolled in a graduate department and was duly taught the method and theory of the leaders of the discipline by apprentices, themselves aspiring to leadership. Failure was often a matter of not showing the proper attitude toward those who wanted to promote modernist sociology through the process of mentoring. Usually the successful candidate was one who did not show considerable originality or insight but who was most likely to be a carbon copy of a respected mentor.

Apprenticeship is a process of observation and imitation.[3] This process promotes modernism in expecting students to adopt the attitudes, practices, interpretations, and even research agendas of their mentors. Discipleship was the method by which progress was to be made in the discipline. An older scholar would recommend a younger one who had appropriately adopted the professional attitudes of the mentors.

The revolt against modernism in sociology was slow in coming, mainly because so many professors were trained in the modernist mode and almost none in the postmodern. Modernists held to the credentialing process, refusing to allow postmodern thinkers to hold forth from podiums in their universities. Requiring a doctoral degree as the criterion for hiring assured that only modernists would find their ways into the classrooms where students would be affected. New faculty were continually hired by the old criterion, namely, being wed to the modernist agenda. Dozens of new departments of sociology were opened after World War II, and modernist professors sought to promote their own students as the best candidates for the positions opened up in these departments. Where they could not control the hires, they erected criteria for judging departments; this again gave the advantage to the modernists.

By the late 1950s Reece McGee and Theodore Caplow could talk about departments of the first rank and those of "Siberia." Their rankings reflected the emerging perception that the better sociology departments were mainly in the East, and the Midwest, a few were in the Far West, and two or three were in the South. Other departments, they thought, offered graduate degrees that were embarrassments to the profession; these centers of American sociology were referred to as Siberian teaching posts.[4] Some academics thought that a social science report similar to the Flexner Report of 1910 was needed. That report noted that many medical schools were not meeting standards and to preserve the integrity and professionalism of medicine they needed to meet uniform criteria.[5]

POSTMODERNISM: SIMPLY ANOTHER VARIETY OF MARXISM?

Within academic sociology there was a tug-of-war between the functionalist perspective and conflict perspective. The functionalists sought to explain order, equilibrium, and deviance; conflictists, in contrast, purveyed the idea of class antagonism. For conflictists, deviance was also a function of class struggle. In the sense that functionalists and conflictists (Marxists) were trying to explain deviance—individual in the case of the functionalists and group in the case of the conflictists—they were working from the same premises, those projected as founded upon order and social coherency. Thus, both functionalism and Marxism were modern in that they held to rigid concepts of explanation and causation. By so doing they became essentially frozen in time and increasingly had to justify their own theoretical orientation by reference to previous features of their schema. There was almost dogmatic adherence to these grand theoretical paradigms, and sociological practitioners took their positions in either of these camps or perhaps identified with a very few others.

Because postmodernists did not automatically endorse modernist sociology, as their normal training would predispose them to do, they were thought to endorse the Marxist approach, and many were considered Marxists, there being little place for scholars with positions not within the extremes of the functionalist or Marxist camps. Essentially, the modernists had forced all sociological mainstream actors to choose up sides within the parameters of functionalism or Marxism. There did not seem to be many alternatives to the adoption of either of these orientations, although with Merton one might adopt the idea of the "middle range," or positions somewhere between the two, to account for smaller aspects of societal activity and behavior. Perhaps the very idea of critical, and even radical, sociology came to be identified with Marxism and socialism.[6]

Of course, postmodernism was not thought possible in American sociological scholarship because of the inability of Americans to read foreign languages well, thereby preventing their understanding the subtleties of the European works outside the modernist mode. The hold of modernism was so strong that no alternative to it seemed credible. Perhaps the first alternatives to modernism were based upon humanism and grew out of the alienation of such writers as Richard Wright (*Black Boy* and *Native Son*), who bitterly criticized the system envisioned through the lives of such protagonists as Bigger Thomas. In academic sociology, it was probably Gunnar Myrdal's *An American Dilemma* (1944) that departed from the modern and posited that the discrepancy between creed and deed with respect to the interethnic problem was essentially moral, helping to create a wedge for the alternative sociology of postmodernism.[7] Where critical and radical sociology tried to gain a foothold, both were assumed based upon Marxist thought, which in its most radical form, was seen as revolutionary.

The arrogance and ethnocentrism of departments of the first rank and their graduates, along with expanded enrollments necessitating newer departments, created a false sense of status among newcomers into the academic marketplace.

New graduates thought they were losing in status by having to teach in schools below the stature of those from which they graduated. The best of the graduates were taken by departments in the ranks they sought; the others went sullenly to the schools and departments thought of as Siberia. There they tried as hard as possible to purvey modernist sociology but found the atmosphere unreceptive.

Students were more attuned to getting jobs in bureaucracies, social welfare, and institutions than in becoming sociologists of the modernist trend. The jobs they sought did not require orientations commonly associated with modernist sociology. Since few students were listening to the scholars in the departments in Siberia, the opportunity was created to move beyond the limits of thought, theory, and philosophy posed by modernism. It was in these Siberian departments that inroads were being made into the canon that had become modernist sociology. The sheer numbers of these departments and the number of students they taught helped revise the attitude toward modernist sociology and helped pave the way for its eventual overthrow.

For students of the Siberian departments, and many of their schools met the same criteria, sociology became a service major, not merely to be taken as a vehicle to the acquiring of a job but as a means through which society could be altered. The very subject matter studied sensitized the student toward change and away from the value neutrality that had come to characterize modernist sociology. All the categories and groups studied by the modernists were problematic, and their theoretical foundations were not inherent in the theories themselves.

Postmodernist scholars were ready to go beyond description and nomenclature and toward the advancements of prescriptions for the correction of social ills. Where sociology would not yield to a program of change advocacy, students began to defect from the field and into those fields that promised to promote change toward a more egalitarian society. Since so many fields had adopted the modernist agenda and approach, it was difficult to find any place where advocacy could be proffered.

The tug between postmodern advocacy and modernist value neutrality came to a head in the issue of credentializing. Modernist scholarship, seeing that postmodernism was gaining a foothold, began to try to control the direction the field was taking by insisting that before any suggestions could be made toward change, the individual must have certification through credentialing. Every avenue of change was thus blocked by imposition of a credentialing process that literally made it illegal to practice any degree of advocacy.

The debate between the modernists and the postmodernists was waged at the level of credentializing, but it was really a contest of ideology; the programs of both modernists and postmodernists were not fully grounded in theory or predictive accuracy. The modernists were more structuralist than the postmodernists, and they sought answers to social problems in their respective theoretical leanings, which, again, were more ideological than scientific. Though very aware of the contest over ideology that would be reflected in research support, sociology as a whole was largely unwilling to engage in this level of debate and generally withdrew from the fight, leaving the large funded research and studies to be carried out by disciplines that were willing to go postmodern rather than holding to the relatively inflexible modern.

The failure of sociology to receive grants in the numbers it had received in the past, say, twenty years reflected changes in discipline ideology and structure. Old sociology continued to purvey the modernist thrust, which had plainly lost currency and was unwilling to meet the competition posed by postmodernism[8] with its emphasis away from structure and macroanalyses to smaller units of analyses, even down to the individual.

NOTES

1. Max Weber, *The Protestant Ethic and the Spirit of Capitalism* (1905), trans. Talcott Parsons (New York: Charles Scribner's Sons, 1930).

2. Robert K. Merton, "Puritanism, Pietism and Science," in *Social Theory and Social Structure* (Glencoe, IL: The Free Press, 1957).

3. Edward Myers, *Education in America—A Unique Experiment* (London: Twentieth Century Press, 1912), p. 6.

4. Theodore Caplow and Reece McGee, *The Academic Marketplace* (New York: Basic Books, 1958).

5. A. Flexner, *Medical Education in the United States and Canada: Bulletin of the Carnegie Foundation for the Advancement of Teaching* (New York: Carnegie Foundation for the Advancement of Teaching, 1910).

6. Nicholas C. Mullins and Carolyn J. Mullins, *Theories and Theory Groups in Contemporary American Sociology* (New York: Harper & Row, Publishers, 1973), pp. 270–286.

7. Gunnar Myrdal, *An American Dilemma* (New York: Harper & Row, 1944).

8. Frederic Jameson, *Post Modernism or the Cultural Logic of Late Capitalism* (Durham, NC: Duke University Press, 1990); Jean Francois Lyotard, *The Post Modern Condition: A Report on Knowledge* (Minneapolis: University of Minnesota Press, 1984); and Kegan Doyle, "The Reality of a Disappearance: Frederic Jameson and the Cultural Logic of Post Modernism," *Critical Sociology,* no. 1 (1992): 113–127.

15

Technicism, Conservatism, and the Curriculum: The Loser Sociology

Like so many other liberal arts disciplines, sociology made the fundamental mistake of thinking that there is something inherently interesting about the field. These disciplines had secure positions in the academic spectrum. They had gained places in the decision-making circles of their schools and could argue for students on the basis of the need for students to take their courses because they would lead to better general education.[1]

After the overthrow of religious orthodoxy in education or the banishment of its most stouthearted proponents to private and parochial schools, liberal education began to compete for the attention and resources of students. The growing affluence of the United States meant that there was less concern with the basics of survival. Now there could be some attention given to the larger questions of life: questions about beauty, the arts, values, and meanings, questions that could not be easily entertained when such emphasis was placed on conquering the wilderness. By the late nineteenth century, the most successful Americans had become individuals who valued liberal education after they had made great fortunes in their businesses. They became the leaders of academics in that their decisions greatly influenced the way students were trained.

Copying the successful entrepreneurs meant following a trail of liberal arts and then applying general brilliance to the accumulation of fortunes. Controllers of academics came to believe that liberal education was beneficial in the making of more liberal people. This type of education was seen as the solution to most of the problems of the American public.[2] Liberal education meant an inquiry into the lighted and darkened corners of society. All topics would be explored because they were considered equally valuable, at least to some segments of the society. Only the narrowness imposed by those professors who were very narrowly trained prohibited an objective inquiry into a variety of subject matter.

The mark of an educated person was a liberal education, which, it was believed, made an individual more intellectually expansive.

An appeal of liberal education was in the reading and discussion of books that provided food for thought and reflection. Interpretations were something like Freudian ink-blot tests because each person's opinion was as valuable as anyone else's. Answers were not final; they were matters of discussion, with the quality of the discussion determining whether the answer was correct or incorrect. These discussions were stimulating, and classes were also. Students could establish themselves by the position they took and could become known on that basis. Students gained confidence and knowledge through these discussions. They wanted to participate in classroom work and often went to classes because they were interested in the ferment of opinions. They did not have to force themselves to participate because now subject matter was inherently interesting.

The essays students wrote defending or expanding their positions were important in helping them clarify their own thought. At the same time, they helped uncover literary and other talent. Papers were to be turned in to instructors who spent considerable time grading them. Probably as much as 50 percent of the work of college professors was the grading of student papers. Difficult, often boring work, it had to be done, for there was no other way a professor could gain insight into the thought processes of students, as well as seeing whether the students exhibited basic academic skills.

On campuses today there are fewer faculty members who consider their work with students the main part of their job.[3] Such educators were stand-up teachers with little to go on other than their own ideas, the books they had read or written, and the teaching challenges presented by the students. Walking through a prominent college of education on a heavy teaching day yielded classrooms in which stand-up professors were holding forth on matters such as theory and pedagogy of education. Students were enthralled in the debates over ideas, the clashing of which could occasionally lead to minor confrontations. Ideas were important, and professors who traded in ideas were always highly valued by students. Such faculty members are becoming more difficult to find on campuses today, causing a change in the entire character of students.

Students seeking exciting professors who are walking/talking encyclopedias (and who are thought to have all the answers) today are finding more specialized instructors who are generally much younger. They often instruct their students from computer terminals with little interchange and clash of ideas. More students and professors today consider themselves educated if they are able to master some of the more sophisticated computer programs.

Book knowledge takes a lower place because as one student put it, "Book knowledge people don't have common sense." Students holding to this concept probably missed the idea that book knowledge means dealing with ideas and not necessarily with things. The revolt against ideas no doubt relates closely to the success of technical people, who displaced the idea people as controllers of the thoughts of students. If students place more emphasis upon technology or mastery of things than on mental expansion through involvement with ideas, it is probably due to the aggressiveness of the technicists, who see that they can gain control of the educational apparatus and assure the training of students according to their standards.

Technical people claim that the education of today and tomorrow must be technical; that is, it must contain a much lower loading of ideas. People who know how to do things, that is, people who have a technology, are assumed educated. That is probably why such fields as engineering, agriculture, architecture, medicine, and even law, all claiming practical components, are much more remunerative than the liberal arts fields that stress working with ideas. Liberal arts proponents claim that liberalism was more desirable than narrowness, and they even insisted that a person was not properly educated unless liberally educated.[4]

By a gradual process the technical wing of education grabbed control of the curriculum and actively propagandized against the merits of a liberal education. Today, typically university leadership is greatly biased toward technical education, with persons in the liberal arts trying to keep from being submerged totally under the juggernaut of the technicists.

One of the propaganda moves of the technicists is to publish the starting salaries offered in technical fields compared to those offered in the liberal arts. The figures encourage students to move toward the technical fields, where they do not have to deal much with ideas. Their education becomes technique, or procedure, more like bricklaying or truck driving. If students learn the procedure, they may become certified without their ideas changing. One student, for example, declared that he reads only computer books. Another, claiming that street smarts are more valuable than book smarts, said he reads only one popular magazine.

The idea people, or liberal arts aficionados, are unable to convince students of the value of a liberal arts education mainly because they are unable to show that idea people as a category are highly paid. Students are unimpressed by the small salaries that even highly degreed liberal arts people receive. As this book was being written, a student who was in my university's master's program in sociology some twenty years ago came by the office to visit. He had his family with him. He was asked when he planned to come back to complete his master's degree. He quickly said he didn't think he would, since he was now making $49,000 per year in the trucking management business, running computers. The bottom line is income. Evidently society does not want students who have much liberalism. If it did, there would be a greater expression of that interest in the form of higher salaries for liberal arts graduates. The evidence accumulates that too much liberal arts training can be damaging to one's economic health.[5]

The exchange of technical education for liberal education came about after World War II. Until that time liberal education at America's most prestigious schools had higher value than the most technical education. It was a long time before a technical degree from MIT (Massachusetts Institute of Technology) outranked, say, a history or a political science degree from Harvard or a Cal Tech certificate over a preaching certificate from prestigious Brown University. Liberal education had to be downgraded if the growth of right-wingism was to be promoted. Students today place as much value on being narrow and right wing as they did in years earlier when being liberal and a little to the left was popular. This shift is attributable to the control of the country by conservatives, a polite moniker for being politically and socially right-wing.

To hold control the right wing must support a curriculum that stresses its values. Technical education is the best vehicle for promoting right-wing sentiments; its curriculum places little emphasis upon the student's engagement with ideas. A large impetus was given to the development of understanding of human behavior through manipulation of rewards and punishments through the vehicle of operant conditioning, an idea advanced largely by B.F. Skinner.[6]

Sociology has been as much affected by the onslaught of the technicists as the other fields. The stand-up professors in this field are finding it more difficult to interest students who have equated education with technique and manualism, and any discipline without a specific technique is at risk at a time when great emphasis is placed upon conforming to the norm of the factory. Students are clones of each other; they are interchangeable, unique ideas and interpretations have not been encouraged but squashed or removed altogether.

So similar have student become that they may be graded by the same examination, whether by intelligence test or some other. The students who do not score as high as the others are not necessarily different. They simply require further processing toward conformity to the mold now in vogue. They have common values. Certainly it was a master stroke to foster sufficient similarity to enable the use of a uniform yardstick by which to evaluate students. Their processing to conservatism predictably came with the demotion in the significance of ideas. Very many of the students who would have studied sociology converted to newer fields such as criminal justice, which provided them with more of a technical base and which decreased the need for their dealing with problems at the level of ideas.[7]

There is currently no strong voice for liberal education in the United States, no voice at a level high enough to effect a policy.[8] At the level of collegiate and university administration, liberal education has given way to the technical, which is reflected in the increasing unwillingness of students to expand or modify their thoughts through grappling with ideas. Ironically, one of the most liberalizing fields in the curriculum was sociology, now all but succumbed to the idea that the discipline is a scientifically based technology and not one concerned with the big ideas and problems that have challenged the best thinkers of the country.[9] Today some of the most widely used books in sociology are those that stress the technical aspects of data processing, with scarcely a mention of sociology as a core content area.[10] Yet the material that has given sociology its excitement is all about ideas that lead to practices that have made differences in how men and women lead their daily lives.[11]

At the base of much of the problem with modern sociology is its measurement of human group behavior—essentially, its assigning values to variables and treating them as if they were isomorphic with behavior. The practice of measurement in social relations has become confused with the logic of measurement. Whereas the practice is well understood in the processes of arithmetic and statistics, hard questions have seldom been asked about the fundamental value of social measurement. To understand the attitude toward measurement better, consider its earlier development in the sister discipline of psychology.

Quantification was beginning to occur in psychology in Germany by the end of the 1880s. It was called the new psychology because it was experimental. H.L. Helmholtz and Wilhelm Wundt had set the stage for experimental work in psychology in the 1850s and 1860s.[12] There followed a steady trail toward the incorporation of measurement in psychology to divorce it from philosophy and even British empiricism which dated back to John Locke's tabula raza, Bishop Berkeley's emphasis on experience, and David Hume, David Hartley, James Mill, and John Stuart Mill. Experimental psychology reached America in the work of William James at Harvard. James had brought the idea from Germany, where he had studied at the University of Berlin.[13] The story of the move of American psychology to empiricism and measurement is told candidly by Edward G. Boring.[14]

Sociology moved toward quantification about the same time as psychology. The new sociology was a departure from the speculation of philosophy, but unlike psychology, which could break its data down into small units encompassed within individuals, sociology was interested mainly in group interactions. For a long time sociologists wanted to know what members of groups thought about a particular problem or some other group. Since literacy had greatly increased by the turn of the century, a favorite tool of study became the questionnaire, which enabled more individuals to give more input than possible through participant observation and the case study.

In participant observation, the researcher joins the group to be studied, gains the confidence of the group, and as a member of that group engages in its usual rounds of activities. The researcher's findings are submitted to the group for its correction and approval, out of respect for the group and out of the idea that the group knows more about itself than the researcher. Similarly, the case study concentrates upon a particular group, usually as a representative of a class, and delves deeply into its inner workings. However, in contrast to participation, the researcher remains outside the group. What emerges is a comprehensive study of the group or even of an individual who could be considered a representative of the group.[15] Measurement can be used in each of these methods of study, but measurement need not be thought of as an improvement in the method of study.

Description was long considered the most important sociological tool. In this, sociology was very close to anthropology, which widely used that method. The richness of description gave studies their flavor and enabled those reading about groups to believe they understood them better. Words were very familiar to individuals, and the images they conveyed were in closer agreement than the images that were to be offered later through the use of measurement. The earliest sociological studies were descriptive and, some say, speculative. Of these descriptive studies, perhaps the most popular were those regarding stratification. There may have been something intuitively interesting about a discussion of the class systems, in local areas and nationally.[16]

Just why studies began to take a quantitative turn is speculative. However, around the turn of the century the British statistician Karl Pearson tried to integrate studies by offering all a possibility for the use of more precise reasoning.[17] As early as 1925 George Counts sought to assess occupational status.[18] In 1928 quantitative studies in the area of social stratification began to appear.[19] Probably when sociologists began to contest over the matters of status and placement, because there was no agreement on what others had said or were saying about this highly discussible issue, they started to seek out more precise means of answering questions. Social stratification studies were perhaps among the earliest of the sociological studies to become highly quantified.[20]

NOTES

1. Liberal education probably got a start with the American and French Revolutions when there was a turn to consideration of such issues as the basic rights of persons, liberty, and equality. Whereas the more privileged conducted parlor talk about these rights, the common people were in no position to take these issues to heart. There is not much discussion of the place of liberal education in the important volume edited by John Barnard and David Burner, *The American Experience in Education* (New York: Franklin Watts, 1975).

2. General education and liberal education came to be viewed as practically synonymous and now constitute the basis of the first two years of education in the typical American college curriculum. Study of the social, natural, and physical sciences, mathematics, and the humanities are thought of as the broad liberal arts. See Chris A. De Young and Richard Wynn, *American Education*, 7th ed. (New York: McGraw-Hill, 1972), pp. 302–303.

3. Page Smith, *Killing the Spirit: Higher Education in America* (New York: Penguin, 1990), is very critical of the dash into research and the retreat from teaching so characteristic of many professors today. See especially pp. 199–222.

4. Smith conveys the excitement of the use of ideas in various aspects of teaching, but especially in respect to the lecture. Ibid., pp. 211–213.

5. It may be damaging in the sense that liberal arts graduates are in less demand than those trained in the sciences and cannot command the salaries of technically trained people. In many cases, though, persons in liberal arts working in the more technical departments earn more than those of equivalent training who work in liberal arts departments. A sociologist working in the College of Agriculture may earn thousands of dollars more yearly than one working in the sociology department.

6. For his basic views on the application of technology to human conduct, see B.F. Skinner, *About Behaviorism* (New York: Random House, 1976); *Science and Human*

Behavior (New York: Free Press, 1965), and *Beyond Freedom and Dignity* (New York: Random House, 1972).

7. It is well known that criminal justice majors have now greatly outrun sociology majors numerically. Some say this is because there is less emphasis upon the manipulation of ideas than in the former case. The emphasis upon technique is not all that great at the undergraduate level. The student may thus complete a curriculum, receive a degree, and not grapple seriously with ideas.

8. James B. Coonant, president of Harvard, a scientist himself, thought so strongly about the value of a liberal education that he thought the West's "liberal and humane tradition" was "basic to civilization." Cited in Smith, *Killing the Spirit,* pp. 141–142.

9. The major courses of the sociology curriculum are now those of methodology, statistics, and computers; all are joined together in the emphasizing of technique with less attention to grappling with ideas. Students hear less and less about the ideas of sociology and more about the various features of this or that computer program that enables this or that statistical analysis for this or that data set.

10. One such book is by Kenneth B. Hoover, *The Elements of Social Scientific Thinking*, 4th ed. (New York: St. Martin's Press, 1988). Hoover's text is merely illustrative of this focus.

11. Consider the tension created between conflict perspectives encouraged by the thought of Karl Marx, with its stress on the division of society into two warring classes, and the functionalism of Robert K. Merton and Talcott Parsons, who emphasize that society is made up of groups that work together to sustain the society instead of promoting its disintegration. Because these positions are opposite and competing for the thoughts of discussants, they generate substantial discussion. See R.P. Cuzzort and E.W. King, *Twentieth-Century Social Thought*, 4th ed. (Ft. Worth, TX: Holt, Rinehart and Winston, 1989), p. 354.

12. See Edwin G. Boring, *History, Psychology, and Science: Selected Papers* (New York: John Wiley & Sons, 1963), p. 159.

13. Ibid., pp. 161–162.

14. Ibid., pp. 163–164, especially as the work and influence in this kind of psychology by James Cattell is stressed.

15. For an overview of doing sociological writing, see Judith Richlin-Klonsky and Ellen Strenski, eds., *A Guide to Writing Sociology Papers*, 2nd ed. (New York: St. Martin's Press, 1991).

16. Nearly all academics have wanted to know how those above them have behaved, for by emulating them it might be possible to move up in social rank. The importance of etiquette has long been stressed in American mobility. See Anna Steese Richardson, *Standard Etiquette* (New York: P.F. Collier & Co., 1925), pp. 1–9.

17. Karl Pearson, *The Grammar of Science* (London: Adams & Charles Black, 1900).

18. George S. Counts, "Social Status of Occupations," *School Review,* 33 (January 1925): 16–27.

19. F. Stuart Chapin, "A Quantitative Scale for Rating the Home and Social Environment of Middle Class Families in an Urban Community," *Journal of Educational Psychology,* 19 (February 1928). See also V.M. Sims, *The Measurement of Socioeconomic Status* (Bloomington, IL: Public School Publishing Co., 1928).

20. See especially Harold M. Hodges, Jr., *Social Stratification: Class in America* (Cambridge, MA: Schenkman, 1964), for an excellent comprehensive history of the studies of stratification up to the 1960s.

16

Dethroning the Old Gods

Reading books and articles published in the 1970s provides an opportunity to look backward to understand what was thought to be important. Then the salient feature was the rise of ethnic power, or ethnic sloganeering, which came into being with the decline of the Vietnam War. Ethnicity was something that people had long denied because of the thrust of assimilation or pursuit of the "American way of life." People look to return to their "roots," in so doing finding great security in the historicity of their ethnic origins. Being ethnic was not only the socially correct thing to do but also the best way of proving to others who were trying to be something else than who they were that they were really misguided.

Ethnics were really people from Europe who had other than British names. Their grandparents ordinarily did not speak very good English. Usually they were Catholic or Jewish and largely working class. They came from large families whose members worked together in everything that mattered in life. What held them together, they claimed, were love and history.[1]

Ethnicity was the god of the old sociology. Every way of studying ethnicity became stressed and sanctified. The explanatory factor in nearly every sociological study, ethnicity was a god created by the creators of all gods, the people who control of the means of propaganda and who find that use of a concept or practice has benefit for them. Within the ethnic category was a focus upon ranking. Classes were created within ethnic groups, separating the people within in the same way they were separated outside the group. Intragroup disharmony was as great as that existing between groups.

The concept of ethnicity worked for sociologists in the same way that the stethoscope worked for physicians, as a marvelous job aid. Today a sociologist's badge of recognition is the study of some ethnic group or another, either in whole or part. Ethnicity has been a staple concept of sociology so long that it is symbolically carried around one's sociological neck the way a physician carries around a stethoscope.

Sociology's concern with status was not simply that it denoted social placement. Status was consistent with the idea of hierarchy and dominance. It was a way of locating individuals in the social structure and tying expectations to those placements. Allied with the emphasis on status was emphasis on class. Within each social class were many statuses, all graded, if broadly. One's status was as important as one's class. Never was a low-status individual to be placed over one with high status. Thus, status and class were not to be confused. One could have high-class standing, but that standing would not be worth much without high status. Status was individualized and localized, whereas class was a group phenomenon that could be relatively meaningless in a local area. An individual would rather have high status within a group than have high general class standing and the class not recognized. Obviously, then protection of status was a very important undertaking within the American social system.

Earlier studies of status did not consider that individuals would attempt to affect their status. For instance, it was thought that individuals with high social class standing did not have to worry much about encroachment from below. Their birth and/or their wealth would be sufficient surety that their class and status would be protected. Old sociology taught that much status was ascribed; that individuals took the status of their parents quite commonly. This reasoning promoted the idea that class positions were not likely to change much during the course of one's lifetime. The criteria of birth and wealth were sufficient to bar many individuals from ascending to the highest ranks of class and status.

The rigidities of America's stratified social structure were not satisfactory for whole groups of people who were seeking to improve their standing in society. Assaults were made on the old criteria, which assured that mainly members of old aristocracies controlled upper status recognition and that all newcomers were basically unwashed pretenders to high places.

One way of overcoming these social rigidities was to insist that status, which heretofore had been an unmeasurable quality, become measurable. Status would be measured in terms of objective scores. If women outscored men on, say, medical and law school examinations and got into those schools in numbers and percentages greater than men, would it not show that they were entitled to the recognition that goes with achievement, which, again, was not dependent upon their gender or other connections? Given such objective criteria of status, it would no longer be necessary to resort to the "buddy system" or "the old boy network"; women would not need to seek the sponsorship of some male with a personal interest in their mobility. Individuals could work on developing strong resumes, for these would take the place of apprenticeship and sponsorship.

To elucidate further the hold of persons perceived as giants in sociology, we may take the case of William Lloyd Warner, whose thought has so greatly influenced American impressions of class.[2] Warner was really an anthropologist who early on gained fame studying the aborigines of Australia. When he joined the faculty of the department of sociology at the University of Chicago, he had become fascinated with the caste system of India and other systems of social ranking. Scholars in Europe had used the concept of class in their relatively philosophical studies of society there, but class was never thought of in the way it was in the United States. If anything, there was too much mobility in America to think seriously about a rigid class system.

Warner was impressed with the rigidity of ranking systems and thought the ideas could be transferred to the American social situation. The Lynds had studied class in Middletown some years before Warner began to examine communities in a series of studies called the Yankee City Series.[3] Warner,[4] no doubt understood that there was a lingering acceptance of the concept of class as it existed in the European context. No doubt he felt that such a feeling was present in America. At least it would make good reading.

Warner was opposed to the Marxist position, which perceived class as rigid; he thought he could preserve the idea of class by ranking several classes ranked from low to high. At first Warner had some nine classifications, where each class was divided into three levels: upper upper, middle upper, lower upper; upper middle, middle middle and lower middle, and upper lower, middle lower and lower lower. Warner even sought to make his assignments on the basis of objective criteria. He found that the very concept of class was laden with subjectivity. Later, popular usage collapsed these categories into upper, middle, and lower classes, with the possibility of mobility from one class to the other.

Warner discovered his dilemma, for he could see that class in America was not the same as class in Europe. To remedy this problem, he suggested that each city, town, or village had its own class structure. His cultural relativism, no doubt gained from anthropology, satisfied those persons who were of higher status in their areas but who might be even middle or lower class in other areas. Warner's remedy for having no uniform standard of class from one group to another and from one area to another meant that class had lost its utility; it had no universality.

At the time Warner wrote, social scientists were struggling to achieve scientific recognition by using widely applicable concepts in a universal way. Since, under Warner's logic, class became specific to a particular area, there soon developed within sociology a tremendous focus on class analyses in very many contexts. It seemed that there was no way to bring meaning to class unless in the Marxist sense, for there was too much variation in class structure from one group and time to another. Warner seemed less concerned with finding a universal meaning of class than with showing that different areas had their own class structure. His attempt to show class relativism rendered the concept almost useless; there was very little to tie the classes together. At the same time, the people who were said to be upper class in their limited environments could feel secure relative to those who were beneath them.

Warner was probably as aware as others that class would lose its meaning unless there were some way of tying classes together, as Marx had done, by showing the common interests of members of the upper class in holding their wealth and of the lower class in having that wealth redistributed. Warner did not sanction nationwide or areawide classes, for they would combine their resources. Particularly, he did not want the lower classes to combine their resources, for they might contest with the upper class for redistribution of wealth and opportunity. His interest was in arguing for class as an area-specific reality.

Because Warner's concept of class accorded so closely with what Americans thought of class, leaving it area-specific and without antagonism of the lower class toward the upper class, it was widely endorsed. Warner's concept of class became practically ingrained into sociological thought, and he became something of a high priest of stratification. Ordinary sociology teachers launched into Warnerian stratification without much thought about its validity.

Warner's authority on this topic was practically unimpeachable. In the rush to preserve the cultural relativism of class, its universality was overlooked. Consider that a valid, useful concept, especially a scientific one, must have universal applicability. An example will suffice to illustrate the point. A yardstick of thirty-six inches is commonly used in America to measure an individual or a common object for length or height. In European countries a meterstick may be used. It does not make much difference which stick is used, for an individual will be the same height whichever measuring stick is used, and the values of one stick may easily and exactly be translated into the values of the other. It is the same with money, whose value fluctuates, making an exchange variable. One does not have more wealth in dollars than in yen, for a formula enables the easy translation of one currency into the other. As Euclidean geometry and common sense teach. "Things that equal the same thing are equal to each other."

Now, look at class in the European and the American contexts. If one is in the upper class in Europe, one cannot be in the lower class in the United States, even though one may be perceived to be in the lower class. An upper-class American cannot be lower class in Europe if the concept of class has universal validity.[5] Upper-class status in one context means upper-class status in the other. Lower-class, or even middle-class, standing cannot differ by culture. Incumbents are the same in either culture, the same as an individual is the exact same height in the United States or Europe whether measured with a yardstick, meterstick, or laser beam. A scientific concept cannot have a meaning that differs according to cultural setting although the cultural relativists would demur.[6]

We pose that there is no class system in the United States, although there are many persons with more or less money or access to the good things of life. There is a large folklore built up around the idea of class because it is a comfortable topic to discuss and one over which discussants may disagree at some length.[7] There has been no serious attack on Warner's class system analysis because it has felt so comfortable and accorded so well with what American scholars have wanted to believe; given Warner's classifications, they do not have to do logical or empirical checks to see if class structures are a reality.

Were they so, they would not be greatly different from class structures in other settings. It makes no greater sense to say that a person is upper class at home and lower class away than to say that a pygmy is tall at home but very short away from home. The idea of cultural relativity has taken over to guide thought where empirical or logical checking is required. Perceptions are no substitutes for empirical understanding.

Warner has become an authority as revered as Aristotle. Mention his name, and his eminence provides sufficient authority to serve as empirical reality. When Galileo decided to check the statements wise old Aristotle made 2,000 years earlier, he found that the sage authority was in error and the scientific revolution was on. Likewise, when there is a valid and empirical check on the idea of social class in the United States, and not a deferential bowing to the authority of Warner, it may be found that it is Warner's authority rather than defensible statements about stratification that have been carrying the day.[8]

Related to the idea of class, as put forward by those of the Warnerian school, is the belief that such a system could be implemented in the American context. It was, in fact, a function of generations of teaching to prepare many persons out of the European tradition to believe that transferral of social systems was a simple matter. The old systems of caste and estate are discussed next to show that they both were based upon landholding, which had long determined status and power in old social systems. Because landownership in America did not have the value it had in Europe, the entire stratification structure in the United States was bound to be less rigid than in older European societies.

LAND, STATUS, AND HEREDITARY PEASANTRIES

All stratification in the earliest days of human existence was based on landholding. Early peoples had access to all the land that they surveyed, for it belonged to no one and no one could alienate it. In biblical times land was a resource. It not only was available for grazing but also provided water sources and nuts, berries, fruits, animals, and wood required for sustenance. This, of course, was to change. Land had to be alienated from the group and concentrated in the hands of landlords, who thenceforth would command the people by controlling their livelihood. Since land was the source of livelihood, those who held the land could control those who had no land.

Landlords controlled at first through hired soldiers who served in exchange for security on the manor. Because the landlords were constantly trying to find new sources of money, they eventually charged the soldiers a fee; the soldiers thus became indebted like the other persons on the land who worked for the landlord. The cost of being a soldier or knight continued to rise, thrusting the knights into a different relationship with the landlord.

In time the knights, who could not accumulate property and who could not pay their fees, agreed to serve in positions of fealty. They would subdue weaker persons upon command of the landlords, forcing those conquered to work for the holders of land. In order to acquire larger armies, landlords had to gain control over more land. Their appetites became practically insatiable, and their holdings would extend until they ran hard up against the holdings of some other landlord. Often these landowners combined their resources, either through marriage or through willful subordination if the condition of resistance looked hopeless.

Peasants were at first persons who were conquered and forced to work for landlords at a variety of menial positions. Some tried to rise in the system, but most were unable to do so. Even though ownership of the land circulated within a few families, it did so slowly; and when it did, those most unable to move were tied to the land as peasants. To assure a steady source of cheap labor, the landlords arranged for the hereditary placement of peasants such that they were permitted only limited mobility out of their subordinate positions.

With soldiers and peasants locked into place, the landlords secured their own place and status by making sure that the land remained in the family. The caste and estate systems relied heavily upon the erection of groups hierarchically related to each other and subordinate to the landlords. In both the caste and estate systems, untouchability was elaborated. The lowest members of the caste system were viewed as untouchables, assuring that they would be practically excluded from all but the lowest positions in society. In the estate system, the nobility were the untouchables in that they were insulated from the majority of the society and had very little to do with those lowest down. Their untouchability assured that they would always have the highest positions in the land. The upper members of society, whether members of the knighthood or the clergy, did not have ready access to members of the nobility. The inaccessibility of the nobility gave them the quality of untouchability.

In both of these systems, the holding of land separated the landlords from the general masses of the people of whatever rank. Since the financial cost of maintaining social distance was increasing, the landlords had to find ways of convincing those lower down the social ladder that their positions were natural. Elaborate rules of association developed, the principal rule being one of mystification, particularly with respect to the behavior of the landlords, who had somehow become ensconced at the apex of the caste or estate systems.

The peasants were happy merely to be in the presence of their landlord or the landlord's representative, and they cherished every moment and memory of that association, for it was quite infrequent that these higher-ups condescended to associate on a nonritualistic basis with the persons of a lower class. Today almost any English working-class person will take off a day from work in order to stand on a street to get a glimpse of the Queen or some member of the royal family. Likewise, a large number of the lower-class in America will eagerly seek glimpses of the president and first lady.

It is probably in the Catholic countries that the mystical carryover from feudal times is greatest. The pope is the mythical supreme landlord. Wherever he travels, hundreds of thousands of people with feudal mentalities turn out to see him and to listen to his words. American landlords, though with holdings much smaller than those of the medieval lords, were not unknown to assemble their slaves at the big house or in another common spot in order to address them or confirm their exalted status.

In caste societies such as those in the Orient and, especially, India, landlords held onto power and status much longer than they did in Europe. They fought very hard in Europe to preserve their status based on the old ground of landownership. In the New World land meant a lot less, for there was much of it, and caste and estate had a more difficult time getting started. The Americans were probably the original fighters against the control of the landlords, although the colonists attempted to install the European system in the New World. When they were unable to entice enough European peasants to the New World, mainly as indentured servants, they sought to displace them and bring in a new peasantry, a people who would have to be trained into the hard labors of servitude. These persons were called slaves, but their role was to provide the basis upon which a hereditary peasantry would be built, as had been the case in the older caste and estate societies.

It proved impossible to convert the slaves or other captured people to a permanent peasantry. In Latin America, conquistadors subdued the Indians and attempted to make of them peasants and mine workers under the control of an hacendado or jefe, who was to enforce the rules of labor and social placement common during the Spanish feudal system. The Indians resisted both peasantry and slavery, however; they were not prepared psychologically to acquiesce to a system that had taken Europeans over 500 years to accept as the correct social order. In North America, where the Native Americans were obvious candidates for peasantry, they proved to be too intractable for the work of field and mines. In a continuing attempt to establish a peasantry, African slaves were introduced more than 100 years after they had been brought to Latin America. The attempt, though a long one, was even more trying, and its failure was almost inevitable.

Peasantries were difficult to establish in the New World because the people who were candidates did not have the requisite mentalities. They had been members of tribes of various sizes. Tribesmembers were tied together nebulously, having at best a very simple political organization. The chief or headman did not have a great deal of power. Very often there was no army to enforce chiefly desires. Importantly, a chief did not own much more than the other tribespeople, and there was no real need for peasants to defer to chiefs as was done in caste and estate systems. Tribesmembers were essentially independent families making their living in traditional ways that did not depend upon political organization for the maintenance of that tradition.

Even though tribal warfare was not uncommon, the people who were captured in warfare were not put into the service of the chiefs who were their captors. They were not generally reduced to a hereditary peasantry. There were no means of enforcing their peasant status, and the cost of keeping them was prohibitive. Incorporating them into the structure of the conquering group was found more useful.

The case of the Baganda of Uganda is instructive.[9] When the British entered Uganda in the 1860s, they found intralacustrine kingdoms that were highly developed politically. The Baganda had, through warfare, gained control of territory around the western edge of Lake Victoria and had taken over a variety of lesser groups. The Kabaka (King) of Buganda demanded little of these conquered tribes. They could maintain their own languages, continue their methods of making a living, and basically give lip service to the suzerainty of the Kabaka. None of the captured tribal groups was pressed into work directly in support of the Kabaka. The king was not really interested in much beyond having the people recognize him as the regional chief, paying him off with occasional cattle, goats, bark cloth, trinkets, and other produce. The Kabaka did not live measurably better than the typical tribesmen and women.

When the British came as other than missionaries, the first thing they did was to get an agreement from the Kabaka that he would be the chief of all the surrounding tribes. He was placed as a vassal to the British. In exchange he was given more scrumptious living arrangements, along with title to much land in his province, and provided a much larger retinue of servants. His subchiefs were to organize the territory so that the people would work and bring in coffee, tea, hides, and other produce that would be transferred to the British for sale in Europe. The British directed the Kabaka to erect a peasantry on the order of that with which they were familiar in Britain. This was the only system that they fully understood.

The efforts of the Europeans, of which the British example is illustrative, to establish peasantries in Africa were unsuccessful, and everywhere they resulted in severe internal fighting among the tribal Africans. The fighting became known as tribalism, but it was fundamentally a response to the attempts to convert heretofore free men and women to unfree peasants. The mentalities of Africans were never such that they could fit comfortably into peasant status.

Europeans and some Asiatics had no trouble accepting the peasant role, in either the estate or caste systems, because they had for generations, for hundreds of years, adjusted and became accustomed to the requisite mentalities. Peasanthood was not merely an economic and social status; it carried with it a particular mental set that justified or gave credence to the social placement of the individual, allowing that individual practically no opportunity to see or think beyond those boundaries.

A peasantry would be impossible to maintain without constant reinforcements of place. The lowest-status people, in the Indian caste system, the outcasts, were denied common schooling and then told that their social positions were religiously based; that they would receive their rewards in the afterlife. They were told by Krishna and other religious leaders to view their positions as worthy and to see their lives as fulfilled even though they were to carry out tasks others were unprepared to undertake. Of course, if the outcasts did not carry out their tasks, they would be coerced by the next level, the soldiers, who were in the employ of the landlords, the heads of their respective castes. The warriors, always above the outcasts, protected their landlords, often serving without expectation of upward mobility.

It was relatively easy for the British to move into India, pay off the ruling caste members with cash and the promise of greater status and higher standards of living and establishing indirect rule through native institutions. The people had already been prepared psychologically. For literally hundreds of years the people had been psychologically prepared to participate in a system based on hereditary landownership and the consequent peasantizing of the local people. There never were more than 2,500 British soldiers required to control 250 million Indians in the caste system, as Lord Lugard discovered.[10] His attempt to establish a hereditary peasantry and landownership system in Nigeria failed badly; nor did these attempts at European rule through indigenous institutions prove workable in any part of Africa.

In the 1820s, when the Americans sent former slaves back to Africa, the plan, though not publicly stated, was to reduce the local people to a peasantry. The former slaves from America gained control of Liberia, and whether they intended it or not, the outcome was a concentration of wealth and power in the hands of their descendants and the making of a poor class in Liberia, a class vassal to the African-Americans. The 1970s saw revolutions against these interlopers; they were displaced from rulership, and indigenous Africans were reinstated into positions of control. Most associated with this ongoing revolution, was Master Sergeant Samuel Doe.[11]

NOTES

1. See Barbara Mikulski, "Proud to Be Polish," in Drew McCord Stroud, ed., *Viewpoints: The Majority Minority* (Minneapolis, MN: Winston Press, 1973), pp. 94–98.

2. For a cogent discussion of the whole field of social differentiation, see Karre Svalastoga, "Social Differentiation," in Robert E.L. Faris, ed., *Handbook of Modern Sociology* (Chicago: Rand McNally & Co., 1964), pp. 530–575, but especially pp. 538–541, where Warner's method of computing ranking is presented.

3. See Robert S. Lynd and Helen M. Lynd, *Middletown* (New York: Harcourt, Brace & World, 1929), and their *Middletown in Transition* (New York: Harcourt, Brace & World, 1937).

4. See William Lloyd Warner and Paul S. Lunt, *The Social Life of a Modern Community* (New Haven, CT: Yale University Press, 1941), and their *Status System of a Modern Community* (New Haven, CT: Yale University Press, 1942).

5. The idea that class exists in the United States is basically a proposition about the procedures for determining class, which include an assessment of the validity of the procedures. In no case could a set of procedures yield contradictory conclusions if the concept is a valid scientific or theoretical one. See Alfred Jules Ayer, *Language, Truth and Logic* (New York: Dover Publications, 1946), pp. 5–16, where he shows that equivalency cannot be violated simply by moving into cultural relativity. Thus, the British expression of class and the American expression of class (or expressions of class in any

other culture) entail the same thing, namely, one of the procedures of verification of the thing or things or even values for which class stands.

6. Class seems to be a descriptive term which has not yet reached technical or theoretical utility. See John Wilson, *Language and the Pursuit of Truth* (Cambridge: Cambridge University Press, 1967), pp. 22–25, where the types of words are discussed, along with their places in various kinds of work.

7. Montague believes Warner's status ladder of several easy steps up or down was a view quite compatible with the basic myths of American society. See Joel B. Montague, Jr., *Class and Nationality: English and American Studies* (New Haven: Connecticut College and University Press, 1963), p. 43.

8. Class is just one of the many concepts used conventionally, but such usage need not be confused with statements of empirical fact. Again, according to Ayer, truth must be verifiable by experience. The dictionary could be in any language, for in the translation the meaning would be the same in either language if the *concept* is a theoretical one. Where the meaning of the word is unclear, there must be a dictionary for its translation. See Ayer, *Language, Truth and Logic,* p. 13.

9. Of the many reports on Uganda that tell the story of the former kingdoms, see D.E. Apter, *The Political Kingdom in Uganda* (London: Oxford University Press, 1961), Grace S.K. Ibingira, *The Forging of an African Nation* (New York: Viking Press, 1973), and Lloyd A. Fallers, *Bantu Bureaucracy* (Cambridge, England: W. Heffer & Sons, 1956).

10. Margery F. Perham and Mary Bull, eds., *Lugard*, 2 vols. (London: Collins, 1956–1960), will inform of the work of this representative of the British Empire in both India and Africa. See also Baron Frederick J.D. Lugard, *The Dual Mandate in British Tropical Africa* (Hamden, CT: Archon Books, 1965).

11. Basil Davidson, *Modern Africa: A Social and Political History*, 2nd ed. (London: Longman, 1990), offers a convenient capsule story of the history of political, economic, and social changes that have taken place in Africa.

17

Vernacular Sociology

Vernacular sociology is grounded in the needs of people to understand their own social environments. It does so in terms that are understood by the people, terms that they use in their everyday lives. The subject matter of vernacular sociology is life as it is experienced by individuals and groups. It is not necessary that the experiences be recorded by persons formally trained in the social sciences, for it is believed that any interested and literate individual may accurately record an event or tell a story that can be used to illustrate a point clarifying some aspect of social understanding. The assumption is that general education has proceeded to the extent that levels of sociological knowledge and understanding are very widely available and that more ordinary citizens may contribute to the advancement of the discipline and to their own knowledge.[1]

This type of sociology takes the subject matter of the discipline out of the hands of a few persons and makes it available to the many. It does not assume that the discipline is a fraternity of like-thinking individuals trying to fit their thought into a few well-established traditions. It brings to the discipline a degree of freedom that was not possible when the old sociology, with its relatively fixed approaches to the understanding of society, was in vogue. Therefore, it allows all ideas opportunities to compete in the intellectual marketplace on a more equitable basis. Social backgrounds of observers are less important in this type of sociology than in the old.[2]

Vernacular sociology introduces a larger variety of material into the discipline and enables greater flexibility in teaching. It allows the instructor freedom to tailor a class in general sociology to the needs of the students or other constituents instead of forcing them to confront a fixed subject matter. Vernacular sociology does not depend upon mass-market textbooks that are more schemes for class management than means of extending students' knowledge about how society operates. Often mass-market texts give the impression that there is a degree of certitude about the way society operates and that the answers are contained within the pages of the hardbound volume. They generally discourage discussion between instructor and student and reduce sociology to the teaching of many hundreds of students at a time.

The United States has always had a vernacular sociology, but there was no way of escaping the hold of the old masters, many of whom were taught because they were already in place and the opportunities to challenge them few. Once in place a paradigm became extremely difficult to displace, even when its credibility was in doubt. Paradigms hold people to the extent that virtual revolutions are required to make changes. Vernacular sociology allows the students to learn about society in a most natural way, in a way appealing to their interests.[3] It keeps the subject matter localized but does not limit the student, who can range over many social experiences to a depth interest determines as satisfactory.

The presentation of much of the old sociology was politically motivated. Questions and answers were to be considered in the light of what the political situation would tolerate. This meant that some questions could not be approached or some answers could not be given because they were perceived as politically unacceptable. Vernacular sociology does not have these reservations. All topics are open for discussion. Political considerations may be a part of the discussion on the same basis as the topics themselves, but they are not grounds for the exclusion of some topic or the tailoring of answers to fit the political needs of the time.

The scholar Thorstein Veblen almost 100 years ago proposed a model of the understanding sociology might yield if it were divorced from its European ancestors. One of the most exciting means of understanding how society works is through the life story. Its popularity earlier under the impetus of the Chicago school was greater than it is today. But as C.W. Mills has argued, it will be very difficult to distill societal operation from figures and secondary sources without great loss of meaning. The new sociology will use the methodology of the life story to encourage students to talk to the older generations to a much greater extent than they do presently.

The following section, which is a story of a professor's rummaging through the smokehouse of his boyhood home, is intended to provide an introduction to the excitement of vernacular sociology. It enables students to visualize changes in the social and economic status of their family as evidenced by materials retained and discarded over many years. Students can then question whether these changes were reflective of the larger society or segments of it.

RUMMAGING IN THE SMOKEHOUSE

I was visiting my childhood homestead recently and found myself rummaging around in the old storage shed. It had not been used for many years. It was built back in the late 1940s to serve as a meat curing shed, which we called a smokehouse. It was about fifteen by twenty feet, without windows. When the shed was being built, I wondered why it had no windows. The partition in back took up only about four feet. Inside that section were some benches built up to support boxes that held salted pork. The intention was to smoke the meat whenever a hog was slaughtered.

We never got around to smoking any meat from the time we moved into the house in 1947 until the present time. It is now very clear that we will never use the little shed for that purpose. Once or twice there were a few pigs salted down and sugar cured, but we never got around to smoking. We began to graduate from high school in 1948 and began to move away from home. My father was now engaged in other work for cash and did not have to rely as much upon the hogs we commonly raised for food and supplemental cash. He eventually recognized that he did not like to kill hogs. He never did, and he managed to have someone else in the community do it for us for part of the meat. By 1950 it was easier to sell the hogs he raised and buy the meat the family needed.

The smokehouse began to fill up with stuff that needed to be stored. Rakes, hoes, paint brushes, buckets, step ladders, tools of many sorts, all accumulated in the smokehouse so that it became virtually impossible to enter and exit comfortably. Stuff hung on the walls or found storage on the floor. My father tried for some time to keep the meat section open, but soon he just gave in and admitted that there would not be any use for the smokehouse other than for the storage of stuff that was accumulating in the family.

Nobody ever wants to throw anything away in my family. So a fairly good accounting of the progress of the family can be seen by rummaging through the shed. As stuff became less useful, it was relegated to the shed in order to make room in the house. Of course, the house would be almost overrun with relics before the hard decision was ever made to transfer some of the stuff to the shed.

The few times we had meat in the smokehouse were enough to make it smell as if you wanted to go inside. The salt and the sugar cure made very attractive smells. After a few weeks of being in the salt, the hams were hung up, suspended from bailing wire driven through the shank of the ham. If the weather remained cool, the meat would cure, and we would go out and cut off a few pieces just to snack on.

The red-eye gravy that was made from the hams was always a treat when it was served with the piping hot biscuits from the wood burner that was in the kitchen. We knew when we could expect to have ham and red-eye gravy because we usually had to cut up a special batch of stove wood so that the skillet would be heated specially to accommodate the ham and the sugar and water put in the pan after most of the ham had been cooked. The gravy was burned just right for sopping with the biscuit bread and the blackstrap molasses that we usually had to go with the ham.

But those days of ham and gravy from our own meat were pretty few. Even the homemade sausage met the same fate. Only a year or two after we moved from town to our little fifteen acre place did we have the pleasure of making sausage from the slaughtered hogs. It was much cheaper to buy meat from the butcher shop and sell our own pigs for cash. So, in time, the smokehouse continued to fill up with stuff from the house.

Somewhere in the mid–1940s when my mother did domestic work, having lost her teaching job, some of the people she worked for had children somewhat older than ourselves. They were facing the same problem of what to do with things their children had outgrown. Their own storage sheds and attics were getting filled up. These employers were getting desperate for space and often gave us things they simply had no further use for, even if it the things made them nostalgic. We got books, old clothes, shoes, and even bicycles, those big old balloon-tire bikes that must have weighed a ton; we used a little ingenuity to get the bikes running, but did not feel they were so great.

Youngsters were changing to skint-tire, lighter-weight bikes with several speeds. These were more feasible as the roads became smoother. The balloon-tire bikes had been used mainly as vehicles of transportation and not particularly for sport. When people could afford automobiles, they abandoned the bicycles. They became instruments of play for the youngsters. These single-sprocket vehicles did not provide much of a mechanical advantage, and young boys could be seen toiling to make the wheels roll, for so much energy was required to use the bicycles. The advantage was that once they got rolling, they coasted longer than the skint-tire bikes. Of course, we judged the quality of a bike by how far it would coast off the long Highway 65 hill on the northeast side of the town. Some of those old bikes were old when we got them, and they required repaint- ing and other maintenance. Quite often they were not put into running shape; and after leaning against the house in the rain and the elements, sometimes for years, they might be transferred to the smokehouse with the hope that they would later be restored to running shape. They seldom ever were.

One could tell what the early styles in clothes were by looking in the smokehouse. The quality of clothes made was seldom an issue. They were usually good and heavy, of broadcloth, wool, or tightly woven cotton. There is no way that these clothes would ever wear out. They just went out of style, and people got tired of wearing them. They were too good to throw out. They were kept in the house for years and then, when they had to be removed to make space for newer styles, usually after years, they were stored on nails in the smokehouse. Sometimes they were just laid on boxes or on whatever else was in there. The intention was always to put them on hangers, to arrange them, to find somebody to give them to. But it never did happen and they hung forlornly in the smokehouse. Only the oldest members in the house knew what they meant or to whom they belonged. Young people wondered why anyone would keep all these old clothes, which would never be used.

Shoes, rubber boots, and other footgear were placed in the smokehouse on about the same schedule as old clothes. In time the footwear drew up or de- hydrated for want of use. A pair of shoes was simply too good to throw away, yet no young person who could wear the shoes was willing to do so. Older people were not so much in tune with fashions and saw nothing wrong with these perfectly good shoes and clothes. Nobody was wearing keen-toe two-tones with wing-tips anymore. Seniors, of course, castigated the young people for having too much and not appreciating what they had.

In the smokehouse I found some old Sears Roebuck catalogs. They suggested how prices have changed over the years. It was unbelievable how cheap merchandise was thirty or forty years ago. We could not afford an abundance of these goodies even then. Prices were never low enough for some people. We could not have afforded much, for there was seldom enough money in the house for the necessities, to say nothing about the luxuries. The catalog was much thinner than one might find today, suggesting that the number of items available was somewhat smaller. Guns, medicines now considered illegal, elixirs, and all sorts of equipment could be bought by mail order. Ingenious youth went from door to door taking orders for merchandise, filling out order blanks for old people who could not see or read too well. They would then go to the post office and buy money orders to mail to the company for the merchandise, which would come directly to the purchaser, or sometimes to the bus or train station. The youth made money running the errands, not off the merchandise.

Hanging on one wall was a number 2 washtub, the kind we bathed in on the weekends. The kitchen door had to be shut after the last meal and the room converted to a bathroom. If several people in the house needed baths, sometimes bathing could be done in other rooms. Needless to say, some bathed more quickly than others, and only critical spots were hit as the water cooled.

On another nail hung an old washboard. I can't remember the last time it was used. We got running water in 1956 and a wringer-type washer a year or so later. That meant the demise of the wash pot and the rub board. The wash pot sat outside, and after a number of years the cast iron utensil was converted to a big flower pot. We had no further use of the rub board, and there was not enough copper or brass in it to sell at the junkyard. Even so, it was hard to forget those raw knuckles that were produced as clothes were cleaned with lye soap and elbow grease using the tub, the wash pot, and the rub board.

Moving some of the things around in the smokehouse, I came upon a "smoothing iron." I picked it up, and looked it over carefully; it brought back memories of how our mother washed our clothes and did a special job of starching and creasing our khakis and shirts so that we would look sharp to step out on Saturdays and Sundays. That iron had to be heated on the wood stove and tested to see that it was the exact temperature not to burn clothes of different weaves and weights of cotton and wool.

There was no known formula and no thermostat for determining the correct temperature of the iron. The best method was to wet the finger with the tip of the tongue and touch the finger rapidly to the iron. If the finger stuck, the iron was too hot. If the heat was not felt, it was too cool. Some of us tried to beat the iron by dropping water on it to see how it fried or ran off the smooth side of the iron. Precautions never assured that ironed clothes would be perfect, although quite a number of them were. When the iron was used for doing clothes for people across town, more care was taken, since good work meant repeat business.

The best memory I have of that iron was when it was heated on winter nights, wrapped in old sheets or other discards, and placed in the bed to warm it for us, there being no stove in any other rooms than the sitting room and the kitchen. A warm night in the bed made it that much harder to get up in the morning when the heat would have escaped. That is why we wore long-handle underwear to bed. It might get a little warm at night, but you were thankful you had them on when you hit the cold floor at five o'clock the next morning to make a fire in the heater, the cookstove, or both.

Hidden in one of the corners of the smokehouse was an old double-blade axe. The handle had been broken out so long ago nobody remembers. It must have happened just about the time we got butane gas for cooking. That meant we had to cut less wood. The butane was so convenient for mother that I guess we got spoilt. We soon began working to get it for the rest of the house. We promised ourselves we would not overuse it, for gas was costly. We would leave the heating stove up for a while, just in case.

It must have been around 1957 when we got the house plumbed for gas. Chips from the old woodpile were picked up until not a single one was left. Old boards, boxes, paper, and other combustible materials were used, and the axe was getting less and less of a workout. The file was put somewhere on a ledge but could never again be found. Everybody at home was working, and nobody had time anymore to cut wood for the heater. We would just buy butane, even on credit. There were not too many trees left around the place, and nobody was selling pole wood anymore. People were moving into new houses, and fireplaces were getting to be fashionable as status symbols. This drove up the price of firewood. I don't know what happened to the heater and the wood-burning cookstove. I think my father sold them for a few dollars to someone farther out in the country. They never did make it to the smokehouse.

Once the roof of the house had to be repaired, and while the carpenter was up there my father told him just to go ahead and tear down the chimney. We stacked up the bricks under one side of the house, and I suppose they are still there. By that time, we had gone over completely to butane and were moving toward natural gas.

In the older homes, generations may come and go and the smokehouse remains. Sometimes it might get a new roof or a coat of paint. People just do not have the heart to tear it down because it has too many items of potential use. Moreover, it is hard to convince the older members that the things inside should be discarded and the smokehouse razed. Surely somebody somewhere could use those items inside. The smokehouse looks so incongruous with the architecture of the community. Nobody had been seen going into some smokehouses for years. Often they are padlocked, and nobody knows where the keys are. After the departure of the last old members, nobody will have any idea of what is in the smokehouse, which will have been downgraded to a shed.

THE SOCIOLOGIST AS A POPULAR WRITER

Writing for the public is a valuable part of the sociological enterprise. Our imaginations of discipline propriety prohibit more of us from engaging in this work. Several issues usually come up in regard to popular sociological writings. The first issue is the question of content. Some think popular writing requires a lower order of skills than professional writing. In both types of writing, having something to say is basic. A popular writer attempts to tell a story, to make a point, the same as a writer for professional journals. He or she must observe, gather data, make interpretations, draw conclusions, extrapolate, and hypothesize. The popular writer cannot misrepresent the facts and is bound by the same ethical considerations as the writer for professional organs.

Perhaps the shortest popular writing is a letter to the editor. But even it must be timely, informative, and clear. It must speak to a problem, make a clarification, or raise an issue. Letters to editors must be graded and meet rigid standards regarding style, language, choice of subject, and length, to name a few. They suffer high rejection rates.

The features page of the newspaper is an attractive vehicle for purveying sociological knowledge. Articles are not automatically accepted for publication on these pages. To get published on the pages of prestigious papers, one must exhibit knowledge of a more specialized field of interest to the reading public. Not everything written, even by syndicated columnists, is accepted by newspaper editors.

Writing in national circulation papers or magazines is more difficult than writing for state or local ones. In national circulation organs the competition is truly keen, and only a small handful of those with sharply honed skills can crack this club. The author appearing in these organs on a regular basis will have greater recognition. In time a name is associated with thoughts, and that recognition is almost as important as what is being said.

There are many styles of doing sociology. It is an enterprise rather than a specific activity. A style of work is a means to the ends of observing, discovering, and reporting on social behavior. Writing in the popular media enables the sociologist to participate in issues to a greater extent. Newspapers are published daily or weekly, magazines monthly, perhaps, whereas academic journals are published quarterly. An issue is often raised and resolved before a sociological journal article is read by reviewers. What the scholar wants to say about an issue must wait sometimes years before gaining a hearing. Slow printing means the sociologist is generally out of touch with the present scene; he or she then gains a reputation of talking to dead issues.

A second issue in popular sociological writing is language. Objectors to popular sociology claim that the language of the discipline is not being protected when there is communication with nonprofessional audiences. But is any more being said by use of the stilted jargon of the academic social scientist? Any discipline strives for communication in a commonly accepted language. Even medical doctors know there is no point in using a long Latin name when all you mean is aspirin. For sociologists, *gesellschaft* means "they are not close friends." *Proletarianization* means "working for a living." What passes for an exact technical language in sociology is a jargonized language that obscures communication, practically assuring that no one will read the work. Impact is lost through the talking and writing of sociologese.

A third issue for popular sociologists who write is procedure. Popular-writing sociologists are accused of being less professional than those sociologists writing in the journals. This view grows out of seeing sociology as a set of procedures instead of as a part of a broad intellectual tradition to which no fixed criteria may be applied. Popular writers use their style because they feel that what they are trying to achieve dictates the style. They do not use many statistics but are aware of the need to process data through statistical analysis. A big difference between popular and academic sociologists is the greater compulsion by the latter to present their methodology and statistics. Popular writers have access to and expertise in the use of the very same procedures.

A sociologist must be free to choose the method required to exhibit an understanding of society. No single style or medium is always more appropriate than another. Presently, though, popular sociologists are discriminated against in departments whose members want to impose a style of work on all. By so doing they hope to use an inflexible yardstick to measure productivity and, therefore, to judge in a quantitative way that which is truly qualitative.

NOTES

1. One of the clearest calls for this type of sociology, which he calls "public sociology" or "lay sociology," is found in Herbert Gans, "Sociology in America: The Discipline and the Public," *American Sociological Review,* 54 (1989): 1–16.

2. The various approaches to the study of society, especially the conflict, interactionist, and functionalist, are familiar to members of the discipline. However, for an overview of these approaches, see George J. Bryjak and Michael P. Soroka, *Sociology: Cultural Diversity in a Changing World*, 2nd ed. (Boston: Allyn & Bacon, 1992), pp. 10–25.

3. A good example of vernacular sociology is seen in the work of Melissa Fay Greene, *Praying for Sheetrock* (Reading, MA: Addison-Wesley Publishing Co., 1991), a story told in a natural manner covering many sociological insights into how McIntosh County, Georgia, actually operated. The author accomplishes her mission by using the language of ordinary discourse.

18

European Sociology in
the American Context

The American lead in the teaching of sociology rankled Europeans who thought that theorizing was a domain in which the Americans should be subservient to the Europeans. Part of the reaction was based upon ranking people according to intellectually, an idea whose greatest flowering was in Europe, and not only among its university thinkers. What of substance could the Europeans learn from the Americans, was the basic question, even when not so bluntly asked? After all, were not the Americans the intellectual offspring of the Europeans? Had not they learned nearly all they knew from Europe, particularly if it had to do with science, high culture, and values? Had they ever created thought on their own? Even in the natural sciences had they not capitalized upon the basic knowledge the Europeans had produced in science?

The Americans used the natural bounty of their country as the foundation of their development. There was no mystery to American advancement; simply, Americans had use of large territory and untapped natural and human resources at a time when the rest of the world was woefully short of these. Most ruling groups in Europe had used up the human resources of the territory long ago. Productivity and creativity had fallen to low levels and survived mainly through a division of labor that assured that practically no surplus could be created. Where the typical European mind was strangled by a closure of environmental and social choices, the American options were being opened.

In Europe there was a kind of hereditary assurance of social and economic placement. As Vilfredo Pareto, another European, could remark, there was a "circulation of elites." He might have noted that there was also a circulation of the peasantry from one generation to the next for it was very difficult to experience mobility, individual or intergenerational. Peasants never had a chance in European society and an incredibly large proportion of all the people of any European province or capital were peasants, even up to World War II. Their only hope was to emigrate to the New World for options were practically closed off in Europe. Whether they went for religious or economic freedom was not the issue. There was little opportunity for achievement in the Old World. The system of class and means of hereditary ascription of status were too rigid.

European sociology was easily imperialized to America through people who felt inferior to the upper classes of Europe. They would carry that sense of inferiority with them for literal centuries. Anything he Europeans sent over to America was accepted and uncritically approved, including sociological theory. The intellectual hold of the Europeans over the Americans was practically total.

When America became a major economic and military force in the world, it became imperialistic in other ways. It used its productive and economic capacity practically to overwhelm the world while emplacing an ideology favorable to itself. All countries of the world, save the United States, were backward after World War II, in the sense that their economies had been destroyed, along with the hopes of their people. Most depended heavily upon the United States, a characteristic of relative underdevelopment. They all needed help. In the field of education America simply dumped books by the truckloads off on Third World peoples who were hungry for knowledge and technology. By the mid–1950s, or early 1960s, American knowledge had bombarded the world like a blitzkrieg. Only when the defeated and used-up countries could get back on their feet were they able to counter U.S. economic overlordship, which included academic hegemony. For a long time after the war little had been said because it was neither polite nor politic "to bite the hand that was feeding you."

But the reaction to America's lead in various fields was sure to be challenged. American sociology, which had become the method by which the discipline was studied in the world, was not safe from scrutiny by Europeans not wishing to concede leadership to the Americans, particularly when they knew of American intellectuals' Achilles Heel. One attack on American sociology came against the Chicago school, which was the only serious effort at American social science theorizing. Ian Taylor, Paul Wilton, and Jock Young, all from English universities, write:

> "Social disorganization," however much it continued on as a research tradition in American criminology, was nevertheless unsatisfactory in two important respects. Methodologically, the theory, at least as used by Shaw and Mckay was, as David Downes (1966a, p. 71) has pointed out, essentially descriptive and tautological.

Delinquency rates led to disorganization rates which led to delinquency rates. There was no way to reconcile the question of pathology and diversity. Under Clifford Shaw and Henry D. McKay's concept, social disorganization was, from another viewpoint, simple cultural pluralism, where different groups emphasized different values.[1] The real question posed by the ecologists of the Chicago school was not how to explain social disorganization and delinquency, but to explain the lack of assimilation and greater social inequality of immigrants and unmelted peoples of the Zone of Transition.[2]

There are European attacks on American criminological theorizing in other contexts. Sutherland's claim that criminal behavior is learned in differential association is exposed as crude behaviorism where people do what they do, even crime, because they are reinforced to do so. The theory is tautological in that people get some charge out of what they are doing. According to behaviorism, into which differential association may be translated, people have no values and are propelled through life like Skinnerian rats.

Albert Cohen's boys do not stress school success because they do not see that school success has any payoff in the short or long run; they see people with great learning living in poverty and many with little learning living in luxury. The delinquent subculture that Cohen's boys create is like the working-class utilitarian subculture that today identifies much of the American public, even members of the economic middle class.[3]

European sociology used physical science analogies to cement ideas about social life. This practice was transferred to the United States, where such concepts as functionalism found fertile ground for acceptance. In an illustrative paper Marvin Harris, using a functional analysis concluded that sacred cows have negative and positive functions in the Indian social structural complex. Negatively the cows cause millions of Indians to be severely undernourished because they lack the protein coming from beef consumption. Positively the cattle droppings fertilize fields and the dried patties are used for fuel.[4] The negative and positive functions cancel out each other leaving India static.[5] The suttee functions to make sure that there are no Indian females without males so that prostitution and other vices associated with the mistreatment of women do not arise. The veil, or purdah, in Moslem cultures serves a similar function.

Since demonstrating that a practice serves both negative and positive functions is not an empirical proposition, almost any activity may be assigned these functions. Sumner can report that any culture is relative and that it is the cultural interpretation or meaning given to an action which makes it right. William Graham Sumner can report that any culture is relative and that it is the cultural interpretation of meaning given to an action that makes the action right. Sumner, being impressed by the notions of statics imparted to him by his European mentors, posits essentially a theory of social statics when he informs us that "The mores make anything right."[6] Functionalism was a theory of social statics because it did not contain a program of political action or change.[7]

American sociology did not develop strong schools because there was no idea that captured the imagination of any number of promoters of any concept. There developed styles of work that were associated with American thought but no unique way of addressing the problems and challenges of the real world were offered by these concepts. Social work was the field that sought to distribute to the needy the fruits of an abundant society. Psychology and psychiatry attempted to understand individuals who were making poor psychological adjustments to the social structure of which they were a part. The judicial system criminalized those who were too misplaced to find security through honest work. All these fields worked on piecemeal parts of societal problems but there was no discipline that offered a uniquely American radical critique of the social assumptions in vogue in the country. A critique of American sociology was a critique of European paradigms that had become dominant in U.S. scholarship, since Americans had erected none of their own. They had, with Charles Hampden-Turner, "borrowed the European toolbox."[8]

The Marxist paradigm was exciting for classroom discussion, but very few took even the vast differences in wealth and living standards characteristic of Americans as irrefutable evidence of the existence of a class system. If anything they viewed success as a sign of openness of opportunity or the absence of the reservations of class. No group at the grass roots had ever so thoroughly repudiated a class analysis, even though the students for generations sat passively through lectures using the language of class.

Another reason Americans made no radical critique of European sociology by Americans was because there was no crisis in America that demanded a questioning of the assumptions on which the country was founded, nor were there any assumptions that proved to be ideal in America's operational patterns. Major events like the French Revolution and the Bolshevik Revolution 126 years later, and the rise of fascism in Germany and Italy in the 1920s, forced a rethinking of old European social norms. They demanded a revision of thought. America was never faced with any such calamity, although the country was half-strained or less during the Civil War. World War I, followed by the Depression of the 1930s, did not create the same unsettling attitudes in American scholars as similar events had caused in European scholars, forcing them to reassess the social and economic assumptions of their societies.

Where the science of other cultures, particularly that of Germany and Japan, plunged them into World War II, American science was used mainly to improve the living standards of the people. American science was never closely linked to nationalism, although it tried to be during the early years of the invention of the atomic bomb. Germany and Japan had severe space limitations and the scientific talents of their people could not find expression because people were bound to the older logics and rhetoric, namely, that national eminence and world recognition could come about only through military means and the territorial expansion of colonialism.

The greatest critique of the European masters was not offered by Americans but by the Europeans themselves. The Frankfurt school, begun in 1931, with such scholars as Erich Fromm, Theodore Adorno, Herbert Marcuse, Max Horkheimer, and Franz Newman, attacked the structuralism of the old European masters, particularly those in Germany, arguing that the class concept was important in fomenting anti-Semitism and fascism. In the United States, Herbert Marcuse, after fleeing Germany, held in his *One Dimensional Man* that classes have disappeared because there are no longer a bourgeoisie and a proletariat.

Instead power can be held by persons who have no class standing but who have gained influential positions in industry or government. Such scholars as Raymond Aron and Daniel Bell claimed that differences have been gradually obliterated erasing even the likelihood of class conflict.

WAS SOCIOLOGY NEEDED?

Howard Odum, probably the earliest and most assiduous chronicler of the history of American sociology, notes that in understanding the development of the discipline, the emphasis must be, as in the case of American literature, upon men and women rather than on movements.[9] There was no particular need for the discipline when it was imported to America for the country looked abroad for its sociological as well as other intellectual leadership. Unlike the case of literature, which could be brought over from Europe, where masterpieces had been written before the United States was born, sociology grew up in Europe at about the same time that the United States was undergoing major social changes associated with the late Civil War, least of all the changed status of the former slaves.

But why did America need a sociology? The story of the development of European sociology may be found in the frustrations of scholars who wanted to understand, explain, and eventually offer their services for control of European society. There had been breakdowns and strains in those societies and the scholars were perplexed because people were not behaving predictably. Also, the advances that were being made by scholars in the physical sciences made those who wanted recognition, but who could not achieve originality in those sciences turn to new disciplines. Auguste Comte could not match the notoriety of a Sir Newton or other scientists and philosophers. He wanted not so much recognition but a way of understanding the changes within the French society.

Karl Marx was marginalized within German society, and his thought reflected it. He wanted to get back at the ruling classes in practically any way he could for they had rejected him from membership in it. Marx was never fully accepted in the very class-conscious society of Germany. His history and family background were not auspicious, and he went through life being sensitive about them. Part of his reaction through his writings was to upper-class control of everything meaningful that literally shut him out. He saw no option other than a radical restructuring of society. Of course he did not develop these ideas alone. He had been a member of a group of young Hegelians who had social leanings then considered radical.[10]

Emile Durkheim, like Marx, was trying to overcome ties to the Hebrew religion. Marx's father had been the last to begin to secularize and passed those ideas on to his Karl. Durkheim came from a long line of rabbis but he had tried to secularize, making his religion an understanding of French society rather than the more traditional Hebrew. Both Marx and Durkheim were essentially alienated from their religious roots. They would have been somebodies within traditional Hebrew culture but nobodies within the wider secular culture. Their choices were difficult ones. It may fairly be said that the European founders of sociology had axes to grind with their own societies which prompted them to seek expression in the new discipline coming finally to be known as sociology.

We cannot find any reason that the American founders of sociology had any similar axes to grind with American society. Again, Odum describes them. Franklin H. Giddings was raised on the discipline and fortitude of a New England village family. He came into sociology from the very symbol of American freedom of the press, *The Springfield Republican*. Lester F. Ward was a country boy from the Midwest who worked his way up through formal education and scholarship. Albion W. Small and William Graham Sumner came into sociology from the ministry, preaching that the truth would make one free, morally dominant, and a supporter of laissez-faire. There was nothing radical about George Vincent, a university professor and president, Chautauqua orator, and head of the Rockefeller Foundation. Charles H. Cooley was insulated throughout his career at the University of Michigan. There was no particular social or intellectual agenda that can be found in the activities of E.A. Ross, George Howard, Frank W. Blackmar, U.G. Weatherly, John R. Commons, and Richard T. Ely, all prominent in the founding of the discipline of sociology.[11]

The general point is that there seems to have been no need for the discipline in the early days of its American existence. The founders were not radical. Indeed, most were fairly well ensconced into mainstream American thought, if not at the highest levels. None seems to have been alienated by personal misplacement or even misplacement of the group he was in.

The problems that America faced were generally not problems of structure—technical problems in their truest sense. They were moral problems that grated on the nerves of a people who were steeped more than any other in the world in an emerging egalitarian ethic. The problems of inequality were so precisely because of the twin ethics of emerging egalitarian and a distaste for social inequality.

European sociology, trying to posit the functionalism of a structure of inequality, despite Karl Marx, would eventually be adopted by the dwindling group of Americans who yet hungered for the old European structures of inequality. Because this sociology made so little sense to American students it had to be forced upon them, not as plausible descriptions and answers to problems, but as a canon, dogma, passed from one generation to the next, to be understood reflexively and internalized in the same way.

The fashioning of a new sociology will mean a serious questioning of the suppositions of the old masters. And all of these are not European masters. Many are masters of our own time who have spoken largely out of European contexts. They had such exalted status that they were and are treated almost as gods. We have already discussed how Max Weber was able to convince the scholarly public that there was validity to the supposition that the capitalistic genius of America was due to the presence of Puritanism among the aggressive money-makers and culture builders.

Nobody questioned Weber's premises, even though he could not have talked to a single Puritan. They had all been dead 200 years before Weber ever came to America and wrote *The Protestant Ethic and the Spirit of Capitalism*. He completely ignored that the Puritan impact had lasted only about seventy-five years and there was so much dilution of that influence that it was almost gone long before the Protestant ethic based upon Puritanism was thought about. Yet we go on quoting Weber as though there were some truth to his claim. Weber completely forgot that many of the large fortunes in America were made illegally, something that the Puritans would never admit doing, and many were made long after the Puritan influence had waned. Indeed, it might be argued that had not the Puritan influence been so strong much larger fortunes could have been made because inhibitions to acquisitions would have been removed. There were very few great fortunes in the United States until a score of years after the Civil War, after which there was the rise of the Robber Barons, to whom scholars refer when they are not impressed with the religious qualities of the fortune-makers.

Weber is not the only scholar who posed as an expert when there were no were credible data upon which expertise could be built. If Weber were going to talk seriously about Puritans, he should have talked to someone who was Puritan. If he did it is obscure in his book. If he read many books and papers about and by Puritans that is quite good, but expert findings cannot be fashioned on extinct people, no matter how many books one has read about them. Weber's work rested largely upon secondary sources many of which would be suspect today because they were not written for purposes of hypothesis testing. They were essays and stream-of-consciousness materials, and their scientific validity would be weak at best; but Weber took them as correct estimates of what Puritan life and thought were like.

Are we to believe everything that Cotton and Increase Mather wrote? Or Benjamin Franklin? Our simple point is that it is improper to draw hard and fast conclusions from secondary data. The conclusions drawn could not be at a higher or more believable level than the sources used. Imaginations run wild when the opportunity presents itself to do so.

There is also the matter of Weber's writing in German because he perceived in German. Stepping out of his cultural framework would be just as difficult for Weber as for anyone else. Being a scholar does not excuse one fully from ethnocentrism. How would he know the meaning of the actions of Americans when his framework for understanding was culturally German? Wouldn't Weber be subject to the same questions that anthropologists and others must answer when they study other cultures? How does one guard against selectivity of observation and interpretation?

If Weber did not interview any Puritans, though using Puritanism as a pillar of his proposition to account for capitalism, other scholars were not far behind.

There are plenty of scholars who claim to be experts on slavery when there has not been a possibility of talking to a live slave for 135 years. There is simply nobody left who could school a scholar in slavery. The many books that have been written are selections of the institution. One may become an expert in knowing the books and papers written about slavery, but one could not become an expert in slavery without at least talking to some slaves, even one. Talking to one or to a few slaves could not make the researcher an expert because of the problem of selectivity of information.

The last slave interviewed may have been so thoroughly a part of the general American culture that his or her viewpoints could represent total distortions of the idea of slavery. The WPA (Public Works Administration) Slave Narrative project of the 1930s sought to capture the slave experience sixty years or more after that experience. The people then were at least seventy-five years old, and their memories probably had begun to fail. Interviewers could learn something from seventy-five-year-old people but what they learned would require tempering by the factor of age. Additionally, the seventy-five-year-old former slaves may have been those who managed to survive for one reason or another. There is no way of knowing whether they represented the rank and file of the slave category. They might have been favored by their former owners and may not have wanted to tell all they knew about the institution.

Again, very simply, if one is going to be an expert on slavery, one should have talked to at least one slave. It is not possible to become a true expert on something that is extinct. How would one know that expertise was evident? What tests would there be of the credibility of the expertise?

Some ideas gain the fore for the time that they are relevant and remain long after there are grounds for doubting their relevance. The books that sought to describe black people in terms of their psychologies can be examined in this context. These books, such as William H. Grier and Price M. Cobbs, *Black Rage*, Frantz Fanon's *Black Face White Masks*, John Griffin's, *Black Like Me*, and Abram Kardiner and Lionel Ovesey's *The Mark of Oppression*, are just a few of the literally dozens of books within the category of black alienation. If the black person is not alienated from the system he is alienated from himself. Most likely he is alienated from both. Why doesn't he just go out and shoot himself, since there is no way of escaping the continuous problem of alienation?

No doubt there are people who are separated from the societies of which they are a part, yet some suggestion is found in such books that a whole category of people is alienated, living on the edge of psychological disturbance. Whatever black persons thought, did or even did not do could be attributed to alienation. If they went to school it was because they were trying to prove to someone or themselves that they were as good as other people. If they went to church it was a means of escaping the mind-numbing reality of segregation and an attempt to flee from the alienation imposed by color. Even Kenneth and Mamie Clark's doll studies, beginning in the 1930s, showed that blacks hate themselves by age five or six. The idea of black self-hatred was said to impress the U.S. Supreme Court to the extent that it was moved to rule favorably in *Brown v. Board of Topeka* in 1954 in which racial segregation in public schools was outlawed.

The media had found a use for the term *alienation* and found that it could sell books and information organized around the concept. And sell them they did. The old European masters had struck again, this time in the form of newer people who were purveying old ideas. It was not Jean Paul Sartre and Albert Camus who rediscovered alienation from Marx and Durkheim. The idea had been around a long time. What about the Egyptian soldier who did not want to oppress the Children of Israel as he was told to do by his Egyptian captains? What about the European members of the Underground Railroad who helped slaves escape from the misery of bondage in the South? What of the employer who gave a man a chance to work and then provided him with a wage according to his competency when he could have taken advantage of his inability to defend himself because the law was not on the side of the slave? Was John Brown alienated when he struck against slavery by seizing the arsenal at Harper's Ferry to speed up movement to the Civil War?

Scholars such as Frantz Fanon, in an attempt to stroke the readers of his books so that they will buy others, go to some lengths to argue that black people are somehow alienated people, that they were made so through the experience of colonialization and continued psychological and economic dependency even in their imagined postcolonial freedom. Ralph Ellison took up the chant in his *Invisible Man* and so did Claude Brown in his *Manchild in the Promised Land*. These books assaulted the mind with the idea that perhaps blacks were a psychologically disturbed people who showed only one side of their faces. One was never able to get into the heads of blacks person because of their alienation and inability to relax.

Ideas may disturb as much as physical reality. Someone said, perhaps it was John Donne, "Stone walls do not a prison make, nor iron bars a cage."[12] A continuous assault of an idea upon individuals will soon result in their believing it if there are no means to counter it. The idea of the confused black man took root in the minds of blacks for they were always facing impossible contradictions. Few scholars were able to counter the images presented. When they wanted to do so they were rejected print and distribution of their ideas.

Alienation may be thought of as a literary gambit to prove a particular point. It grows out of a particular European way of looking at the world, a way that is the product of long-standing in a social situation such as feudalism. The tearing and wrenching of Europeans from the complacency of that system created ambivalence in them. They wanted the security of the feudal structure but the potential freedom that system denied. It was relatively easy to assume that a similar ambivalence was in all other groups when they faced any condition of social change.

NOTES

1. The ecological model of the Chicago school was widely used in studies of crime and juvenile delinquency. Clifford Shaw and Henry D. McKay were two scholars using that framework for analysis. See Clifford Shaw and Henry D. McKay, "Social Factors in Juvenile Delinquency," *Report on the Causes of Crime, National Commission on Law Observance and Enforcement,* vol. 2 (Washington, D.C.: U.S. Government Printing Office, 1937).

2. This was the zone of high degrees of social disorganization surrounding the business district in the old concentric zone theory of the Chicago school. Chauncy D. Harris and Edward L. Ullman, "The Nature of Cities," *The Annals of the American Academy of Political and Social Sciences,* vol. 242, no. 12, and George J. Bryjak and Michael P. Soroka, *Sociology: Cultural Diversity in a Changing World,* 2nd. ed. (Boston: Allyn & Bacon, 1992), pp. 452–453.

3. Albert K. Cohen, *Delinquent Boys: The Culture of the Gang* (New York: Free Press, 1971), contains an exposition of the delinquent subculture.

4. Marvin Harris, "India's Sacred Cow," *Human Nature* (February 1978); and William Fiegelman, ed., *Sociology Full Circle,* 5th ed. (New York: Holt, Rinehart & Winston, 1989), pp. 31–37.

5. The idea of functionalism is balance in the operation of the parts of society. When all parts are correctly running society has few problems and dislocations.

6. William Graham Sumner, *Folkways* (Boston: Ginn, 1906), made the statement famous. The idea of functionalism is found in Mark Abrahamson, *Functionalism* (Englewood Cliffs, NJ: Prentice-Hall, 1978). The institutions of society are interrelated and tampering with the parts may jeopardize the smooth running of the whole. An excellent book dealing with the questions raised by this theory of sociological analysis is Jonathan H. Turner and Alexandra Maryanski, *Functionalism* (Menlo Park, CA: The Benjamin/ Cummings Publishing Co., 1979).

7. Turner and Maryanski report that practically no scholar today wants to be identified as a functionalist and that continued efforts to use functionalism as a theoretical explanation should be abandoned. Ibid., p. 141.

8. Charles Hampden-Turner, "The Borrowed Toolbox and Conservative Man," in John F. Glass and John R. Staude, eds., *Humanistic Sociology: Today's Challenge to Sociology* (Pacific Palisades, CA: Goodyear Publishing Co., 1972), pp. 120–134.

9. Howard Odum, *American Sociology* (New York: Longmans, Green & Co., 1951), p. 2.

10. Of the many books discussing the life of Marx, see E. Stepanova, *Karl Marx: A Short Biography* (Moscow: Progress Publishers, 1968), and Isaiah Berlin, *Karl Marx: His Life and Environment* (New York: Oxford University Press, 1968).

11. Howard Odum, *American Sociology,* pp. 4–5.

12. John Donne (1572–1531) wrote more than 50 books of sermons, poems, and other works. The quote about stone walls not making a prison has been used so often that proper attribution is difficult. See John Donne, *Sermons on the Psalms and Gospels, with a selection of prayers and meditations.* Edited with an introduction Evelyn W. Simpson (Berkeley: University of California Press, 1967).

19

The Decline of Victorianism: A Walk Through the Century

Although there was no dominating philosophy in the United States during the twentieth century, there were those that sought to fill the bill. Most of these were inherited from nineteenth century Europe. The literary tradition that existed in Europe among the upper classes promoted the impression that great debates over philosophies were advanced among the elites. The French Revolution of the last quarter of the eighteenth century was not much debated by ordinary Frenchmen or Europeans who were not members of the literate and privileged classes. These people were not a part of any of the significant debates. They were so far down in the social structure they did not consider it their duty to debate what was happening in the larger French society. In nineteenth-century Europe the same condition prevailed, and even though the literarians and academics debated issues and sharpened their verbal swords so that they could split verbal hairs, the ordinary Europeans were ensconced in positions that allowed them little time for such leisure activity.

In the United States, although colleges, newspapers, and publishing companies had been opened literally from the beginning of the country, a tradition of literary or academic discussion was a long time in developing. Most people were too busy trying to make a living or to accumulate wealth to have much time for or interest in esoterics such as philosophizing. The man in the forest with an axe in his hand or the farmer holding the plow had as much practical knowledge as learned preachers and doctors. If anything, formal learning had a low priority in the country, and it was again, a long time before strong men preferred to go to school than to go to work. Boys who went to school were not being men. If they were they would be out doing what men have always done— working at jobs "real men" did. Boys who went to school were effeminate or too weak to carry out a day's physical labor in the male tradition.

America had no salon culture, no subculture whose major business was idle speculation and conspicuous exhibition of leisure, as in Europe. The principal book read, if people read at all, was the Bible, which, it was assumed, contained the knowledge essential to living in the New World. There was no need to debate philosophies, for philosophers themselves had low status—they were men who did not wish to put in a hard day's work in the fields, mines, forests or at a trade that required hard work to master.

All that was to change with the Industrial Revolution, which found a substantial flowering in America. By the opening of the twentieth century the United States had made inroads into mastery of the subcontinent. Prosperity was enjoyed by a greater proportion of the population than elsewhere in the world. Hard work was losing its lure. Living was becoming easier. By 1899 Thorstein Veblen could write his acerbic *Theory of the Leisure Class* which showed that there was emerging a class whose lifestyle was in some ways similar to that of the old leisure classes of Europe, from whom the new American leisure class had taken its cue. These now comfortable Americans had managed to accumulate wealth, to send their children to finishing schools and colleges, and to enable their offspring to worry less about where they would get their next crusts of bread. Great fortunes had already been made by the Rockefellers, Fords, Morgans, Carnegies, Goulds, Kennedys—some of the most notable of the wealthy. Others also exhibited the basic tenets of Protestant Christianity, capitalism, and social Darwinism in the pursuit of wealth. Persons with nowhere near the wealth of the Robber Barons began to imitate the leisure-class lifestyle. Max Weber was fascinated by what he saw in the country, namely, that ordinary families were showing signs of prosperity; he tied their ethics and behavior to European Calvinism which stressed hard work, rationality, saving, and rejection of the enjoyment of worldly accumulation. Unlike the leisure classes of Europe, the American Protestants who had experienced prosperity came to believe that they were not true to their religion or faith if they enjoyed their prosperity.

The theories of Weber and Veblen sought to describe and explain the behavior of prosperous Americans. Veblen's *Theory of the Leisure Class* was probably more widely discussed than Weber's *Protestant Ethic and the Spirit of Capitalism*, both being published close to the turn of the century. Veblen spoke derisively of the Robber Barons and the wealth accumulators who conveyed to the general public the idea that work was for the amassing of wealth so that one could vacate the work role and enter the role of consumer. Consumption, not work, became the evidence of success. By contrast, Weber whose work was finally translated in the early 1930s by Talcott Parsons, claimed that work conveyed a sense of nobility, or religious dedication, and when held as a facet of personality, was sure to lead to salvation in the next life, if not wealth accumulation in this life.

By the time Weber came into relatively widespread readership, Veblen's *Leisure Class* had lost some of its acerbity. The book was still interesting, but it did not command the attention of an extremely large following. Students in college sociology courses spent a little time considering Veblen's theses about "conspicuous leisure" and "conspicuous consumption," but their discussions were being promoted mainly by the small group of critical scholars emerging in the country. Veblen no doubt did not reach very far into the general public, and neither did Max Weber some thirty years later when the *Protestant Ethic* was translated.

Men like Lester Frank Ward, William Graham Sumner, and the physician Asa Gray argued for social Darwinism, as it had been argued for in Europe, and their thought carried over into the twentieth century, although few outside the classrooms gave them serious attention.

If anything, the twentieth century opened with a great burst of optimism, exemplified largely by achievements in industry. Perhaps the best example of expanded hope was the opening of the Ford automobile plants in Detroit, Michigan, with the offering of five dollars per day to workers. This permitted the first real opportunity for large numbers of immigrants and native peoples to own homes, automobiles, and more expensive furniture and to show some of the trappings of leisure. Expansion in the Ford output, duplicated in other industries, meant that raw materials had to be secured from afar. That meant work for miners and steel mill workers, and it led to mobility for skilled and unskilled workers alike. Industrialization greatly affected the South, drawing thousands of sharecroppers from the southern farms. These laborers took the lowest jobs in the industrial cities, replacing earlier workers who had moved higher into the skills and management structures. Farmers in the South had to diversify their offerings from single crops, such as cotton, to various food crops to feed the populations in the growing cities and towns.

Basically, then, the beginning of the twentieth century did not offer new thought but dragged the Victorian philosophies from the earlier century into the present. If anything, the consuming discussion in the United States involved neither the class exploitation ideas of Karl Marx, nor the social Darwinism of the Europeans such as Herbert Spencer, nor the fundamental evolutionism of Charles Darwin himself. The dominating discussion was the status of the freedmen, the former slaves who escaped shackles because of the Civil War. This debate was commanding because interest in the problem was consuming. Not only were former slave owners discussing what strategy to adopt to recover their fortunes, but new players were trying to figure ways of leveraging the labor of the approximately 5 million former slaves and freemen in the country at the opening of the twentieth century. The freedmen themselves took larger roles in their development. There were memorable discussions, in retrospect, in the early parts of the century, such as women's suffrage and temperance, but they did not become dominating; they lasted only for a short time and were then replaced by new concerns and discussions. In the first quarter of the twentieth century one of the most memorable debates was between Booker T. Washington and W.E.B. DuBois over the direction that freedmen education should take. Booker T. Washington made a plea for "practical education" for the freedmen, whereas the highly intellectual DuBois pleaded for "classical" or literary education as the best hope for the gaining of full citizenship by the freedmen.

The status of black Americans continued to excite discussion and quite possibly has dominated discussion for the entire century. Early on, and especially around World War I, there emerged some hope that the concept of Marxian social class conflict could be used to explain the plight of black sharecroppers in the South, of the entrapped miners, of the industrial common laborers, and of the immigrants heaped very near the bottom of the social structure, living meagerly in their ghettos. When any of these groups tried to organize, or unionize, with the help of what were called communists and sympathizers, whether in the cities of the North or in the deltas of the South conflict broke out. The most violent conflict of the first twenty years of the century took place in the unlikely little delta town of Elaine, Arkansas. Riots lasting about a week there ended in the deaths of some twenty-five persons killed in the melee.[1]

Despite the conflict existing between labor and management, despite the difficulties of the Depression of the 1930s, communists and socialists were unable to make much headway in recruiting people to their philosophy. Their lack of success deprived the movement of a philosophy that could easily be appealed to by either the literati or the general public. No overarching philosophy trilled off the lips of nonliterary persons in the way Victorian thought summarized the ideas and feelings of Europe of the nineteenth century.

In the 1930s some writers tried to pull America's heartstrings by writing about the tragedies of the Dust Bowl and the Depression. John Steinbeck's *Grapes of Wrath*, (1937), especially, exemplified books about the movement of Okies—Oklahoma farmers to the so-called Promised Land of California displaced from their small, 160-acre farms—moved a few people to tears but did not move them to make radical social changes.[2] Upton Sinclair's exposé *The Jungle*, an essay about the packinghouse industry and its excesses as it owners sought to make profit, largely encouraged Congress to pass the Pure Food and Drug Act.[3]

Midcentury saw a brief discussion of communism as a threat to democracy, a concern fueled by the success of the Russian Revolution in 1917 and fear that collectivism might spread to democratic countries. Most Americans knew little about this foreign doctrine of collectivism; to them, the government's efforts to intervene in their lives during the Depression were not perceived as a basic change in the government's operating procedures and attempts to control the economy. They did not believe that intervention was in conflict with private industry. With 25 percent of the population out of work, hardship was a very present reality. When government aid did come, it was not enough to change the living styles of the people. The aid simply enabled maintenance. The Depression was cured when the United States went to war with the Japanese bombing of Pearl Harbor in 1941 and the subsequent declaration of war on the Axis powers. Even before this time some people had gone back to work as war plants began to turn out material to aid Britain and France against the Germans, who had declared war against England and other countries in its area.

Although it did not truly stretch the productive capacity of the United States, the war did for some time stanch a discussion of major philosophical issues. There was no time for idle speculation. Even the colleges and universities, woefully short of professors and students, went mainly into holding operations. Teaching could not be as challenging without the full contingent of students. Curriculums were shortened and students rapidly processed so that they could take their places in the war effort. There was really very little time or inclination to be concerned with big philosophical issues.

After the defeat of Germany and Japan, came a return to peacetime production. People had done without so long that after the war they were ready to return to civilian consumption. Rationing had made their money almost worthless. Those who were inclined to save, saved heavily. That America might not win the war was inconceivable to them, and so with money saved, they thought, they would be in much better position to accumulate even more afterward. Again, although there was some anxiety about the Russians and the carving up of territory they jointly liberated with the Allied powers, ordinary Americans did not worry much about the likelihood of communism or bolshevism. The persons with had a better understanding of what all that meant would have to communicate it to the public. Because after the war the Soviet Union was much weaker than the United States, a few radicals thought any problem the Soviets created could be settled militarily. Cooler heads prevailed, and by the early 1950s a cold war had developed between the Soviet Union and the United States.

In the attempt to alert Americans to the serious threat of communism, space was created for the rise of those who practically made careers out of "baiting the Russians," or at least showing how Soviet and communist sympathizers were threats to the security of the American people. This fear of communism came to a head in the thought and behavior of Senator Joseph McCarthy of Wisconsin in the early 1950s.

Even though there was off-and-on conflict with the Russians over philosophy from the end of World War II, it did not reach the proportions predicted. One or the other of the superpowers—the Soviet Union or the United States—generally gave ground. Meanwhile both nations kept their nuclear arsenals pointed toward their adversaries.

The Indo-China War involved the United States from about 1954, when the French were expelled from Dien Bien Phu. Conflict broke out between the communist or socialist Vietnamese and the capitalist Vietnamese. The United States supported the capitalist Vietnamese against the Viet Cong communists. There ensued an eight-year war that was not endorsed by many young people in the United States. The Vietnam War fostered an alienation that became the topic of scholars such as Erich Fromm, writing books like *Escape From Freedom*.[4] Alvin Toffler's *Future Shock*, Eldridge Cleaver's *Soul on Ice*, and Alex Haley's *Roots*, and Malcolm X's *Malcolm X*, provided interesting reading for largely youthful college students who felt alienated and became radicalized. Among young people, Patty Hearst became the symbol of alienation. She alleged that the Symbionese Liberation Army had kidnapped and brainwashed her into cooperating with them in robbing banks. The Symbionese Liberation Army believed that by destroying the economic foundation of America, represented by the powerful banking industry, they would cause capitalism to fall and the country would be changeable. As sympathetic as individuals might have been for Miss Hearst, they could not accept her machine-gun brandishing behavior and found instead that hers was a form of alienation. She and the Symbionese Liberation Army represented persons who needed real, rather than symbolic, enemies against whom their aggression could be vented.

Alienation was possible partly because there were no credible enemies. Immigrants were being assimilated; blacks were being given more of their due. The old teachings of hatred and aggression were being done away with—legally and often morally. American prosperity left little room for hatred and aggression against others. Although all these previously excluded groups may not have have been loved, there at least was the idea that the playing field should be somewhat level, that is, without all the advantages going to one team. Without any group against which to display acceptable or credible aggression, youth turned on themselves, using drugs, drinking, and in general following lifestyles that did not have the approval of their parents. Some young people drifted into cults, which signaled their dissatisfaction with the values of society at large; they sought satisfaction in lifestyles and behaviors lacking high status in the general culture.

The erasure of objects of old-fashion hatred, against whom aggression could be vented, left thousands with the same old inclination to exercise hatred and aggression but without anyone or any group against which to vent these these urges. During the last century, wars, riots, and violence against ethnic groups and various minorities, were practically acceptable reactions to hate objects, and indeed there was some degree of theoretical support for these attitudes: colonialism, the sharecropping system, the slums, unemployment, and lack of health care. Much of this animus carried over into the new century, but its force was noticeably diminishing. Theories of assimilation, the melting pot, laws stressing human equality, anxiety about people on welfare, as well as programs aimed at including all who had been excluded, helped to undermine any tendency to overt aggression against those disliked. As well, the civil rights movement helped to promote an attitude of nonaggression by seeking to get otherwise excluded persons into social the system so there would be no reason to treat them differently from others. Although progress was slow, even tortuous, for some years, time finally proved the acceptability of the civil rights agenda. Hatred and aggression seemed to diminish. The millennium, however, had not arrived. In many individuals there remained such a strong urge to hurt, hate, and aggress that they did not know how to act when there were no culturally acceptable objects against whom aggression could be vented. Scholars such as Erich Fromm, holding to Durkheimian reasoning, tried to show that modern society, with its emphasis upon impersonality, depersonalization, and decreasing primary contacts, promotes alienation. Although they are probably right in their assessment, it cannot be overlooked that those against whom hatred and aggression could be exhibited were being incorporated into mental frameworks that left little space for these values.

This emphasis on alienation brought on by rapid change—exhibited in the thought of Alvin Toffler, author of *Future Shock*—held on for perhaps as much as a decade and then was dropped. Students remained radicalized for only a few years. When they were out of college they cleaned up, for the most part, changed their rhetoric and orientations, and began to fit into the middle-class niches for which their parents thought they were preparing in the first place. The literature of alienation and radicalism remained, but it was not taken all that seriously by adults in decision-making positions.

FROM PERSONAL ALIENATION TO SYSTEM ANALYSES

There have been dramatic swings of attitude toward societal changes in America. As the Victorian values of the last century receded, others arose to take their place, only to be superseded themselves. When individual alienation as an idea ran its course, other explanations for societal change had to take its place. By the early 1960s, writings began to emphasize that the United States was literally breaking up, at least in terms of its institutional structures. Subcultural groups, it was pointed out, had decaying families. Michael Harrington opened the discussion with a salvo entitled *The Other America* (New York: Macmillan, 1963), in which he showed that poverty and privation existed in the "poor half" of America. Harrington's book so touched the authorities that they began to study the matter further. For them poverty was inconsistent with the goal of sharing the general prosperity available to all. Perhaps the most provocative book in this line was that of Daniel Patrick Moynihan, whose work *The Negro Family: The Case For National Action* (Washington, D.C.: U.S. Department of Labor, 1965), sparked debate that lasted for more than a decade. The black family in general was found to experience a large number of pathologies, such as absentee fathers, working mothers, poverty, out-of-wedlock children, limited mobility, slum living, and men in jail. There were so many problems with this family that it could be helped only if the government became more involved in a war on poverty. Yet serious pockets of poverty were located in every section of the country and in all ethnic groups. Appalachia, for example, yielded displaced, undereducated, and poverty-stricken coal miners with black lung disease and large numbers of children.[5] Poverty was discovered in small towns throughout the country. Urban poverty was examined meticulously. The structure of society itself was to blame, and the disadvantaged individuals in the society were to be given assistance to move into the middle-class to become productive citizens. The elimination of poverty became a political mission elevated to a religion. The debate caused by the Moynihan book caused a looking backward to find the roots of poverty. For some time Oscar Lewis had been observing similar conditions in the Hispanic population, in Mexico and in the United States, but it was only after Moynihan's work that serious attention was given to Lewis's interpretation.[6] Even earlier scholars had talked about a "culture of poverty."[7] The poor were described as having certain attitudes and behavior patterns that were passed from one generation to the next and which impeded social mobility. Included among these practices and attitudes included the female-centered family (matrifocal), the easy use of physical aggression, an inability to plan for the future, the seeking of immediate gratification, a weak impulse control, and a fatalism toward the future. There was considerable support for the idea of a culture of poverty, as well as criticism of it.[8]

The data of poverty emphasized its epidemiological features. That poverty was extensive was inarguable. If poverty were a reality, its causation would require assignment. The Victorian values of the last century that placed much stress on personal shortcomings related to the competitive struggle could not carry the day. Darwinism and Marxism were no longer united as they had been in the nineteenth century, they were at loggerheads in the twentieth century. A rejection of Darwinism meant at least a partial acceptance of Marxism or a location of the problem of poverty in the behavior of industrialists and capitalists who squeezed out additional profits by ignoring those individuals who could not help them do it. Those unwilling to train, retrain, or develop attitudes functional for assignment in the capitalistic enterprise would have to seek alternatives for survival. The language of class struggle was used sparingly, although when it was used, it was used shrilly.

A number of scholars and activists thought that greater responsibility for the elimination of poverty rested with the larger system, and not so much with the upper class' unwillingness to share profits and prosperity. C.W. Mills's claim that an industrial-military complex, or power elite, made the important decisions in the United States made some sense and at the same time did not point to a Victorian class actually hostile toward the poor. For Mills and his followers, it was a matter of power. There was no contradiction of the reality that power was concentrated in a few hands, but the lower classes had more power than they thought—if they would use it at the ballot boxes to put into office those who represented their interests. Even though the lower classes worked for persons who had great power and influence, they still had an independent ballot. Threats that they use their ballot as specified by those for whom they worked had a limited degree of force, for by now there were some safeguards against the summary dismissal of persons who failed to support certain political candidates.

The 1970s found a slightly new form of attack, partly on the individual and partly on the system. It was recorded by Professor William Julius Wilson that ghetto poverty was due not to old fashioned discrimination but to structural changes that had happened in American society.[9] The old sweaty jobs in the factories, mines, and fields were gone—mechanized, automated. The economy had made strong moves toward postindustrialization and many parts of it were moving into the postmodern phase. In the vernacular of the time this was known as a high-tech economy where knowledge of computers was essential to getting a job of even the most unskilled sort. Wilson noted that there was a growing black "underclass" characterized by unemployment, lack of skills, broken homes, and welfare dependency, while being "frozen" in lower-class status. As Michael Harrington had noted in 1963, there were two Americas: one rich and another poor Wilson noted also that there were two black Americas: one rising and affluent; another socially immobile, poor, and frustrated.[10] Since there are many programs to assist those who wish to climb out of poverty, Wilson suggested part of the onus for not doing so must lie with the individuals themselves. If the opportunities are there and individuals cannot be encouraged to take advantage of them, their remaining in poverty cannot be wholly attributed to the system.

Into the 1980s the problems of the ghetto continued. The so-called war on poverty declined. It became more difficult to convince people that there was much wrong with the system. Poverty and crime reflected personal choices individuals made to evade the norms of society, it was believed. There had already begun, by the early 1970s, a government initiative called the Safe Streets Movement. It recognized that crime had made the streets no longer safe and enjoyable by local community people, especially the middle class. There was simply too much violence. Basically, crime was rampant. The problem of poverty and crime was approached during the Supreme Court administration of Chief Justice Earl Warren: The system, especially the justice system, needed to be more responsive to the poor. Claims were made that the system was unfair to poor people. The Omnibus Crime Bill, otherwise known as the Safe Streets Program, sought, among other things, to give police officers more human relations training. By understanding their clients and the social conditions from which they came, police officers would be more humane and not contribute to the crime rate through their own reactions. Warren, through his office, insisted that due process of law be carried out as prescribed by the Constitution. This meant that police authorities could no longer be as arbitrary in the handling of alleged criminals as in the past. Nor would those in prison be brutalized with impunity. During Warren's tenure, capital punishment was practically outlawed in *Furman v. Georgia* (1972).

When the crime rates did not drop appreciably as a result of the millions of dollars spent through the Omnibus Crime Bill, the public did not remain sympathetic. There was a turning back toward Victorian punitiveness. The ban on capital punishment was lifted, and in 1978 Gary Wayne Gilmore was executed in Utah; thus began a trend toward capital punishment in more than half the states. By the mid-1980s prison building had become a growth industry. On any day there were over 1 million people in some stage of the criminal justice process.[11] Conservative estimates were that around 2 percent of the total U.S.

population had spent at least three months in a jail or prison (see *Uniform Crime Reports*, various years). Local and state judges were elected, and federal judges who voiced a readiness to support capital punishment appointed. Victorianism seemed to be making a comeback as individuals were charged with responsibility for their own problems, with less emphasis given to the impersonality of the system.

Force would assure conformity to political dictates. Perhaps the outstanding symbol of the willingness to use force was in respect to the continuing hostility toward communism exemplified since the cold war began in the early 1950s. John F. Kennedy, the U.S. president, had threatened the Soviets, possibly with a nuclear attack that would pit one nuclear force against another, if they did not remove the nuclear weapons from Cuba. The Soviets claim to have done so, averting large-scale disaster. Reagan's attack on the tiny West Indies island of Grenada in the 1980s, ostensibly to prevent the Soviets from building an airstrip to support planes armed with nuclear weapons, as well as his support of the Contras in Nicaragua, exhibited a continuation of Victorianism.

Barbara Ehrenreich called the 1980s a "decade of greed."[12] She thinks that Americans are notorious for their lack of class consciousness or even class awareness.[13] Even though the gaps were widening between the lower- and higher-income groups, those of lower income had little inclination to turn on those in the upper-income categories. Instead of attacking the system, as predicted by the Victorian Marxists, they began to attack themselves. Excesses of every kind became common. Suicides, AIDS, crime, and other indices of self-destruction increased. There was little willingness of more students to study hard, to work their way through school, to learn to accept responsibility. They turned instead to drugs, drink, cults, and other deviant personal lifestyles. Individualism took over as youth sought their own identities, which increasingly were separated from the groups in which they were socialized. New programs, such as those for the gifted and talented, had to be created with the hope that there would be less of a hemorrhaging of talent as youth in other countries took over academic leadership from the Americans.

The election to the presidency of George Bush in 1988 was determined in part on his pledge to get tough on crime. His making Willie Horton—a scapegoat symbolizing the necessity for his political ascendancy—paid large dividends. Bush brought a return to Victorian values, trying to raise them to new respectability. A sense of hatred and punishment was in the air. He attacked Panama, ostensibly to prevent drugs from reaching the United States. Hundreds of Panamanian lives as well as millions of dollars in destruction of property were lost. Later, Bush attacked Saddam Hussein's Iraq in retaliation for his incursions on Kuwait to reclaim property that had been seized earlier by the British in the establishment of Kuwait as a colony.

In the election of 1992, the people turned on George Bush, giving the gavel of the presidency to Bill Clinton. Clinton did not win by a clear majority. Still around were some of the old Victorians who wanted to use the old methods of control; manipulation, hatred, bigotry, and the power of finance to gain their way. The Baby Boomers, numbering some 78 million people, no doubt helped Clinton win, signaling a shift in the philosophy of social mobility. The Baby Boomers were socialized to much greater state participation in their mobility than any previous generation, and certainly not the generation of their parents and grandparents. Now, instead of seeing the state apparatus as controlled by a power elite, they see the state as a source of opportunity and a platform of security. Less punitive than their Victorian parents and grandparents, they see lack of success as a personal problem.

Victorian thought will not die, however. In the last part of the twentieth century, it is still gasping for breath. Some groups continue trying to place blame for their lack of success on others. Especially notable are the fear of white males who fear being cast into a defensive posture and probably positions of poverty by the elevation of, or even the giving of opportunity to, minority groups and women. Like the Victorians of the last century, they are willing to lash out at those they believe responsible for treating them as the equals, and not the superiors, of everyone else.

AN AFTERTHOUGHT

Victorian thought promoted government as the preserve of men of learning, leisure, and landholding—that is, members of the upper classes. The fundamental hostility of the nineteenth century served to legalize the low positions in which colonialized people found themselves. Darwinism, law, science, and religion came together to support the widespread inequality present in European society. The principal vehicle for the maintenance of this thought was the class system. Classes were determined by a number of circumstances—birth, intelligence, and experience. Only members of the higher classes were thought to possess sufficient intelligence and "good breeding," to make responsible decisions in business, the professions—including the military—or government. No member of the lower classes was expected to achieve anything important, nor even to aspire to achievement higher than common labor. In whatever sphere, the higher classes were expected to have the highest positions. Such thinking was the legacy of the feudal period when nobles and peasants alike knew their places in the social system. This thought hardened into dogma that by the nineteenth century characterized an age and came to be called Victorianism.

Before the American Revolution there had been a growing belief that self-government is the natural order of governance everywhere. People ought to be free to decide how they want their government to be structured and who should represent them. Decisions affecting the lives of the people should be made through the participation of as many of the citizens as possible. No person in good standing as a citizen should be excluded from participation in government. Whenever the United States took over new lands, those lands were given the right to self-government. Perhaps the earliest example of the application of this philosophy was in the 1820s with the opening of the colony of Liberia. The freed slaves from the United States were to serve as the leaders of the Liberian colony only at first, for they were to prepare the natives for participation in their own government. The record shows that this did not happen as speedily as anticipated. The Afro-Americans established themselves as a privileged class—some called them a caste—and represented the large expatriate businesses making substantial profits at the expense of the natives. Rancor between the Afro-American overlords and the natives continued for more than 150 years until the Afro-Americans, themselves representing recessive Victorianism, were overthrown in the 1970s.

The twentieth century did not witness strong U.S. support for colonialism. The Spanish-American War, on the eve of the opening of the new century, resulted in the nominal self-government of the appropriated former Spanish colonies. Although the leaders of these colonies were generally corrupt, gathering wealth largely by representing American interests, they encouraged significant local participation. Some colonies newly out of slavery found most working people willing to accept the way the government operated so long as they themselves received enough to remain relatively satisfied. These people of ordinary standing had not been trained to expect much more. Like the sharecroppers in the American South, they considered their new status a quantum improvement over their former slavery. It would be some time before they connected their own standing with their nonparticipation in the political process. When they made the connection, they would initiate suffrage movements to boost participation in the processes that determined their status and their prosperity. Their awakening interest would be consistent with the teachings of the Americans, many of whom had, at least theoretically, if not practically, rejected Victorianism.

Throughout most of the twentieth century the most visible evidence of the continued rejection of Victorianism was the tendency to promote government by the people. Victorianism arose under other headings such as totalitarianism, represented in the first three-quarters of the century by fascism and communism. Sometimes distinguishing between these concepts was difficult. Victorianism was a naked exemplification of Darwinism—that those who were best fitted both survived and ruled. Totalitarianism suggested the same, namely, that the class of people best fitted by strength would both rule and survive. The Victorian capitalists employed the very same arguments, claiming that those most successful economically were best prepared both to rule and to survive.

American insistence on self-government of the colonies, however the colonies were structured economically, meant a continued fight for colonial self-rule. From the end of World War II, such has been the program of the United States. Some observers have suggested that as a dominant economic and military power, the United States wanted the colonies free to exploit them. Just as cogent is the argument that there was an increasing rejection of Victorianism, that the anti-Victorian sentiment of the last century was gaining strength as the twentieth century continued.

NOTES

1. See Carey Wayne Rogers, "The Southern Tenant Farmers' Union as a Social Movement: Conflict in a Plantation Society," M.A. thesis, 1980, Department of Sociology, University of Arkansas, which contains much information and bibliography on problems leading up to the Elaine Riots and subsequent matters in its several decades aftermath)

2. John Steinbeck, *The Grapes of Wrath* (New York: The Viking Press, 1939).

3. Upton Sinclair, *The Jungle* (New York: The Viking Press, 1946).

4. Erich Fromm, *Escape from Freedom* (New York: Holt, Rinehart and Winston, 1941).

5. Helen Matthews Lewis, Linda Johnson, and Donald Askins, *Colonialism in Modern America: The Appalachian Case* (Boone, NC: Appalachian Consortium Press, 1978).

6. Oscar Lewis, *Five Families: Mexican Case Studies in the Culture of Poverty* (New York; Basic Books, 1959).

7. Oscar Lewis, *Five Families: Mexican Case Studies in the Culture of Poverty* (New York; Basic Books, 1959).

8. See Paul B. Horton and Chester L. Hunt, *Sociology,* 5th Ed. (New York: McGraw-Hill, 1980), p. 322. See also John H. Burma, ed. *Mexican Americans in the United States: A Reader* (Cambridge, MA: Schenkman Publishing Co., 1970), pp. 17–28.

9. See his *Declining Significance of Race* (Chicago: The University of Chicago Press, 1978).

10. See in Paul B. Horton and Chester L. Hunt, *Sociology* (New York: McGraw-Hill, 1980), pp. 365–366.

11. Michael S. Bassis, Richard J. Gelles, and Ann Levine, *Sociology: An Introduction* (New York: Random House, 1980), p. 232.

12. Barbara Ehrenreich, *The Worst Years of Our Lives* (New York: Harper Perennial, 1981), p. 206.

13. Ibid., p. 206.

Twenty-First Century Sociology

Many of the concepts that have dominated sociology in the past century will require modification or scrapping altogether during the next century. Of the many
terms that will no longer be viable, some are based upon the need to preserve
the originators of these terms rather than upon their viability in modern life.
Most sociologists grew up on certain positions posited by heroes of the discipline. There is tremendous emotional investment in these figures and their
positions. Partly out of deference to them, their concepts continue to be discussed even though their utility is in obvious dispute. The relationship of groups
to each other has changed so drastically that old concepts are not widely applicable. The age of mass communication has dawned and is in full flower, breaking
the isolation of practically all groups wherever they may be found.

The old conflict sociology assumed that groups were homogeneous and that
their interests were opposed to those of other groups unlike themselves. Groups
were seen as absolutely constructed such that there was no overlap between. For
instance, the bourgeoisie and the proletariat were defined without common
ground so that there was no possibility for members of these two classes to work
together. The concept was Darwinian in that one group had to destroy the other,
according to the social science construction. Yet there is much evidence that the
bourgeoisie and the proletariat were not mutually exclusive, except in the minds
of the constructionists.

Every army has a division between officers and soldiers of common rank.
In the construction of traditional social science, these are castes with such rigid
rules of association that groups of one category are prohibited by law from close
association with the other, either on or off duty. Members of one rank do not
automatically consider themselves in conflict with members of the other rank.
Indeed, there exists the possibility for close relationships across the ranks.
Members of the higher ranks look forward to the admission of members from

lower ranks and to the retirement of those above, for in this way the system remains fluid.

In plantation societies tenants may have much interest in the success of the landlord and they may actually work harder because they see that their success is largely dependent upon the landlord's success. One reason landlords were so harsh on their tenants, especially with respect to work hours and productivity, was that they were trying to break even, not necessarily to make an enormous profit.

In the modern poultry industry the workers look daily at the stock reports of their companies to see if they are making or losing money. Contrary to the conflict paradigm, the workers, wage and salaried, are interested in the growth and success of the company. They are not against the owners' making large profits if their own efforts are rewarded. With opportunities for everyone to be rewarded, they see no point in destroying the plant in order to destroy the owners, as the classic conflict confrontation dictates.

Many twentieth-century concepts were enunciated during a time of reduced communication and group insularity. One such concept was that of the primary group. Charles Horton Cooley, an early sociologist of the Chicago school, defined the primary group as one in which individuals associated because they liked each other.[1] They had no other purpose for association. Cooley used neighborhood play groups and even gangs to illustrate primary groups. As well, nuclear families were thought to be primary groups because they associated intimately and were deeply involved in each other's activities. Cooley could not foresee the communication and transportation revolutions that cut the ties of close relationships of all these group members. They may associate with people at some remove from their immediate environment, and their attachments may be primary but their associations secondary. Consider the admirers of, say, Elvis Presley. They may not be familiar with each other but may belong to fan clubs, wear paraphanalia, subscribe to publications about Elvis, and so on. The emphasis is upon the central symbol—Elvis—and not on association with each other.

Today almost nowhere is left for neighborhood groups to form spontaneously, as was possible during the time Cooley and Mead observed. The old ethnic neighborhood bars and clubs are practically gone, although some large cities offer possibilities for them to reemerge. Nearly all the large vacant lots have given way to commercial establishments. Primary ties have been severed by the opening of social structures, by socialization in to the limiting effects of ethnic chauvinism and narrowness, and by the greater geographical and social mobility of potential participants.

Of course, Cooley's idea of primary and secondary groups is closely related to Ferdinand Toennies's *gemeinschaft* and *gesellschaft* and is based upon the assumption of group exclusivity brought about by the greater difficulty of association outside a limited circle.[2] With the circle of isolation broken, groups would not need to interact so intimately, having their personalities shaped in the process. But Cooley commands such loyalty that there is reluctance to tamper with his idea of the primary group, even though today's highly segmented and bureaucratized society shows little evidence of primariness.

Another twentieth-century concept that will require modification is social distance. In the 1930s Emory S. Bogardus at the University of Indiana began publishing reports about the extent to which the majority group allows other groups to approach it.[3] He developed a social distance scale that assigned a numerical distance to correspond to the social distance separating the people. Like much twentieth-century sociology, which was based upon nineteenth-century notions of exclusiveness and separation, Bogardus did not anticipate the changes that would undermine group isolation. The sweep toward urbanization was so great that the exclusiveness inherent in village and small-town life was bound to crumble.

Sociology is a Western discipline in the sense that it developed in the Western environment. It began as social criticism or a clarification of relationships between groups, and intergroup hostility was explained as an example of class hostility. Society was said to be made up of classes that were essentially antagonistic toward each other. It was only because of the relative freedom of speech in the West that such criticism could emerge. In older societies all avenues of expression were rigidly controlled by ruling families, either through government, the church, employment, or landholding. Many individuals did not want to criticize the system because they had been socialized into it and accepted its modus operandi. Things were the way they were, and that was all there was to it. There was little to discuss and even less to criticize. In antebellum America, for example, there was no widely read book that criticized the institution of slavery. Perhaps Harriet Beecher Stowe's novel *Uncle Tom's Cabin* (1952) was the first widely circulated book that attempted to tell of the relationships between slaves and slave masters in the American South.

Such writers as Anthony Giddens (1982) argue that sociology grew out of the realities of the Industrial and French revolutions of the seventeenth and eighteenth centuries, respectively. In the Industrial Revolution the primary mode of production became machine power—really, the use of steam to generate energy to do the work that had before required thousands of hands. The revolution was not only in manufacturing but in agriculture as well. Technology and science aided these revolutions and cause a recentering of populations from countryside to the city and widespread participation in a money economy. The relationship of men and women to the means of making a living changed for the first time in literal eons. Now individuals would not rely largely upon the uncertainties of primary production but would become part of a massive network that produced for the consumption of many, if they could earn enough through work to purchase the civilities and amenities they produced. In those parts of Europe where the Industrial Revolution was strongest, such as in France and England, there were revolutions in social relationships. No longer would the old relationships of rank and status prevail for so many as they had in previous history.

The Industrial Revolution freed peasants from their masters and tied masters to workers in a way never before imagined. An industrialist, even with a large supply of labor, could not be assured of production because workers had rights, although for a long time the rights were not much of an improvement over those that had bound workers to the land through rules of tenure and status. Groups formerly greatly separated were now drawn together to live similar lifestyles.

Twentieth-century sociology was dominated by the thoughts of Marx, Weber, Durkheim, Comte, and Freud, as well as Mead, Cooley, Merton, and Parsons, who took up positions intermediate between the rigid structuralism of Marx and the more limited structuralism of the symbolic interactionists. With some exceptions, sociology was argumentation over this or that interpretation of the work of this or that theorist. Peripheral arguments ensued over the appropriateness of methods to resolve issues separating these dominant individuals. Even though provocative thought emerged from other individuals in subfields of the discipline, much of what they said could be resolved into the thought of the thinkers of the first layer.

Twentieth-century sociology could be conceived as a struggle between the thought of two rival forces: the rigid structuralists, represented by the thought of Karl Marx and his supporters, and the weaker structuralists, represented by the thought of Max Weber and his followers. Within these ranges was found the most vigorous sociological thought, which manifest itself in the study of a variety of problems of society. Whether poverty or prisons, individual or group breakdown, all could be related back to rigid or weak social structure. Neither Marx nor Weber would go away, nor would they become relevant to an understanding of modern social problems. So thorough had been the indoctrination of scholars into this weak structure–rigid structure dichotomy that it served to limit the terms in which discussion could take place.

The Marx-Weber dichotomy was discussed and written about so abstractly that sociology became alienated from the people it was intended to serve. The outstanding scholars gained credibility among other sociologists, but outside the field their influence was small, if any. Although Marx and Weber had long passed from the scene, others carried their thoughts forward, causing them to gain a larger hold on academic sociological thought after their death than they had had during their lives. Although not all sociologists subscribed to every Marxist or Weberian proposition, the most thoroughly indoctrinated literally treated such thought as dogma and insisted that their students do the same under pain of not securing their degrees and placement in positions of influence after graduation.

Sociology in the twenty-first century will call for a greater use of the means of socialization that were practically discarded during the twentieth century, namely, emphasis upon structure and a scientific approach to the solution of practically every problem. The twentieth century was a period of suspicion of everybody. Science itself was an attempt to cast doubt upon the familiar by showing that its foundation was flawed and its unanticipated consequences greater than ever believed. Science sought to establish itself as having answers to an increasingly greater number of human and environmental problems.

In the first half of the twentieth century George S. Lundberg wrote a small book asking "Can Science Save Us?" Perhaps he thought it could, for the problems which Lundberg saw were those of technology, which depended heavily upon science. Twentieth-century sociology found it difficult to divorce itself from its emphasis on structure and therefore upon the belief that science and technology held the answers to all human problems. A great participant in this enterprise in praise of science, sociology led in the attempt to show that human problems were fundamentally technical problems that could be corrected by application of technical and scientific solutions.

As the century draws to a close there is a turning back to the ordinary means of solving problems. It is increasingly evident that nature contains the corrections to many of the problems faced by humankind. Homeopathic medicine came to the fore; natural cures through the use of herbs, exercise, and the ingesting of foods containing nature's vitamins and minerals, have begun to compete with the high-priced medicine promulgated by the scientific and medical communities. As well people around the world have become more aware of the importance of the ecological environment. Destruction of the environment anywhere may affect people everywhere; pollution in one country may have severe consequences for people in another. Even political problems, it is recognized, are not limited to the borders within which they occur.

The countries of the world have become linked such that in no meaningful sense can they be considered independent of each other. Starvation in, say, Somalia or the Sudan is as much a problem of the developed countries as of the affected countries themselves. Ordinary citizens ask daily, "What are we going to do about hunger and starvation in the Sudan, about war in the Balkans, about earthquakes in Mexico, or about student uprisings in China's Tiananmen Square? And what are we going to do about population explosions in the countries of the Third World, which are having trouble feeding themselves?" Communication and interdependence have been shrinking the world in the latter part of the twentieth century to perhaps half its size at the opening of the century, and it is getting smaller. Only after World War II and the subsequent cold war of the 1940s through the 1960s was this interdependence fully realized.

Sociology's emphasis upon structure during the twentieth century led to a focus upon institutions that seemed to give stability to society. The larger units of analysis were the family, religion, politics, education, and economics, whose values and processes were detailed; but these institutional analyses were unable to tie nation-states together. The institutions, it was thought, behaved uniquely enough in the various cultures to distinguish them, establishing basic differences, while at the same time all were participating to a greater or lesser extent in the technological, ecological, political, and economic culture of the world.

Twenty-first century sociology will address global problems, with the idea that the world is the arena in which these problems will be played out. Because there will be more attention to global problems, however, the local environment will not be overlooked as much as it had been in twentieth-century sociology. People do live, for the most part, in local settings. Accordingly, stress on understanding environments with which one is not familiar, and is not likely to be so, will give way to bestowing more attention on the local environment. Twentieth-century sociology has sought to overcome parochialism and ethnocentrism by rewarding very lightly those scholars who have studied local environments, instead giving disproportionate attention to scholars focused on distant cultures and environments.

Twenty-first century sociology will be more interesting to all than was the twentieth-century variety, with its unending hunt for laws having the degree of certitude suggested by the physical sciences. This variety generated within the profession almost a century-long sense of guilt surrounding the issue of predictive accuracy. When pushed into a corner, the social scientists have fallen back on the timeworn thesis that social behavior is vastly more complex than the data of the physical sciences. Issues such as how subjects feel about being studied, as well as what researchers value have come to the fore. These can affect outcomes. Every social science finding can be contradicted by those who, for whatever reason, do not wish to agree with it.[4] Hypotheses have been accepted or rejected largely through argumentation, not through the introduction of critical experiments. Very few of the meaningful hypotheses have been resolved other than by disputation.

Twentieth-century sociology has not been acceptable to the people at large, for it has portrayed them as prisoners of society.[5] The idea that they do not have the control over their lives they thought they had has been somewhat disconcerting. They have wanted to destroy the bringers of bad news. Unless sociology can tell people how positive they are, instead of how negative and lacking in individual freedom they are, the discipline itself will remain castigated. Prisoners of society have little choice but to remain so, for they are born into a society that is determined to exercise maximum control over them.

In a sense society has demanded that it not be informed of its dysfunctional features. Is not the way people behave sufficient evidence of their freedom? Sociology has had to find a way not to alienate people by telling them what they do not want to hear, the corrections of which would prejudice their freedom. Sociology has therefore become locked in struggle with disciplines that have moved into the void to tell people that they are not social prisoners, obeying the largely preset dictates of the groups to which they belong; that they have made their own choices in the freest of manners.

Disciplines such as psychology, social work, and even medicine have reinforced the concept of individual freedom and have therefore reduced the element of society's control upon individuals. With society no longer responsible for imprisoning individuals by its demands, sociology has found itself without much of a visible role. The larger society demands that the groups within it be downgraded, if not destroyed. People less and less expect to find status in group membership. The group has no longer a practically complete hold over the individual. The ethic of individuality has taken precedence over that of community or social control. The job of sociology has, then, become one of contributing to the liberation of the individual by improving our understanding of how society works. But there may be actual hostility and resistance to understanding how society works, both of which may be manifest in attempts to lower the quality of sociological offerings and even to stigmatize the work of sociologists not operating in "bad faith."[6]

A 1994 *Newsweek* article on suicide discussed the suicide of a prominent grunge rock musician Kurt Cobain.[7] The article cited Emile Durkehim's study of suicide, in which the emphasis was on social integration. The article noted, however, that newer research stresses improper brain function, whether due to genetics or defective brain chemistry, as a factor in suicide. The victim is not mentally wired up like other people and is therefore unable to think normally or rationally.

The latter explanation seeks to trash the sociological explanation of suicide and institute in its place a technical, mechanical, calculable concept made up of variables whose use promise a high degree of predictability. The nonsociological explanation suggests that a child with an unusually wired brain can no more avoid self-destruction than a moth can avoid the attraction of a light or than a brick, unaffected, can avoid falling when dropped. Such reasoning converts sociological causation to sociobiology. Society loses its force as an explanatory medium, or even as a seriously contributing variable, and with it the discipline of sociology is downgraded.[8]

NOTES

1. See Gordon D. Morgan, "Is the Group Obsolete" (Fayetteville, AR: Department of Sociology, University of Arkansas, 1994).

2. See Ferdinand Toennies, 1887, translated 1957. Anthony Giddens, *Sociology: A Brief but Critical Introduction*, 2nd ed. (New York: Harcourt Brace Jovanovich, 1982).

3. Emory S. Bogardus, "Social Distance and Its Origins," *Journal of Applied Sociology* 9: 226; and "Racial Distance Changes in the United States during the Past Thirty Years," *Sociology and Social Research* (November-December 1858): 127–135.

4. The best inquiry into the question of how any discipline lays claim to knowledge is seen in Laurence Bonjour, *The Structure of Empirical Knowledge* (Cambridge, MA: Harvard University Press, 1985), which discusses many issues relevant to assessing the meaning of statements claiming to represent empirical reality.

5. Peter L. Berger, *Invitation to Sociology: A Humanistic Perspective* (Garden City, NY: Doubleday, 1963).

6. See Bennett Berger's definition of sociology as "bad faith" in R.P. Cuzzort and E.W. King, *Twentieth-Century Social Thought*, 4th ed. (Fort Worth, TX: Holt, Rinehart & Winston, 1989), p. 259.

7. *Newsweek* (April 14, 1994), pp. 44–49.

8. Disciplines struggle among themselves for public recognition. If sociology does not expect to get "trashed," it must make a more sincere effort to be useful to the people

who have generously funded it, which means it must be of some use to the public at large. Other signals have been sent about the problems of the discipline. See Irving Louis Horowitz, *The Decomposition of Sociology* (New York: Oxford University Press, 1993), where discipline problems and concepts are elaborated.

21

Sociography: A Final Thought

Historians have a field called historiography, which inquires into the social context in which historical findings and writings are conducted.[1] The premises upon which the central findings of the discipline are made are continuously examined and reexamined. It is fully understood that each generation redefines the definitions and directions considered central. In the field of sociology there is no reference to sociography in one of its earliest and probably its principal dictionary.[2]

A typical student in sociology is not exposed to an inquiry into the social context in which the major paradigms of sociology were produced, although there may be some attention to rebuttals to statements by detractors of certain positions. There may be a few references to the turmoil occurring in the wake of the French Revolution, which prompted Auguste Comte to consider the utility of a discipline called sociology, which Henri Saint Simon (1760–1825) earlier called social physics. Europe was thought during this time to be attempting a move toward modernization, or at least industrialization, which would be based on a change from the more static societies of a decaying feudalism. A few statements about the social context, or even the personal biographies of Karl Marx, Emile Durkheim, and Max Weber, may be offered, after which there is concern with the content of their theses.[3] An earlier approach to understanding the discipline was to trace its development over time, showing how sociology moved from essentially armchair speculation and folklore to science.[4]

There is no fundamental understanding of why sociology emerged as a discipline in the United States.[5] Perhaps the best argument is that it was copied from Europe and transported to America. Reasons for the emergence of various approaches are more obscure. Why, for instance, did there emerge in America an emphasis on symbolic interactionism or functionalism, and what were the social contexts in which they arrived? There was a better understanding of the need to resist collectivist doctrines, which stood a good possibility of claiming the attention of immigrants who did not understand democratic or individualist possibilities.[6]

American sociologists, led at first by morally oriented midwestern preachers espousing individualism, thought they could talk about the problems of the immigrants, whether the newcomers hailed from Europe or Asia or the South; they expected to discuss the growing technological change and economic upheaval and then encourage immigrants to change. The perspectives they fostered, like Topsy, just "growed." Sociology's earlier emphasis upon social Darwinism, might have been expected, for at the time, toward the end of the last century, when the discipline was getting started, social Darwinism was a dominant perspective used largely to justify colonialism and the capture and exploitation of the "backward" peoples of the world.

It was evident in retrospect that upper-class endorsement was an unintended consequence of sociological theorizing, even when it came from what appeared to be persons imbued with great moral principles. Slowly it came to be understood that sociological theory was not just the handmaiden of the ruling cadre. Such theory was not necessarily malicious, though it could have been had it supported ruling-class positions. Upper-class endorsement was the way theorists thought because they could not divorce themselves from the conditions in which they themselves had been socialized. They saw things and made conclusions in the only way they knew.

Even though sociologists, like other scholars, personally may have abhorred the shabby treatment of persons lower down the social ladder than themselves, few could see these people as equal to themselves. Scholars, like others, were essentially prisoners of their own times and experiences and had no framework for seeing this experience in any other light. They tried to socialize their students into slightly greater liberal views than they held themselves, yet they could not entertain or be more liberal toward or promote such views in those beneath their social level.

American sociology grew up in the period of change from agrarianism to industrialism. At the end of the Civil War the nation was largely agrarian, and half or more of all adults were self-employed.[7] By 1920 the United States had become an urban nation in which most persons worked for employers. Only about 29 percent of Americans were self-employed, and only about 11.7 percent of the adult labor force worked on farms. From 1865 to 1920 the labor force became concentrated in the primary (extractive) and secondary (manufacturing) sectors of the economy.[8] The change from agrarianism to urbanization was perhaps more rapid in the United States than in Europe, for America faced fewer problems with the breaking of old entrenchments.[9] The American frontier provided opportunities unimaginable in Europe.

The moralism of early American sociologists encouraged them to see the underclasses, of whom they generally wrote, as cases for change into mainstream America. Yet sociologists never developed a basic appreciation for these people, who were always seen as in need of modification and change. These lowly subjects would have to be taught, even against their will, to accept the dominant values of middle-class society, for there was little space for the appreciation or toleration of those with truly deviant lifestyles.

If and when the deviant people were studied, it was for the purpose of either demonstrating their deviation from mainstream norms or showing that they were increasingly alienated and discriminated by an uncaring system. In America there were to be no authentically different cultures and subcultures, only people who adhered to a broad middle-class standard represented by a suburban home or its city equivalent, one or two cars, color television, secure income, and a variety of personal options to improve the quality of life.[10]

The growth of the assimilationist doctrine, initiated with the Civil War, was not carried out in isolation. At the very same time that this doctrine was most prevalent, separatist ideologies were trying to gain headway. Sociography would account for the development of these contradictory doctrines by explicating the context in which they emerged and developed. It was clear to assimilationists, driven by moral and practical considerations, that few immigrant or culturally deviant persons or groups would experience enviable living outside the mainstream. The assimilationists argued that such cultures were too costly and dysfunctional; that they would continuously look with envy upon those who had more. Overall, it might be better to incorporate all newcomers into the assimilationist picture; let them have their chances at social improvement. If they did not make the most of these essentially equal chances, they could fault only themselves.

Assimilation was not only functional but also basically the only doctrine mainstreamers understood—a doctrine learned at home, in their schools and churches, and in mainstream communities. If they were successful, as assimilationists rationalized, they wanted others to be at least almost as successful as themselves.

Sociology was taught by examining the teachings of the masters. The older ones had become so emplaced that their teachings represented canon. Marx, Weber, Comte, and Durkheim became not just ordinary men with something quite ordinary to say about the operation of society. They took on epic qualities, becoming larger than life. They became like great athletic stars fawned over by a doting public. Students aspiring to status as professional sociologists were willing to emulate, mimic and uncritically accept the teachings and logic of the great canon makers. There was no sociologist who had the orientation of a C.S. Lewis, who reports that he realized early that a historian should adopt a critical attitude toward epic material.[11]

A relatively new term in sociology, sociography means an examination of the social context in which sociological research, orientations, theory, and conclusions are based. It takes full cognizance of the fact that the social context is a definer of that which is considered real. It allows for the asking of questions that might not be posed in the usual approach to understanding the operation of society, and it encourages an examination of the context in which answers are offered.

There has long been some sociography in the discipline, but it was not so called, nor was it organized. Classes in the sociology of knowledge enabled the painting of pictures of the context in which major European thought came about. Knowledge, it was realized, was a function of the total social situation. Some aspects of that situation did not affect the origin of knowledge to the extent other aspects did. As early as 1954 Louis Wirth saw a closer interconnection between ideas and situations than had formerly been thought.[12]

Margaret Mead, the eminent anthropologist, was accused of being influenced by Franz Boas, her mentor. She went out and found what she thought she should find. Her training taught her to expect that nurture would be a greater trainer than nature. After Mead's death a controversy emerged over her findings.[13] Mead is important for helping cement the idea of cultural, rather than biological, determinants of social behavior. An alternative view of the origin of social behavior is seen in the rise of sociobiology.[14]

Every culture that has a tradition of literacy and writing has elaborated areas in which thought is scheduled to proceed and those in which it is to be retarded. Basically, certain questions can be asked and others not. Some topics are taboo and others are scheduled for open discussion. For example, Wirth notes that in the early 1950s it was impossible to ask any questions or to seek basic facts about communism without running the risk of being labeled a communist.[15] Likewise, South Africans who wanted to discuss the possibility of black rule ran the risk of being considered "nigger lovers," a term probably borrowed from America. Consider another example: the federal government routinely declares that information about certain individuals and events may be sealed for generations. On the theory that open discussion will not be in the public interest official files on such persons as John F. Kennedy and Martin Luther King, Jr., may not be opened until well into the twenty-first century.[16]

In a diverse culture nearly everything that is said or written has the potential of "stepping on toes." Some group or other will not like what is said or written. In the period following World War II there emerged a great debate over the value of margarine versus butter. The margarine or vegetable fat interests moved into tropical countries and bought up the pineapple groves. They began to claim that animal fat was injurious to health. Research that showed the value of vegetable fat was supported lavishly, whereas research on animal fat was severely downgraded. That equatorial groups eat largely vegetable fats and those at the Arctic and Antarctic Circles live largely on animal fats was overlooked. Neither of these groups evidenced greater degrees of heart or circulatory problems associated with the consumption of either excessive animal fats or vegetable fats.[17]

Certain information is deemed so valuable, so recondite, that it is defined as closely related to national security. Anyone who divulges that information to those defined as "the enemy" or compromises the data any way, may be charged with treason, a capital crime.[18] Depending upon the force or pressure brought to bear on the traitor by those disagreeing, steps may be taken to protect one's right to say what one chooses. This freedom is protected partially by the First Amendment to the Constitution, the freedom of speech amendment. Rules against reckless use of this freedom are elaborated in the rules against slander, character defamation, and libel.

Another attempt to protect that freedom has come through the use of positivism or the scientific method. This entails a series of steps that are agreed upon ostensibly to assure that statements made are methodologically defensible. If objective procedures are used to reach conclusions, the conclusions themselves can not be automatically impugned. Social science has thus become, with Max Weber, value-free.[19] Of course, one of the great critics of value-free sociology was Alvin Gouldner, who argued that value-free sociology is little more than a storybook picture of social research. All social life has political dimensions. Politics cannot be removed from social analysis.[20]

The above examples merely suggest that there is a social context in which knowledge, understanding, and even statements may be written or uttered. Sociography probes for an understanding of that context, particularly as it relates to sociology. The following discussion of the influence of Auguste Comte, the founder of sociology, and Lewis Henry Morgan, the noted ethnologist, is intended to highlight the role that social context plays in the receipt or rejection of scholarly work. Another example is the growth of the women's liberation movement. The intention is not to give a complete chronology of the movement but to illustrate the context in which the movement occurred. These cases illustrate that the decisions of worth are not based wholly upon the value of the work itself.

In the mid-1880s Lewis Henry Morgan, the ethnologist, became a pervasive force in American social science. As an evolutionist Morgan thought that certain forms of social relations went with savagery and barbarism, and others with civilization. Group marriage was associated with barbarism, and monogamy with civilization.[21]

Morgan's evolutionism accorded with the teachings of Charles Darwin, Herbert Spencer, Cesare Lombroso, and others who thought that society changes through progressive stages. The context in which Morgan's thought emerged was clear enough. At that time the world was divided into industrially advanced and backward societies, the latter to be controlled by the former. Social placement was not simply a function of social class and relationship to the modes of work but depended upon the extent to which groups had evolved from savagery to civilization. The more civilized people were the highest evolved, and they were logically determined to be the rulers of those less evolved.

A consequence of this attitude was that sociology became more stagnant, in the sense that studies meant less. The attitude of the times suggested that there would not be rapid change. People would get where they were supposed to be by the evolutionary processes. It was overlooked that change was everywhere raging. It became extremely difficult to introduce new thought into the discipline because the old gods had such a strong hold, maintained largely because there was no sociography, no examination of the context in which theory was formulated.

The discipline continued but without much of a history beyond a recitation of the dates and lives and publications of the most notable people of the discipline. Students could argue over the plausibility of this or that orientation, but they did not seem much inclined or encouraged to understand sociological theory by locating it in the context of history. Perhaps the closest that the ordinary student came to sociography was upon enrolling in the course History of Social Thought. In that course there was a more or less ritualistic marching through the thought of the greater and lesser luminaries of the discipline, particularly those of Europe. Although the course was taught differently in each of the schools, so much time was spent understanding what this or that scholar said that little time was left to understand the social context in which the sayings had been produced.

Take symbolic interactionism, for example. Students are taught that individuals consciously conduct their lives, make choices, and respond to interpretations and meanings assigned to symbols, other people, themselves, events, and social situations. Individuals are more than passive reactors to physical stimuli.[22] This orientation owes much of its emphasis to the work of Chicago school sociology emphasized by such scholars as Charles Horton Cooley.[23] George Herbert Mead contributed to this orientation also.[24]

By the time symbolic interactionism gained a footing, it had to compete with the class-based sociology that was coming to dominate the department at the University of Chicago. In retrospect, it was a clear attempt to break away from the emphasis that suggests that people were creatures of their class positions, a somewhat weaker position than that taken by the strict Marxists. Symbolic interactionism gave more choices to individuals, reduced their alienation, and gave greater meaning to their lives. It was more consistent with the sense of mobility that had come to characterize the midwestern spirit. Nor did it require the discipline, piety, and asceticism of Weberian Protestantism.

Symbolic interactionism could arise only in a context of relative freedom. It would find greater acceptance in the Midwest and the Far West, both of which showed greater social fluidity than either the East or the South. Eastern Rites sociology, itself hostile to symbolic interactionism, had been most reflective of the attitudes that had dominated European social thought.[25] It reflected stratification that was practically taken for granted in the East with its millions of immigrants who somehow understood their possibilities and their places.

The South adopted sociological theory that accorded with its own social and economic orientation. Symbolic interactionist theory would be a long time in gaining a foothold in the South largely because of the entrenchment of caste and class theory, which gave support to its prevailing practices. As early as 1897 Charles H. Cooley, a founder of the interactionist school, had challenged the biologism of the time.[26] However, his research and that of others offering a concept of environmentalism was largely ignored.[27] Gunnar Myrdal's extensive bibliography makes no reference to George Herbert Mead, whose students brought together his work in four volumes, all but one available through the University of Chicago Press.[28] It is probably not an exaggeration to suggest that symbolic interactionism as sociological theory was not consistent with what decision-makers thought was safe and acceptable in the context of the South.

Both Comte (1798–1857) and Morgan (1818–1881) were children of the great period of Western colonialism and imperialism. Both were evolutionists, moralists, and apologists for the order of social systems. Both were relatively aristocratic, Comte having roots in professorial privilege and Morgan in learning and politics, which resulted in his being elected to serve in the New York State Assembly from 1861 to 1867 and in the state senate in 1868-69.[29] Although Comte was twenty years old when Morgan was born, they shared a common epoch. The interesting thing is that Comte is continuously discussed as the father or founder of positivistic sociology, whereas Morgan, also a great positivist in the sense that he insisted upon the acquiring of data, is seldom mentioned. Morgan was probably a more avid believer in the methods of scientific data collection than Durkheim (1858–1917) was to become years later.

References to Comte and even to Durkheim continue, but very small reference is made to Morgan no doubt because Morgan was associated with what eventually became communist ideology. When Frederich Engels, August Babel, and other communists made positive references to Morgan, himself a rich man, whose work seemed to provide a basis for communism, he was dropped by the detractors of communism.[30] Comte and Durkheim became more acceptable to the emerging theory of American sociology than Morgan even though Morgan had said the same thing that Durkheim said later.

The rejection of Morgan for political reasons becomes clear and shows that theory has as much a political dimension as a plausibility of explaining hypotheses. It made little difference that Morgan's social thought was evolutionary. No one was excited when he showed that the Iroquois were patrilineal and that monogamy was a value associated with "civilization." He had been widely praised for his *Systems of Consanguinity and Affinity of the Human Family* by scholars as noteworthy as Sir John Lubbock, president of the Royal Anthropological Institute of Great Britain, Herbert Spencer, Charles Darwin, Henry Maine, Francis Parkman, Horatio Hale, and Oliver Wendell Holmes, Jr. Stern notes that American reviewers were impressed with the bulk and profundity of Morgan's work but thought that the Smithsonian Institution would not be disadvantaged if it did not have the volumes.[31]

Until Morgan's endorsement by the communists, his work was considered academically interesting but with little value beyond that. His rejection afterward clearly showed that scholarship, however careful, was still controlled by powers that could use it to their advantage. By examining the social context in which scholars write and estimating their likelihood of supporting or undermining leading thought justifying the status quo, one can see that the nature of scholastic work is either value-free or politically supported.

Take the case of women's liberation. Modern society has known all along that social roles are not biologically determined but are learned in a context of social expectations. Women, like other categories of people, are trained to play the roles they do. Society controls both the motivation and the alternatives to choose within a fairly well defined and small set of possibilities.[32] Why did the women's movement emerge, then? It was not simply that women decided they could do many of the jobs men do and no longer saw men's jobs as inappropriate for women. A large body of studies documented that women's expectations have been lower than men's and that women themselves have often adopted those limits.[33]

Women's liberation and women's and gender studies had to be created, ratified, and buttressed, for like other innovations of a social nature, they could not be defended wholly on their own. It would be interesting to investigate and understand the social context in which it became academically and politically proper to introduce these relatively new lines of research and scholarship.

There may be vested interests in the perpetuation of questionable sociological findings. Findings in the field of intelligence testing by race and ethnicity are instructive.[34] It remained for Oliver C. Cox to show that there was a political agenda behind the presentation of the picture of black Americans—one that was consistent with the overall capitalist objective.[35] For example, in order to discourage the movement of blacks from farms of the South, where they were ensconced as sharecroppers, to cities where they would compete for better jobs, social scientists perpetuated the idea of the lower intelligence of blacks, an idea many blacks accepted.

Scholars contend over various theoretical positions, but sometimes there are hidden, or even open, agendas undergirding the contentions. A good example is the vitriolic debate over the issue of Thomas Jefferson's alleged thirty-eight year relationship with his slave Sally Heming, a debate that took on its present character within the past two decades.[36]

NOTES

1. Historiography is taught as a survey of the history of historical writing and a study of the important schools of historical interpretation. See *The Graduate School Catalog, 1992–93* (Fayetteville: University of Arkansas, 1992), 124–125, which probably fairly accurately reflects the content of the course at a number of similar institutions.

2. Julius Gold and William L., eds., *A Dictionary of the Social Sciences* (New York: Free Press, 1964).

3. Don Martindale, *The Nature and Types of Sociological Theory,* 2nd ed. (Prospect Heights, IL: Waveland Press, Inc., 1981), offers an example of the way that students, particularly graduate students, are introduced to the field and indoctrinated. Martindale does seek to set the stage for understanding some of the writers and could be considered something of an emerging sociographer.

4. A good example of this approach is seen in Howard Becker and Harry Elmer Barnes, *Social Thought from Lore to Science*, 2nd ed. (Washington, DC: Harren Press, 1952). The encyclopedic breadth of this scholarship is very notable, summarizing a number of separate approaches to this history.

5. The discipline is said to have emerged as a part of the general pattern of movement from religion to philosophy to science, a process most likely to be found in Western countries. See Don Martindale, *Nature and Types of Sociological Theory*, 2nd ed. (Prospects Heights, IL: Waveland Press, Inc., 1981), p. 1.

6. Americanization or assimilationist doctrines were seen as basic bulwarks against the potential collectivism to which eastern and southern European immigrants were susceptible, although there were a variety of other reasons why this doctrine was promoted. See William M. Newman, *American Pluralism: A Study of Minority Groups and Social Theory* (New York: Harper & Row, Publishers, 1973), pp. 53–63.

7. Melvin Dubofsky, *Industrialism and the American Worker, 1865–1920*, 2nd ed. (Arlington Heights, IL: Harlan Davidson, Inc., 1985), p. 3.

8. Ibid., p. 3.

9. This is demonstrated in a very instructive paper by James S. Coleman. See his 1992 American Sociological Association presidential address, *The Rational Reconstruction of Society*, v. 58 (February 1993): 1–15.

10. Although there are great inequalities in incomes and life-styles of Americans, the general drift of the attitudes of the majority of the people is toward the middle-class. Scholars have suggested that the "middle class measuring rod" is the standard by which societal members are measured. Failure to meet these standards are thought to lead to deviance. See especially the thought of Robert K. Merton who discusses the strains to meet middle-class standards, in *Social Theory and Social Structure* (New York: Free Press, 1957), pp. 230–246. Albert K. Cohen is just one scholar who has taken up the argument of the importance of the middle-class standards to youth who are delinquent. See his *Delinquent Boys: The Culture of the Gang* (New York: Free Press, 1971).

11. C.S. Lewis, *Surprised by Joy: The Shape of My Early Life* (New York: Harcourt Brace Jovanovich, 1955), p. 13.

12. See Karl Mannheim, *Ideology and Utopia* (New York: Harcourt, Brace & Co., Preface by Louis Wirth, 1954), xiv.

13. See "The Samoa Controversy: The Interplay of Science and Politics," in John J. Macionis, *Sociology* (Englewood Cliffs, NJ: Prentice-Hall, 1993), pp. 38–39.

14. Perhaps the most vocal spokesperson of the view of a biological determinant of social behavior is Edward O. Wilson, *Sociobiology: The New Synthesis* (Cambridge, MA: Harvard University Press, 1975). See also his 1977 paper "Biology in the Social Sciences," *Daedalus*, 106 (spring): 127–140.

15. Wirth's preface to Mannheim, *Ideology and Utopia*, p. xvii.

16. Federal sources would verify that these files have been closed to public inspection and will not be available for quite some time.

17. The history of the struggle between the economic interests representing animal fats and vegetable fats is scattered but available. The contest is by no means settled. Juniorous Archibald Lee, "Characterization of Serum Low-density Proteins of Rhesus Monkeys," Ph.D. dissertation, University of Arkansas, Fayetteville, 1972. See *Tulsa World*, June 6, 1994, for evidence of the continuing debate on food fat content and the effect upon the human body.

18. A general appreciation of the nature of political crimes, of which treason is a notable example, is found in Robert F. Meier, *Crime and Society* (Boston: Allyn & Bacon, 1989), pp. 249–256.

19. Weber's 1918 call for a value-free social science is reported in John J. Macionis, *Sociology*, p. 37.

20. Alvin Gouldner, "The Sociologist as Partisan: Sociology and the Welfare State," in Larry T. Reynolds and Janice M. Reynolds, eds., *The Sociology of Sociology* (New York: McKay, 1970), pp. 218–255.

21. See Bernard J. Stern, *Selected Papers. Historical Sociology* (New York: Citadel Press, 1959), pp. 163–184, where much of the thought of Lewis Henry Morgan is capsuled.

22. Rodney D. Elliott and Don Shamblin, *Society in Transition: A Humanist Introduction to Sociology* (Englewood Cliffs, NJ: Prentice-Hall, 1992), pp. 97–104.

23. Charles Horton Cooley, *Human Nature and the Social Order* (New York: Scribner's, 1902).

24. George Herbert Mead, *Mind, Self, and Society: From the Standpoint of a Social Behaviorist* (Chicago: University of Chicago Press, 1934).

25. This term is used to suggest a kind of sociology practiced largely in the major schools along the East Coast. It looks to the European context as frameworks in which American society might be interpreted.

26. Charles H. Cooley, "Genius, Fame and the Comparison of Races," *Annals of the American Academy of Political and Social Science* (May 1897): 317-358.

27. A summary of the debate in research over hereditary or nature versus environment or nurture is found in Gunnar Myrdal, *An American Dilemma* (New York: Harper & Brothers, 1944), p. 91.

28. The work of Mead is found in Arthur E. Murphy, ed., *The Philosophy of the Present* (Chicago: Open Court Publishing Co., 1932); Charles W. Morris, ed., *Mind, Self and Society* (Chicago: University of Chicago Press, 1934); Merritt H. Moore, ed., *Movements of Thought in the Nineteenth Century* (Chicago: University of Chicago Press, 1936); and Charles W. Morris, ed., *The Philosophy and the Act* (Chicago: University of Chicago Press, 1938).

29. Bernard J. Stern, *Selected Papers. Historical Sociology* (New York: Citadel Press, 1965), pp. 163-184.

30. Ibid.

31. Ibid., p. 173.

32. See Jo Freeman, "The Social Construction of the Second Sex," in Scott G. McNall, ed., *The Sociological Perspective* (Boston: Little Brown, 1977), pp. 119–132.

33. Ibid., pp. 119–132, offers a very extensive bibliography on the status and role of women.

34. Myrdal, *An American Dilemma*, pp. 144–149, presents some early findings on the nature of psychic intelligence, including intelligence test differences between blacks and whites.

35. Oliver C. Cox, *Caste, Class and Race* (New York: Modern Reader Paperbacks, 1948), especially pp. 523–538.

36. Whether Jefferson was or was not the consort of Sally Hemings, his slave, is not of particular interest. It is important to note that claimants on both sides of the issue had their own reasons for making the statements they did about the learned president's paramourial behavior. See Fawn M. Brodie, *Thomas Jefferson: An Intimate History* (New

York: W.W. Norton, 1974), for the most publicized claim of Jefferson's love for Sally; also see Virginius Dabney, *The Jefferson Scandals* (New York: Dodd, Mead & Co., 1981), for the rebuttal. Sociography would enquire as to the social context in which both of these allegations and approaches were taken to the Jefferson text.

Afterword

Men like Auguste Comte, Herbert Spencer, Karl Marx, and Emile Durkheim played large roles in outlining and legitimizing sociology as an academic discipline. They worked to sell sociology to the academy, which had viewed the new discipline as an illegitimate child—an unpromising upstart. The story of adhering to the most rigid methods of reasoning, the using of data, and making decisions based upon scientific rather than philosophic foundations is the story of the development of sociology as a discipline in modern times. However, the transporting of sociology to America is not related to the establishment of the discipline. There is no evidence of a need for sociology in the American colleges. Nothing social needed explaining or even studying, according to the thought of the time. Social life was not problematic. Its outlines were seen in the morality of the time.

The framing of sociology in the United States was done mainly at the University of Chicago under scholars such as Albion Small, Charles Henderson, William I. Thomas, and G.H. Mead, although such founders as Charles H. Cooley held forth at other schools such as the University of Michigan. We can obtain details of that framing, learn how various men were recruited to the early department, and vicariously share the triumphs and tragedies they experienced. What is missing throughout these treatises is a statement why anyone thought that the new discipline of sociology would be useful in America. Perhaps it was the tradition of finishing one's schooling in Europe that enabled some students to be put in touch with the emerging sociology of Europe. They may simply have brought the concept back to America to try it out because of its vogue in Europe. Just as a fashion moves from one area to another because of imitation, sociology may have been imitated in America because it was fashionable in Europe.

American sociology was based upon the idea that society originated and is sustained by the characteristics of individuals.[1] This orientation constituted a major difference between American sociology and European sociology. European sociology most generally saw problems in terms of structure. Marx was very much concerned with the exploitation of one class by another, of old implacable relationships between groups. There were things wrong with the organization of societies and groups, the European concept said. The structure was more imperfect than individuals. The European peasant was the embodiment of goodness degraded by the crassness of the ruling lords and barons. Peasants had no choice but to try to alter the structure by physical means, if necessary, because the ruling class would not change to give the peasants more rights and opportunities.

In American sociology the emphasis was just the reverse. There, the individual was viewed as having the problem. There was never admitted to be any problem with the structure of American society, only problems with individuals. The individual approach is used to the virtual exclusion of critiquing the social structure itself. Any examination of the social structure almost immediately moves the critic from the category of serious scholar into that of muckraker.[2]

The old sociology sought to solidify itself by claiming that it was a new field. For the first fifty years or so its concerns were with establishing discipline boundaries, adopting a language and organs in which to communicate with other practitioners and the general public, and finding an appropriate methodology in which to work. Concern was also with determining certification, although this was shown mostly in setting degree requirements for admission to the practice of the discipline.

While these organizational requirements were being met, there arose internecine fights over issues such as whether sociology had applied or theoretical mandates and whether qualitative or quantitative methodologies should hold sway. As these arguments went on, there was little accountability in the discipline. Sociology was literally free-ranging in that whatever a scholar wanted to say was permissible as long as it could be rationalized into a social context for indeed total society was seen as the domain of sociological study.[3]

Through it all there was no real test of the quality of sociology in the sense that it was tested by pragmatic payoff. Students learned of many features of society, naming them meticulously, developing bibliographies on diverse groups and fitting this information into intended theoretical schemas. Social facts were gathered that piled high and deep in offices, for they seemed to portend no line of action. There was literally nowhere to go with the information collected, or even with the "theories adduced." The expertise of many scholars was in raising questions. The list of questions grew, but the number of definitive answers shrank until some of the old questions were simply no longer addressed because new ones had pushed them off the front pages of the discipline.

The discipline had a brief moment in the sun during the 1960s and 1970s as much social change sought for explanation.[4] The tired old conclusions and recommendations of the past were neither impressive nor instructive for the 1980s, however. Departments found themselves in real trouble, even on their campuses as the fight for resources became more Darwinian.[5] Other departments related to the social sciences grabbed the language, methodology, and turf that had been defended by sociology, but they did not recognize the discipline for its contributions.[6]

The problem with sociology was perhaps its leaning toward liberalism while the leadership of the country was going conservative. Sociologists were identified with the underdog and therefore were seen as promoters of liberal causes through their teaching and their research. Not all university or political administrators trusted the sociologists or even the discipline itself. They could get the same interpretations from law, history, human relations, industrial managers, education, psychology, newspaper editors, ministers, and a hundred other sources. They did not have to go to the sociologists, who had become associated with the baggage of liberalism. Where the sociologists were not too liberal, they became too critical. It was better to steer clear of them. Sometimes a few of their more conservative number were placed into positions of leadership so that there might not be a general observation that the discipline and its practitioners were being overlooked and shunted aside.

At the upper levels of the discipline the concern continued to be with the fashioning of theory according to European standards, although based upon data found within the American context. The tenor of European theory was too pedantic for America, a society noted for its pragmatism. Its language separated the readers from the writers and so alienated students that taking advanced courses were not an exercise in the excitement of learning new material but the drudgery of internalizing and interpreting acts and facts within molds set by the old European masters. Students were driven from the classes in droves, and departments had to force them to enroll in the most meaningful courses, not out of interest, but out of fear of not receiving their degrees. Most students considered they had more than enough sociology to last them a lifetime after they completed the introductory course.

The new sociology proposes to return to the discipline the natural interest of students and the general public. Understanding society remains the mission of this focus, which is based on the idea that knowledge of society is valuable in itself; that it is necessary to have studied knowledge in order to participate meaningfully in a democratic society. There will continue to be attempts at formulating theory, in increasing accuracy in prediction, and in sharpening methodology; but all these will be taught and written about in terms that will make the discipline more accessible to the public at all levels. The new sociology will stress understanding society by study of the local environment utilizing examples out of the experiences of students and greatly broadening the kind of information that will be considered sociological. It will remove the artificial restraints placed on the discipline by forcing research to proceed in a certain format and to be published in certain formats and media.

A new sociology is necessary because of the failure of the old one to address the current problems of American society. These are not the problems forecast and studied philosophically and empirically by the students steeped in the methodologies and theories appropriate for an earlier time. It is necessary also because leaders of current society are unwilling to permit what they see as a continued waste of money on the study of things that are not problematic in the country. The pragmatism of Americans demands that there be some result, some benefit, derived from study that utilizes funds that could go for more useful study. American leaders demand the same degree of accountability in all the disciplines. All the problems of society have been studied literally to death; yet there are more of them than ever before, and this is not simply because of liberal disciplines such as sociology. The relativism and liberalism of such disciplines have helped mold generations of students into values far beyond those of the counterculture of the 1960s, when students thought they had legitimate demands when they went naked, smoked pot, and behaved as though their personal deviation would be enough to change societal norms. That many members of the counterculture are today in positions of influence but have not appreciably humanized society, and have in many cases even giving up trying, confirms the earlier supposition that their deviance in the 1960s was a simple excuse to engage in a variety of sublegal, undervalued, and even illegal behavior under cover of claiming to want legitimate social change and human equality. Today these high-salaried former counterculture members are stronger believers in social-class than their lineal forbears, who often found conflict between the creeds they professed and the deeds they carried out.

The new sociology will abandon many of the assumptions about society that have been generated or supported by the old sociology, assumptions that have remained neither provable nor unfalsifiable. It will not be necessary to repeat the mistakes of the past nor to perpetuate the very questionable stereotypes of the past.

The new sociology will have to struggle with the old in order to gain access to sociological turf. There will be an insistence that all interpretations be cast in the old molds. Instructors will be pressured to discuss traditional topics as the old masters had done for literal sociological generations. The hold of tradition will be so great that even persons who are inured to the old masters' inability to explain current reality will be under psychological as well as other pressure to use the convenient old explanations. And the old explanations are convenient. They are known and well understood by present instructors, who have no viable alternatives to the thought of the old masters. In that they were not given alternatives or encouraged to view data in new ways, the instructors have literally been brainwashed. Admitting that we have been presented a single diet for many years and that our whole psychologies, as well as our physiologies, have become adjusted to that diet will be difficult to do. Resistance will occur naturally, though. Struggle to prove the suzerainty of the old sociology with its emphasis on European paradigms and thought, will continue. Textbook publishers will reject the new sociology because it is new. They will try to illegitimize it as without foundation within the ancient academic traditions, and those scholars crying out for new approaches to understanding society will be postured as charlatans who are not central to the discipline in the first place.

Students will be the most receptive to the new sociology, for they are the least steeped in tradition and therefore more open to change. They will look forward to a more flexible course, one that speaks more to the needs and realities with which they are familiar.

NOTES

1. Although the concept of group is basic in sociology, so that the influence of the group is noted, it is seldom that the group bears responsibility for the deviance of individuals. Thus the individual is the focus of most attention in actual social circumstances. If a child is socialized into an environment of violence and adopts that attitude seemingly naturally, when he or she becomes a violent older person little attention is given to his or her socialization. The tug is between the individual and the environment, with the individual held accountable for his or her actions. That different groups make and inhabit different social environments is the essence of the "natural area." See Leonard Broom and Philip Selznick, Sociology: *A Text with Adapted Readings*, 5th ed. (New York: Harper & Row, 1937), p. 525.

2. Muckrakers have been severe critics of society. Probably because sociology has asked that individuals objectively examine their own beliefs and values, with the strong possibility that their conclusions may not support their previous beliefs, sociology could be seen as potentially destabilizing of the status quo. The individual may discover that the choices made are without the influences of many external forces. See Joel M. Charon, *Ten Questions: A Sociological Perspective* (Belmont, CA: Wadsworth Publishing Co., 1992), pp. 235–244.

3. Sociology had such wide boundaries, allowing it to address so many undefinitive answers that the discipline was often equated with the purveying of common sense. To counter that argument an orientation within the discipline emerged that was called "radical empiricism," exemplified in the work of such scholars as George Lundberg, Stuart Chapin, Stuart Dodd, and James S. Coleman. See George A. Lundberg, Clarence C. Schrag, and Otto N. Larsen, *Sociology* (Glencoe, IL: Free Press, 1958), for impressions of how this wing of sociology was presented. Empiricism has held sway to the present in the form of extreme quantitativism, which was thoroughly criticized by scholars generally on the left. See C. Wright Mills, *The Sociological Imagination* (New York: Oxford University Press, 1959), for his notable critique of empiricism.

4. The issues over civil rights, riots, protests, and such, were addressed by sociologists who for a moment seemed to have credibility. By the mid-1980s the public was paying less and less attention to what sociologists were saying or to their research. Of more than 150 sociologists in the Los Angeles area, not a single one had any inkling of what was going on in the ghetto before the riot of 1992 erupted, although the ghetto had been studied for some fifty years. The precise meanings of the studies of these scholars remain unknown at this time.

5. We use the term Darwinian as a metaphor for "struggle" to see which explanation or hypothesis will survive through discussion in the classrooms in which the ideas

of the discipline are most considered.

6. The subject matter that had been the domain of sociology has been spread around the campuses and freely incorporated into other departmental teaching. In many colleges it is impossible to distinguish among subject matters. Dissertations in colleges of education and in many departments of the colleges of arts and sciences could easily be substituted for dissertations and theses in graduate sociology departments. The spread of the subject matter of sociology to other disciplines, of course, has a weakening effect upon regular sociology departments and in some cases has led to their constriction and even to their downgrading.

Bibliography

Abrahamson, Mark. *Functionalism*. Englewood Cliffs, NJ, 1978.

al-Khalil, Samir. *Republic of Fear: The Inside Story of Saddam's Iraq*. New York, 1989.

Anderson, Charles H. *Toward a New Sociology*. Homewood, IL, 1974.

Apter, D.E. *The Political Kingdom in Uganda*. London, 1961.

Ayer, Alfred Jules. *Language, Truth and Logic*. New York, 1946.

Balkan, S.R., R.J. Berger, and Schmidt, J. *Crime and Deviance in America: A Critical Approach*. Belmont, CA, 1980.

Barnard, John, and David Burner. *The American Experience in Education*. New York, 1975.

Bassis, Michael S., Richard J. Gelles, and Ann Levine. *Sociology: An Introduction*. New York, 1980.

Becker, Howard, and Harry Elmer Barnes. *Social Thought from Lore to Science*, 2nd ed. Washington, DC, 1952.

Bellah, Robert N. "Civil Religion in America." *Daedalus* 96: 1-21 (1967).

Bendix, Reinhard. *Max Weber: An Intellectual Portrait*. New York, 1960.

Berger, Bennett M., ed. *Authors of Their Lives: Intellectual Biographies by Twenty American Sociologists*. Berkeley, CA, 1990.

Berger, Peter L. *Invitation to Sociology*. Garden City, New York, 1963.

Berlin, Isaiah. *Karl Marx: His Life and Environment*, 4th ed. New York, 1978.

Bismarck, Otto Furst von. *Otto Furst von Bismark: The Man and the Statesman*. New York, 1899, 1968.

Bloom, Allan. *The Closing of the American Mind*. New York, 1987.

Bogardus, Emory S. "Racial Distance Changes in the United Statess During the Past Thirty Years." *Sociology and Social Research*, November-December 1958.

_____. "Social Distance and Its Origins." *Journal of Applied Sociology* 9: 226.

Bonadeo, Alfredo. *Corruption, Conflict, and Power and in The Work and Times of Niccolo Machiavelli*. Berkeley, 1973.

Bonjour, Laurence. *The Structure of Empirical Knowledge*. Cambridge, MA, 1985.

Boring, Edwin G. *History, Psychology, and Science: Selected Papers*. 1963.

Bottomore, T.B., ed. *Karl Marx: Selected Writings in Sociology and Social Philosophy.* New York, 1956, 1964.

Branch, Taylor. *Parting of the Waters: America in the King Years—1954–1963.* New York, 1988.

Brodie, F.M. *Thomas Jefferson: An Intimate History.* New York, 1974.

Broom, Leonard, and Peter Selznick. *Sociology: A Text with Adapted Readings,* 5th ed. New York, 1973.

Bryjak, George J., and Michael P. Soroka. *Sociology: Cultural Diversity in a Changing World.* Boston, 1992.

Burma, John H., ed. *Mexican Americans in the United States: A Reader.* Cambridge, MA, 1970.

Burnham, Kenneth E. *God Comes to America: The Father Divine Peace Mission Movement.* Boston, 1979.

Burns, E. Bradford. *Latin America: A Concise Interpretive History,* 4th ed. Englewood Cliffs, NJ, 1986.

Cannandine, David. *The Fall of the British Aristocracy.* New York, 1992.

Caplow, Theodore, and Reece McGee. *The Academic Marketplace.* New York, 1958.

Chambliss, Rollin. *Ibn Khaldun: Social Thought.* 1954.

Chapin, F. Stuart. "A Quantitative Scale for Rating the Home and Social Environment of Middle Class Families in an Urban Community." *Journal of Educational Psychology* 19 (February 1928).

Charon, Joel M. *Ten Questions: A Sociological Perspective.* Belmont, CA, 1992.

Claypole, William, and John Robottom. *Caribbean Story: Book One: Foundations.* Essex, England, 1990.

Cohen, Albert K. *Delinquent Boys: The Culture of the Gang.* New York, 1971.

Coleman, James S. *Introduction to Mathematical Sociology.* Glencoe, IL, 1964.

Commission on Population Growth and the American Future. *Population and the American Future.* Washington, DC, 1972.

Comte, Auguste. *The Positive Philosophy.* London, 1982.

Conyers, James E. Unpublished paper on Ibn Khaldun. Pullman, Washington, 1958–59.

Cooley, C.H. "Genius, Fame and the Comparison of Races." *Annals of the American Academy of Political and Social Science,* 1897.

_____. *Human Nature and the Social Order.* New York, 1902.

Coolidge, Calvin. *The Autobiography of Calvin Coolidge.* New York, 1921.

Counts, George S. "Social Status of Occupations." *School Review* 33: 16–27 (January 1925).

Cox, Oliver C. *Caste, Class and Race.* New York, 1948.

_____. "The Modern Caste School of Race Relations." *Social Forces* 21: 218–226 (December 1942).

Cuzzort, R.P., and E.W. King. *Twentieth-Century Social Thought,* 4th ed. New York, 1989.

Dabney, V. *The Jefferson Scandals.* New York, 1981.

Dahrendorf, Ralf. *Class and Class Conflict in Industrial Society.* Stanford, CA, 1959.

Davidson, Basil. *Modern Africa: A Social and Political History,* 2nd ed. London, 1990.

De Young, Chris A., and Richard Wynn. *American Education,* 7th ed. New York, 1972.

Douglas, Jack D. *Introduction to Sociology: Situations and Structures.* New York, 1973.

Doyle, Kegan. "The Reality of a Disappearance: Frederick Jameson and the Cultural Logic of Post Modernism." *Critical Sociology* 19(1): 113–127 (1992).

Dubofsky, Melvin. *Industrialism and the American Worker, 1865–1920*, 2nd ed. Arlington Heights, IL, 1985.

Durkheim, Emile. *Rules of the Sociological Method*. Chicago: University of Chicago Press, 1938.

_____. *Suicide*. Translated by George Simpson. New York: Free Press, 1951.

Ehrenreich, Barbara. *The Worst Years of Our Lives*. New York, 1981.

Elliott, R.D., and D. Shamblin. *Society in Transaition: A Humanist Introduction to Sociology*. Englewood Cliffs, NJ, 1992.

Erikson, Kai T. *Wayward Puritans: A Study in the Sociology of Deviance*. New York, 1966.

Fallers, Lloyd A. *Bantu Bureaucracy*. Cambridge, England, 1956.

Fancher, Raymond E. *Pioneers of Psychology*. New York, 1979.

Fanon, Frantz. *Black Skin, White Masks*. New York, 1967.

Faris, Robert E.L., ed. *Handbook of Modern Sociology*. Chicago, 1964.

Farley, John E. *Sociology: Annotated Instructor's Edition*. Englewood Cliffs, NJ, 1990.

Fiegelman, William, ed. *Sociology Full Circle*, 5th ed. New York, 1989.

Flexner, A. *Medical Education in the United States and Canada: Bulletin of the Carnegie Foundation for the Advancement of Teaching*. New York, 1910.

Frazier, E. Franklin. *The Negro in the United States*. New York, 1949.

Freeman, J. "The Social Construction of the Second Sex." In S.G. McNall, ed. *The Sociological Perspective* (pp. 119–132). Boston, 1977.

Friedrich, Carl. *The Philosophy of Hegel*. New York, 1953.

Fromm, Erich. *Escape From Freedom*. New York, 1941.

Gans, Herbert. "Sociology in America: The Discipline and the Public." *American Sociological Review* 54: 1–6 (1989).

Giddens, Anthony. *Sociology: A Brief But Critical Introduction*, 2nd ed. New York, 1982.

Glass, John F., and John R. Staude, eds. *Humanistic Sociology: Today's Challenge to Sociology*. Pacific Palisades, CA, 1972.

Gold, Julius, and W.L. Kolb, eds., *A Dictionary of the Social Sciences*. New York, 1964.

Gordon, Milton. *Assimilation in American Life*. New York, 1964.

Gouldner, Alvin. *The Coming Crisis in Western Sociology*. New York, 1970.

_____. "The Sociologist as Partisan: Sociology and the Welfare State." In L.T. Reynolds and J.M. Reynolds, eds., *The Sociology of Sociology* (pp. 218–225). New York, 1970.

Graduate School Catalog, 1992–93, The University of Arkansas, Fayetteville, AR, 1992.

Greene, Melissa Fay. *Praying for Sheetrock*. Reading, MA, 1991.

Guralnik, David B., ed.-in-chief. *Webster's New World Dictionary of the American Language*. New York, 1979.

Harris, Chauncy D., and Edward L. Ullman, "The Nature of Cities," *The Annals of the American Academy of Political and Social Sciences* 242, no. 12 (November 1945).

Harris, Marvin. "India's Sacred Cows." *Human Nature*, February 1978.

Haskell, Martin R., and Lewis Yablonsky. *Crime and Delinquency*. Chicago, 1970.

Hawthorn, Geoffrey. *Enlightenment and Despair: A History of Sociology*. Cambridge, England, 1976.

Herndon, James. *How to Survive in Your Native Land*. New York, 1971.

Herskovits, Melville. *The Myth of the Negro Past*. New York, 1941, 1942.

Hill, Mozell, and Bevode C. McCall. "Social Stratification in Georgia Town." *American Sociological Review* 15: 727–729.

Hobbes, Thomas. *Leviathan*. Oxford, 1909.

Hodges, Harold M., Jr. *Conflict and Consensus: An Introduction to Sociology*. 1974.
_____. *Social Stratification: Class in America*. Cambridge, MA, 1964.

Hooton, Ernest A. *The American Criminal: An Anthropological Study*. Cambridge, MA, 1939.
_____. *Crime and the Man*. Cambridge, MA, 1939.

Hoover, Kenneth. *The Elements of Social Scientific Thinking*. New York, 1988.

Horowitz, Irving Louis. *The Decomposition of Sociology*. New York, 1993.

Horton, John. "The Dehumanization of Anomie and Alienation." *British Journal of Sociology* 15: 283–300 (December 1964).

Horton, Paul B., and Chestern L. Hunt. *Sociology*, 5th ed. New York, 1980.

Humphrey, N.D. "American Race Relations and the Caste System." *Psychiatry: Journal of the Biology and Psychology of Interpersonal Relations* 8: 379–381 (November 1956).

Hunter, Herbert M., and Sameer Y. Abraham, eds. *Race, Class, and the World System: The Sociology of Oliver C. Cox*. New York, 1987.

Ibingira, G.S.K. *The Forging of an African Nation*. New York, 1973.

Jacoby, Russell. *The Last Intellectuals: American Culture in the Age of Academe*. New York, 1989.

Jameson, Frederic. *Post Modernism or the Cultural Logic of Late Capitalism*. Durham, NC, 1990.

Johnstone, Ronald L. *Religion in Society*, 4th ed. Englewood Cliffs, NJ, 1992.

Kephart, William M. *Extraordinary Groups: The Sociology of Unconventional Life-styles*. New York, 1976.

Kerr, Clark. *The Uses of the University*. New York, 1963.

Khaldun, Ibn. *Muquddimah*. Translated by Franz Rosenthal, 1958.

Kuhn, Thomas. *The Structure of Scientific Revolutions*. Chicago, 1962.

Ladner, Joyce, ed. *The Death of White Sociology*. New York, 1973.

Laffan, G.D. *The Serbs*. New York, 1989.

Lee, J.A. *Characterization of Serum Low-Density Proteins of Rhesus Monkeys*. Ph.D. dissertation. University of Arkansas, 1972.

Leveritt, Mara. "Retaking Control." *Arkansas Times* 14–17 (January 7, 1993).

Lewis, C.S. *Surprised by Joy: The Shape of My Early Life*. New York, 1955.

Lewis, Helen Matthews, Linda Johnson, and Donald Askins. *Colonialism in Modern America: The Appalachian Case*. Boone, NC, 1978.

Lewis, Oscar. *Five Families: Mexican Case Studies in the Culture of Poverty*. New York, 1959.

Lombroso, Cesare. *L'uomo delinquente*. Torino, Italy, 1896–1897.

Lowry, Ritchie P., and Robert P. Rankin. *Sociology: The Science of Society*. New York, 1969.

Lugard, Frederick J.D. *The Dual Mandate in British Tropical Africa*. Hamden, CT, 1965.

Lundberg, George A., Clarence C. Schrag, and Otto N. Larsen. *Sociology*, 3rd ed. New York, 1958.

Lynd, Robert S., and Helen M. Lynd. *Middletown*. New York, 1929.
_____. *Middletown in Transition*. New York, 1937.

Lyotard, Jean Francois. *The Post Modern Condition: A Report on Knowledge*. Minneapolis, 1984.

Machiavelli, Niccolo. *The Prince*. 1513.

Macionis, J.J. *Sociology*. Englewood Cliffs, NJ, 1987, 1993.

Malthus, Thomas R. *An Essay on the Principle of Population*, 2 vols. London, 1958.

Mannheim, Karl. *Ideology and Utopia*. London, 1929, and New York, 1936.

Manning, Kenneth R. *Black Apollo of Science: The Life of Ernest Everett Just*. New York, 1983.

_____. *Karl Marx: Selected Writings in Sociology and Social Philosophy*. New York, 1956, 1964. Translated by T.B. Bottomore.

Mannoni, O. *Prospero and Caliban: The Psychology of Colonization*. New York, 1964.

Martindale, Don. *The Nature and Types of Sociological Theory*, 2nd ed. Prospect Heights, IL, 1981.

Mason, Theodore O., Jr. "Between the Populist and the Scientist: Ideology and Power in Recent Afro-American Literary Criticism or 'The Dozens and Scholarship.'" *Callaloo* 11: 606–615 (Summer 1988).

Masson, Jeffery M. *The Assault on Truth: Freud's Suppression of the Seduction Theory*. New York, 1984.

Mathbane, Mark. *Kaffir Boy*. New York, 1986.

Mathiesen, Thomas. *The Politics of Abolition: Scandinavian Studies in Criminology*. New York, 1974.

McCaghy, Charles H. *Deviant Behavior: Crime, Conflict, and Interest Groups*. New York, 1976.

McMurray, Linda O. *George Washington Carver: Scientist and Symbol*. New York, 1981.

McNall, Scott G. *The Sociological Perspective*. Boston, 1977.

Mead, G.H. *Mind, Self, and Society: From the Standpoint of a Social Behaviorist*. Chicago, 1934.

Meier, R.F. *Crime and Society*. Boston, 1989.

Merton, Robert K. *Social Theory and Social Structure*. Glencoe, IL, 1957.

Merton, Robert K., Leonard Broom, and Leonard S. Cottrell, Jr., eds. *Sociology Today*. New York, 1959.

Mills, C. Wright. *The Sociological Imagination*. New York, 1959.

Montagu, Ashley. *Man's Most Dangerous Myth: The Fallacy of Race*. Cleveland, OH, 1950.

Montague, Joel B., Jr. *Class and Nationality. English and American Studies*. New Haven, CT, 1963.

Moore, M.H., ed. *Movements of Thought in the Nineteenth Century*. Chicago, 1936.

Morris, C.W., ed. *Mind, Self and Society*. Chicago, 1934.

_____, ed. *The Philosophy and the Act*. Chicago, 1938.

Mullins, Nicholas C., and Carolyn J. Mullins. *Theories and Theory Groups in Contemporary American Sociology*. New York, 1973.

Murphy, A.E., ed. *The Philosophy of the Present*. Chicago, 1932.

Myers, Edward. *Education in America—A Unique Experiment*. London, 1912.

Myrdal, Gunnar. *An American Dilemma*. New York, 1944.

Newman, William M. *American Pluralism: A Study of Minority Groups and Social Theory*. New York, 1973.

Odum, Howard. *American Sociology: The Story of Sociology in the United States through 1950*. New York, 1951.

Park, Robert E., and E.W. Burgess. *Introduction to the Science of Sociology*. Chicago, 1921-1924.

Parsons, Talcott. "Max Weber and the Contemporary Political Crisis." *The Review of Politics* 4: 168–69 (1942).

Pearson, Karl. *The Grammar of Science*. London, 1900.

Perham, Margery F., and Mary Bull, eds. *Lugard*, 2 vols. London, 1956-1960.

Popenoe, David. *Sociology*. New York, 1971.

Reid, Sue Titus. *Crime and Criminology*, 6th ed. Fort Worth, TX, 1991.

Richards, Dona. "The Ideology of European Dominance." *The Western Journal of Black Studies* 3: 224–250 (Winter 1979).

Richardson, Anna Steese. *Standard Etiquette*. New York, 1925.

Richlin-Klonsky, Judith, and Ellen Strenski, eds. *A Guide to Writing Sociology Papers*, 2nd ed. New York, 1991.

Robbins, T., et al., eds. "The Last Civil Religion: Reverend Moon and the Unification Church." *Sociological Analysis* 37: 111–125.

Robert, Sara Corbin. *Robert's Rules of Order*. Glencoe, IL, 1970.

Rogers, Carey Wayne. "The Southern Tenant Farmers' Union as a Social Movement: Conflict in a Plantation society." M.A. thesis, Department of Sociology, University of Arkansas, Fayetteville, AR, 1980.

Rose, Jerry D. *Introduction to Sociology*, 2nd ed. Chicago, 1974.

Rusche, George, and Otto Kirchheimer. *Punishment and Social Structure*. New York, 1939.

Russett, Cynthia Eagle. *Sexual Science: The Victorian Construction of Womanhood*. Cambridge, MA, 1989.

Schroeder, Henry. *History of the Electric Light*. Washington, DC, 1923.

Silverberg, Robert. *Light for the World: Edison and the Power Industry*. Princeton, NJ, 1986.

Sims, V.M. *The Measurement of Socio-economic Status*. Bloomington, IL, 1928.

Sinclair, Upton. *The Jungle*. New York, 1946.

Skinner, B.F. *About Behaviorism*. New York, 1976.

_____. *Beyond Freedom and Dignity*. New York, 1972.

_____. *Science and Human Behavior*. New York, 1965.

Smith, Page. *Killing the Spirit: Higher Education in America*. New York, 1990.

Sorokin, Pitirim. *Social and Cultural Dynamics*. New York, 1937, 1941.

Spencer, Herbert. *The Principles of Sociology*. London, 1893.

_____. *Principles of Sociology*, 3 vols. New York, 1925.

_____. "Progress, Its Law and Cause." *Westminster Review* 67: 445–485 (1857).

Spykman, Nicholas J. *The Social Theory of Georg Simmel*. Chicago, 1925.

Stanfield, John H. In "Race in Science." *Contemporary Sociology: A Journal of Reviews* 13: 684–685 (November 1984).

Stepanova, E. *Karl Marx: A Short Biography*. Moscow, 1968.

Stephan, A. Stephen. "Hymns: Making the Irrelevant Relevant Through Ecology." *The Hymn* 25: 6–9 (January 1975).

Stern, B.J. *Selected Papers. Historical Sociology*. New York, 1959, 1965.

Steinbeck, John. *The Grapes of Wrath*. New York, 1939.

Stowe, Harriet Beecher. *Uncle Tom's Cabin* (1852). New York, 1952.

Stroud, Drew McCord, ed. *Viewpoints: The Majority Minority*. Minneapolis, MN, 1973.

Sumner, William Graham. *Folkways*. Boston: Ginn, 1906.

_____. *Social Darwinism: Selected Essays*. Englewood Cliffs, NJ, 1963.

Sumner, William Graham, and Alfred Keller. *The Science of Society*, 3 vols. New Haven, CT, 1927.

Sutherland, Edwin H. "White Collar Criminality." *American Sociological Review* 5: 1–20 (1940).

Sykes, Charles J. *Profscam*. New York, 1989.

Tawney, R.H. *Religion and the Rise of Capitalism*. New York, 1926, 1947, 1961.

Taylor, George Coffin, and Smith, Reed. *Shakespeare's Hamlet*. New York, 1962.

Thomas, William I., and Florian Znanieckin. *The Polish Peasant in Europe and America*, 2 vols. New York, 1927.

Toennies, Ferdinand. *Gemeinschaft und Gesellschaft*. 1887. Translated 1957.

Tulsa World, June 6, 1994.

Turner, Jonathan H., and Alexandra Maryanski. *Functionalism*. Menlo Park, CA, 1979.

Vander Zanden, James W. *Sociology: The Core*, 3rd ed. New York, 1993.

Veblen, Thorstein. *The Theory of the Leisure Class*. New York, 1899.

Walker, Alice. *The Color Purple*. New York, 1981.

Warner, William Lloyd. "American Caste and Class." *American Journal of Sociology* 42: 234–237 (September 1936).

Warner, William Lloyd, and Paul S. Lunt. *The Social Life of a Modern Community*. New Haven, CT, 1941.

_____. *The Status System of a Modern Community*. New Haven, CT, 1942.

Warren, Carol A.B. *Sociology: Change and Continuity*. Homewood, IL, 1977.

Weber, Max. *The Protestant Ethic and the Spirit of Capitalism*. New York, 1904–1905. Translated by Talcott Parsons, 1930.

_____. *Wirtschaft und Gesellschaft* (Translated by Talcott Parsons and A. M. Henderson as *The Theory of Social and Economic Organization*. New York, 1947.

West, James. *Plainville, USA*. Chicago, 1945.

White, Andrew D. *The History of the Warfare with Science and Theology in Christendom*. New York, 1899, 1986.

White, Ellen G. *The Great Controversy*. Phoenix, Arizona, 1967.

Wicker, Tom. *A Time to Die*. New York: Quadrangle/New York Times Book Co., 1975.

Wilson, Edward O. "Biology in the Social Sciences." *Daedalus* 106, no. 4: 127–140 (fall 1977).

_____. *Sociobiology: The New Synthesis*. Cambridge, MA, 1975.

Wilson, James Q. *Thinking About Crime*. New York, 1975.

Wilson, John. *Language and the Pursuit of Truth*. Cambridge, England, 1967.

Wilson, William Julius. *The Declining Significance of Race*. Chicago, 1978.

Wirth, Louis. *The Ghetto*. Chicago, 1928.

Zietlin, Aeschylus M. *Plato's Vision: The Classical Origins of Social and Political Thought*. Englewood Cliffs, NJ, 1993.

Subject Index

Name Index

About the Author

GORDON D. MORGAN is Professor of Sociology at the University of Arkansas. He has studied sociology for over forty years; concentrating on ghettos, educational sociology, prisons, the Caribbean, and Africa.

ISBN 0-275-94999-0

HARDCOVER BAR CODE